D1572671

Dastan-e-Ghadar

Dastan~e~Ghadar

THE TALE OF THE MUTINY

◆—⚫——⚫—◆

ZAHIR DEHLVI

Translated from the Urdu by
RANA SAFVI

PENGUIN BOOKS

PENGUIN BOOKS

USA | Canada | UK | Ireland | Australia
New Zealand | India | South Africa | China

Penguin Books is part of the Penguin Random House group of companies
whose addresses can be found at global.penguinrandomhouse.com

Published by Penguin Random House India Pvt. Ltd
7th Floor, Infinity Tower C, DLF Cyber City,
Gurgaon 122 002, Haryana, India

First published in Penguin Books by Penguin Random House India 2017

English translation copyright © Rana Safvi 2017
Maps copyright © Zunaira Naqvi 2017

All rights reserved

10 9 8 7 6 5 4 3 2 1

The views and opinions expressed in this book are the author's own and the
facts are as reported by him which have been verified to the extent possible,
and the publishers are not in any way liable for the same.

ISBN 9780670088911

Typeset in Adobe Caslon Pro by Manipal Digital Systems, Manipal
Printed at Thomson Press India Ltd, New Delhi

www.penguin.co.in

To the memory of
Abu Zafar Sirajuddin Mohammad Bahadur Shah Badshah.
May history give you your due.

Contents

Translator's Introduction

In 1837, when Mirza Abu Zafar, the eldest son of Akbar Shah II, was crowned emperor of the Mughal Empire—with the title of Abu Zafar Sirajuddin Mohammad Bahadur Shah Ghazi—little did he know he would be the last of the line.

He was an accomplished poet and his nom de plume or *takhallus* was *Zafar* (victor), and though victory eluded him, we still remember him as Bahadur Shah Zafar. He was born in 1775 to Akbar Shah II and his Rajput wife, Lalbai. Though not the favourite son or heir apparent, a twist of fate brought him the throne and another took it away.

When Bahadur Shah Zafar ascended the throne at sixty-two years of age, the glorious days of the Mughal Empire had ended. In 1803, Delhi, the capital of the Mughal Empire, had come under the control of the British, and Sir David Ochterlony had been appointed the British Resident. In effect, this meant that administrative control rested with the Resident, and so it was he who took all major decisions—while Mughal Emperor Shah Alam's influence extended over a rather limited area in Delhi. As the saying went:

> The kingdom of Shah Alam
> Is from Delhi to Palam

But even that was slowly taken away, and in 1813, the tradition of offering *nazr* was stopped. Coins were no longer minted in the imperial mint of the Mughals, and in 1835, the face of the Mughal emperor was removed from the coins.

The emperor became just a pensioner of the British and received a stipend of Rs 12 lakh per annum in 1813, which was increased to Rs 15 lakh per annum in 1833. Eventually, the emperor was also divested of his command over the Red Fort, and nothing could happen without the British Resident's acquiescence.

Pious and spiritually inclined, the last emperor spent his time contemplating God and writing mystical poetry, one of which describes his plight:

> Either you should have made me a royal officer
> Or you should have given me a crown like a beggar's bowl

In 1856, Lord Canning wrote to the British Resident of Delhi: 'A lot of the elements of the glory of the Badshahi have finished . . . It is, therefore, not difficult to think that on the death of the Badshah by just a few lines on paper the title could be abolished.'[1] With the death of Emperor Bahadur Shah II, the royal family would have to vacate the Qila-e-Moalla too.[2]

Though the imperial star of the Mughal Empire was fading, its cultural star was at its zenith. Bahadur Shah

Zafar's reign saw an extraordinary renaissance in arts and culture. I don't think any other court can boast of hosting poetic luminaries like Mirza Ghalib, Sheikh Ibrahim Zauq and Momin Khan Momin in one gathering. There were many other major and minor poets flourishing under the court's patronage. The emperor was no mean poet himself!

The language we know now as Urdu—originally called Rekhta—developed with poets writing their verses in it. Urdu and Persian writers received state patronage and encouragement. The *Ganga Jamuni tehzeeb*, or syncretic culture of Hindustan, saw the emperor participating in each and every festival of Hindus and Muslims alike. There was a sense of togetherness and pluralism. In fact, Bahadur Shah Zafar is responsible for founding the first Ram Lila Committee in Delhi, and Eid, Bakr Eid, Holi and Diwali were all celebrated with great pomp and show in the Qila-e-Moalla. His Hindu subjects would also partake in the *jharokha darshan* ceremony after praying at the Jamuna early in the morning.

In many of the Urdu accounts of Shahjahanabad, there are descriptions of genuine grief at the fate of Bahadur Shah Zafar. I could feel a palpable sense of anguish among Hindu and Muslim citizens for the emperor after his exile. They cried for Bahadur Shah Zafar with the same sense of grief as for one's own relative.

The Doctrine of Lapse promulgated by Lord Dalhousie overturned the recognition of adopted sons of Indian rulers. The kingdoms of those Indian rulers who died childless would lapse to the East India Company. In 1856, the very popular Nawab of Awadh was removed from the throne by the British on trumped-up charges of incompetence and was in exile in Calcutta in 1857.

Meanwhile, amongst the common people across the rest of India, there had been unrest simmering for some time. There was a general fear amongst the Indians that the British were interfering in their religious and social customs. The attempt to codify law and introduce an English judge alongside a Hindu priest or Muslim maulvi as per need was viewed with suspicion. The advent of missionaries was seen as a direct threat to religion and one of the first targets of the mutiny in Delhi was Dr Chiman Lal, the emperor's physician, who had converted to Christianity.

The soldiers were disaffected at being asked to travel overseas to fight. Most of the Hindu sepoys in the East India Company army belonged to the upper castes. For them, the very act of crossing the sea entailed loss of caste.

The final nail in the coffin turned out to be the greased cartridge that had to be used for the newly introduced Enfield rifles. These cartridges, believed to be greased with cow and pig fat, had to be bitten off before loading the rifle—and this meant bringing them into intimate contact with the soldiers' mouths—anathema for both Hindus (who venerated the cow as a sacred animal) and Muslims (who regarded the pig as a profane beast).

At the time, there was much speculation and gossip that fuelled the notion of a revolution amongst the people. Rumours were rife of an imminent attack by Iran, with help from the Tsar of Russia. The Mughal emperor was suspected of being in touch with the Shah of Iran and plotting against the British. During his trial, the one question asked of all witnesses was whether the emperor had sent an emissary, namely Siddi Qambar, to the court of Iran, asking for help to get the British out of India. There had been a pamphlet put up on the Jama Masjid, purporting to be from the Shah of Iran, asking the Shias and Sunnis to forget their sectarian divide and unite with the common purpose of driving the British away. The pamphlet was soon removed, but it sparked a storm of conjecture and became a steady point of conversation.

It was said that Shah Nimatullah Wali, a fourteenth-century Persian mystic, had made a prophecy in his *qasida* stating that the British rule in India would end. This prophecy began circulating in India after 1850.

It was in this scenario that, on the morning of 11 May 1857, a group of sepoys from the Meerut cantonment of the East India Army came to the Qila-e-Moalla, demanding the restoration of Bahadur Shah II as the emperor of Hindustan. They had revolted against their British officers the day before and killed many of them.

The night the rebel sepoys left for Delhi, the British officers of Meerut managed to send a missive to Simon Fraser, the commissioner of Delhi (also known as the Resident), warning him of the sepoys' advent and asking him to make arrangements to stop them. The letter reached his house at midnight, but he was already asleep. Rumours say he was drunk. His servants refused to wake him up despite the insistence of the messenger. The servants said that sahib was prone to flying into a rage if woken up. By the time he woke up, it was already too late and the rebels had entered Delhi.

When the momentous events of 1857 unfolded before Syed Zahiruddin Hussain Zahir Dehlvi in Delhi, he was twenty-two years old. A poet, he had been a frequent visitor to the Qila-e-Moalla since the age of four and was well-versed with the etiquette of the Qila. He was appointed *Darogha-e-Mahi-Maratib*, which meant he was in charge of the Mughal Empire's fish emblem, which was used on ceremonial occasions and processions. As part of his duties, he had to accompany the emperor whenever he went out whether in official state processions or in public. On other days, he gave attendance at the jharokha darshan and in court.

As Zahir was not a historian but a courtier poet, his book is important not only because it describes the days and nights of tumult, but also because it chronicles the colossal changes wrought by those events and how they impacted his life afterwards. It is an eyewitness account of the cultural zenith that Delhi had reached under Emperor Bahadur Shah Zafar, and the subsequent destruction of that culture. Ghalib called this time *rustakhez beja*, or an unwarranted day of reckoning.

One important event which was thrashed bare by the British during Bahadur Shah Zafar's trial was the murder of the innocent European men, women and children at the start of the 'mutiny'. The British accused the emperor of culpability. This book provides a graphic account of that day, as well as the emperor's attempts to save those innocent Europeans and his own helplessness.

Zahir's book also gives a vivid account of life in the states of Alwar, Jaipur and Tonk where he took up employment. The secular nature of the rulers is well described. In fact, this book is a shining example of the bonhomie that existed between all communities, not just up to 1857, but almost till the end of the writer's life.

An era ended with 1857, and here we can see the changes as described by an eyewitness, a person involved in all the events listed. He wrote this memoir on his deathbed, at the request of friends, probably based on notes. The description

of the *ghadar* and subsequent events are too vivid for him not
to have referred to some notes or diary, which he may have
maintained for posterity.

Zahir was not a historian, and we must keep that in
mind. He mentions only those incidents to which he
was an eyewitness or which he had heard from relatives'
accounts, thus missing out on a few important facts, such
as the activities of Emperor Bahadur Shah Zafar during
those fateful four months in 1857. Zahir does not mention
the emperor's attempts to inspect, guide and motivate the
army present in the Qila through his visits to Salimgarh.
Nor does he mention him going out in procession to quell
disturbances in the city because of the *purbia*s, nor at least
two occasions mentioned by others when the emperor
decided to lead the troops, though both attempts were
aborted midway. He also does not mention Mirza Mughal,
the emperor's son who was appointed commander-in-chief
of the rebel forces until the advent of Bakht Khan, who
replaced him.

A very surprising omission is the trial of Emperor Bahadur
Shah Zafar, which he must have definitely heard about during
his escape from Delhi. The reason for this exclusion could be
that he was not actually present at the trial. But given that
India had formally come under the rule of the British, it is also
possible that Zahir was simply being pragmatic and did not
want to jeopardize his own position or that of his dependants
by voicing his views on the trial.

However, most of whatever he has written has been
corroborated by contemporary accounts, such as that of Jivan
Lal in *Sarguzasht-e-Delhi*.[3] The only chapter which lacks
clarity is the last one, which reflects his bitterness during his
stay in Hyderabad. Here, he even mixes up his first and second

visits when he describes the reception he received. He admits
that the sorrows he suffered had hampered his memory.

His account is very pro-British and mostly blames the
purbias for disrupting the life of the ordinary citizen of
Shahjahanabad. His sympathies are with the emperor but
never with the *baghi*s, as he calls them. This could be because
of the harsh punishment meted out by the British to those
who participated and sympathized with the rebels against
their authority. Another point to remember is that he was
born and grew up when the East India Company was already
ruling Delhi so for him they would have been the real rulers
anyway. In fact, when he returns to Delhi post 1857, after
being given a letter of amnesty, and writes a *shahr ashob*, or
lament of a city on seeing its destruction, he adds a few lines
in praise of Mr Cooper, the deputy commissioner of Delhi at
that time.

This book is one of the earliest autobiographies written
in Urdu. It was called *Taraz-e-Zahiri*, but it became more
famous as *Dastan-e-Ghadar*. Mir Istiaq Shauq, Zahir's
grandson, had given the text to Agha Mohammad Tahir,
grandson of Mohammad Husain Azad, who then published
it in Lahore around 1914. The second edition was published
by Salahuddin Ahmed for Punjab Academy, Lahore, in 1955.
It was in this edition that Asghar Hussain Khan Ludhianvi
edited the headings in the text, and these are still used by Urdu
publishers today. I have retained some of these headings, and
changed a few.

I have used the words 'mutiny' and 'rebels' in my notes
and comments, as those are the words used by Zahir. The
term 'First War of Indian Independence' was coined later by
Indian historians.

Zahir has used a generous sprinkling of poems in his text. I have used the English translations of just a few of these poems and verses which went with the flow of the narrative, and placed the original Urdu/Persian verses in a section at the end. Dr Syed Faizan has translated all the poems and verses from the original Persian and Urdu.

I have used my discretion to edit the text in places to keep the flow and drama of the narrative intact. I would like to end by paraphrasing a line used by Zahir Dehlvi: All mistakes lie on the neck of the translator.

Author's Preface

After praise to the Almighty, this insignificant Syed Zahiruddin Husain Zahir Dehlvi is in service to his friends and benevolent patrons, without exaggeration and with complete honesty towards the loyal and worthy friends who have been asking about the welfare of this contemptible man.

How can I describe the events that occurred in the life of this lowly man? Somehow, I have been going through the motions of life, anguishing over the past and spending my time in prayer.

When the requests to pen my experiences became very insistent and this faqir had no more excuses to offer, and once I had access to some documents and letters, I got down to the task of writing my memoirs, from my birth to this date. This is an absolutely truthful account of the events which took place in my lifetime, presented without artifice, exaggeration or dishonest manipulation.

There is no intent to insult or criticize anyone. Nor do I have anything to do with writing a eulogy or praising anyone.

I don't want any praise, award or compensation.

I have not relied on an elegant style of composition or turn of phrase, and have instead leaned on a simple, truthful style of reporting everything as I saw it. I am weary of oratory and measured speeches.

Even if my writing is against the established norm of the day, I do not care. I am only interested in remaining true to the purpose of my writing. What do I have to do with embellishing the truth?

I am writing down my memoirs in my simple, everyday language. I am not a journalist or a storyteller and I will use my mother tongue, which I have imbibed from childhood, and the style that I learnt from my teachers. I can only write as I have been taught, and even if I now become someone's disciple, what is the use? How can I forget the lessons I have imbibed since childhood? I have used words that I heard from people during these events, and have not changed them. The incidents which occurred during this period, I have seen myself and jotted down faithfully.

All mistakes lie on the neck of the narrator

For instance, I have written down everything that happened during the mutiny and not relied on market gossip.

Dastan-e-Ghadar

1

My Ancestors

That which was heard as if it was seen

The genealogical table of this lowly man, Zahir, goes all the way to Sher-e-Khuda Hazrat Ali Murtaza. My ancestors go back seventeen generations to Hazrat Shah Nimatullah Wali Rahmatallah Alaihi, and eight generations can be traced back to Imam Raza, *Alaihis Salaam*.[4] Shah Nimatullah Wali's grandsons were Shah Nurullah, Shah Habib and Shah Mohibullah. His successor, Shah Khalilullah *ibn* (son of) Shah Nimatullah Wali, was the spiritual master of the king during the reign of Ala-ud-Din Hassan Bahman Shah of the Bahmani kingdom. Thus, his mausoleum was built in Bidar, the seat of the Deccan kings. It still stands there.

My other ancestors were all rewarded with high offices in the courts of the Timurid kings. In the reign of Bahadur Shah Zafar, my father, Hazrat Shah Syed Jalauddin Haider, was given the title of *Hallaj-ud-Daula*,[5] which was further

adorned with the title *Khan Bahadur*. He was also elevated
to the rank of an *ustad* of the emperor. When I was twelve
years old, I was presented in the court. My training to be
a *darogha* began immediately. I was taught the ways of the
court and the art of riding. My commitment to learning
resulted in my getting the title *Raqim-ud-daula Darogha-e-
Qauzbegi Peshgah*. This lowly contemptible person was now
given many important responsibilities.

My Birth

My parents had been longing for a child. Before I was born,
they had lost many children in childbirth and infancy. When
I was born, my elders were ecstatic, and I was brought up
with great love and care. I was the apple of everyone's eye.
During this period, my father held a good post in Lucknow
and my grandfather was the emperor's teacher in the art of
calligraphy.

When I was four years old, I kept my first roza at the
wishes of my mother, who had made a vow to God that I
would keep this fast. My *rozakushai* ceremony, which is
the breaking of the first fast kept by a child in the month
of Ramzan, was celebrated in a grand manner. When I was
four-and-a-half years old, I was circumcised, and that—along
with my *Bismillah* (the ceremony which marks the start of
formal learning)—was celebrated on an extravagant scale. All
the notables of the city were invited and there was dancing and
singing for two days. Money and presents were distributed for
a couple of days. My father would often tell me that on the
day of my Bismillah, my relatives placed 100 gold coins in my
hand. My Bismillah was celebrated so grandly that even my
wedding paled in comparison.

Education

After my Bismillah, I was sent to a school and Ustad Sheikh Safdar Ali was given the task of mentoring and instructing me. Many other children of the same age joined me in the class. After learning the alphabet, I started reading the *Quran-e-Majeed* along with *Pandnama-e-Saadi*. By the time I completed the *Quran-e-Majeed*, I had already finished reading Sheikh Saadi's *Gulistan* and *Bostan*, and moved on to books such as *Bahar-i Danish*, *Yusuf-Zulekha* and compilations of literature and poetry.

I even studied (books written by) Abul Fazl and *Sikandar Nama* (by Nizami Ganjavi) with my late teacher, Sheikh Sahib. I read many other books by the great Persian writers and poets under the guidance of various teachers. After studying Persian books, I studied Arabic texts under Syed Jafar Ali sahib in the madrassa. By the time I was twelve, I had got the opportunity to teach as well. However, once I took up royal employment, I did not get time to complete my Arabic studies in depth.

The Start of My Poetic Career

My initiation into the wonderful world of poetry took place in the days when I used to read *Bahar Danish o Zuleikha*.[6] This is when I overheard an old friend of my father's, Miyan Nabi Baksh sahib, grandson of Shah Naseer,[7] discussing poetry with him when he came to visit. Both of them were sitting in the room where I studied. Miyan Nabi Baksh sahib recited a verse by a well-known poet, and my father praised it saying, 'What an exquisite *matla*. *SubhanAllah!*'

The couplet was:

Let us see till when the beloved's gaze is averted from me
Let me see till when the night and day revolve ceaselessly

When I heard the word matla I was curious, and I went to my father and asked him, 'What does the word matla mean and what is a matla?'

My father explained the meaning of both matla and *maqta*: 'In prosody, the opening verse has a *qaafiya* in both the lines, and that is called a matla. The verse in which the qaafiya comes only in the second line is called a *sher'r*.'[8]

He went on to explain the rules of ghazal writing.

I was able to imbibe all these rules and memorize the verses he recited. I recited an impromptu verse in the same metre and with the same rhyming pattern. Both my father and Miyan Nabi Baksh sahib were very pleased. The latter embraced me and complimented me, saying, 'You will be an incomparable poet.'

The matla and verse I recited were:

Let's see till when the company of the stranger lasts
Let's see till when this having and not having lasts
From the stranger, O beloved, your heart is crystal clear
Till when shall I throw dust on it, dear?

The applause from my elders acted like a match to gunpowder and ignited in me a passion for poetry which kept increasing day by day.

I reached a stage where I started memorizing every good sher'r that I heard. I found many Persian *diwan*s in the library at home. There were commentaries on the poems of the Persian poets as well. I started reading them.

I would learn every Urdu ghazal composed by the well-known poets. *Diwan-e-Nasikh* and *Atish* and various books on different styles of Urdu poetry had just been printed in Lucknow and brought to Delhi. It became my habit to glance through them. I wrote a few ghazals and showed them to Miyan Nabi Baksh sahib. However, my father asked me to refrain from writing poetry even though he himself was an excellent poet. Shah Naseer sahib was my father's student.

In this same period, Hafiz Qutbuddin sahib, who was a student of the late Shah Naseer, held a *mushaira* in the house of Shah Sahib. Since the house where the mushaira was to be held was very close to mine, I attended it. It was here that I read my first ghazal. I became a student of Sheikh Mohammad Ibrahim Zauq *Khaqaani-e-Hind*. The poet Dagh was also part of this mushaira. There were many other famous poets present. I was around fourteen years old at the time. There were numerous mushairas in Delhi even after that, but I did not attend them. I tested my skills on my own.

Though I often got a chance to visit Hazrat Ustad Shah Naseer sahib, I could only show him my ghazals once or twice. However, I was able to benefit greatly from his affectionate company. When I presented my ghazal, seeking his esteemed guidance and correction, he was very pleased with the maqta I had written. He immediately recited this verse:

> The diwan of Zahir Faryaabi
> Steal it in Mecca if you find it[9]

And he blessed me with the words, '*Insha'Allah!* You will become a poet.' It is due to this certificate given by Shah Naseer sahib that I am able to write. After his demise, I wrote a few qasidas and a ghazal.

Alas! All these were destroyed in the turmoil of the mutiny. All that remain are two ghazals, which had become famous and were remembered by people. Even I remembered a few verses, but all the rest were lost. The few I remember are part of a qasida I had written:

> There is nothing unlikely in the season of rain
> The house of the garden becomes like crystal
> The morning breeze blows praises to God
> The breath of the morning dictates into the ears of the flowers
> (For the emperor)

> The breeze is drunk and staggers out in the ardour
> of drunkenness
> Covering the young ones of the garden every time
> (For the heir apparent)

> One month of each year is the month of Ramzan
> Then the exalted God orders us to pursue fasting
> And I have passed four months continuously
> The last month of *Jamadi* to *Shawwal*[10]
> Made me fast for four months continuously
> But I have not got the urge to break the fast till now
> (for Mehboob Ali Khan, agent of the Badshah)

I wrote one ghazal at the request of Maharaja Ajit Singh of Patiala. I was rewarded with a prize of Rs 1000. I received Rs 200 for the matla and Rs 800 for each of the four couplets.

> How should the stricken lover bleed away?
> To the beloved what is a complaint or entreaty, pray?

The other ghazal was

> Love is full of pleasures even when she is suffering
> On both sides the fire is equal in its burning

Only these two ghazals remain from my past writings.

Teachers and Contemporaries

After the death of Hakim Momin Khan sahib and Sheikh Mohammad Ibrahim Zauq, students flocked for guidance to these notable poets: Mirza Asadullah Khan sahib Ghalib, Mufti Sadruddin Khan sahib Azurda, Hakim Agha Jaan sahib Aish, Ghulam Ali Khan sahib Wahshat and Nawab Mustafa Khan sahib Shefta.

We were novices as compared to these great poets. The first rank amongst us novices belonged to Mirza Zainul Abidin Khan sahib Arif.[11]

Syed Moin was on the second rung. The third rung was Hafez Qutbuddin sahib Musheer. He was an accomplished poet with many students and it wouldn't be wrong to include him in the second rung of poets either.

Mirza Rahimuddin sahib Haya was also counted in the second rung of poets. His verse could be compared to that of the master poets.

After these honourable poets came a few young novice poets who were my contemporaries and had a modern outlook. Each was unique in his own way. They included Nawab Mirza Khan sahib Dagh; Mir Mehdi Husain sahib Majrooh;

Syed Shujauddin, popularly known as Umrao Mirza,[12] whose
pen name was Anwar; Mirza Qurban Beg sahib Salik; Maulvi
Abdul Karim sahib Soz, successor of Maulvi Imam Baksh
sahib Sehbai; Hakim Ghulam Maula Qalq; Mirza Pyaare
sahib Shohrat; Mirza Qadir Baksh sahib Sabir; Miyan Khuda
Baksh sahib Tanveer; Ghulam Ahmed sahib Tasveer; Abdul
Qadir sahib Tauqeer; Yusuf Ali Khan sahib Aziz; Maulvi
Amir Mirza Khursheed; Miyan Tashnah sahib (Munshi
Mohammad Ali Tashnah) and Agha Mirza sahib, younger
brother of Dagh Sahib whose pen name was Shaaghil.

Every evening there would be a gathering of like-minded
friends, where we would recite our verses to great appreciation.
This garden of poetry blossomed and flourished till the
mutiny in 1857. I was also a part of this garden.

Alas! What it was and what it has become! After the
mutiny, it disintegrated piece by piece.

The Death of My Mother

I have already talked of the love and care I received from my
parents. My mother loved me and my younger brother, Umrao,
with all her heart and soul. We were the apples of her eye.

I was eight years old when her protective presence was
lifted from our lives and my brother and I were left in the
care of our father. At the time of death, she embraced the two
of us and put our hands in the hands of my father and told
him, 'You have taken care of them with the love of a father,
but now a mother's love is necessary too. They are about to be
motherless. You have to be both mother and father to them.
There is no one else who can give them a mother's love but
you. If you neglect them, I will question you on the Day of
Judgement.'

She recited the *kalima* and left for heaven. My father took her will very seriously and gave us all the love of both mother and father.

This was the first tragedy that struck my life.

There was nothing lacking in my upbringing and I always had the best of teachers. I was very pampered and spent huge amounts of money on pigeon-flying and kite-flying in my childhood. However, my father never once questioned me, and gave me whatever I wanted.

When I reached the age of maturity, I became desirous of learning horse riding. He bought two horses for me and hired an instructor to teach me.

Routine and Pastimes

I would get up very early, and even before the call for the morning prayers was announced, I would ride to my job. Before doing anything else, I would go and join the crowds below the Qila-e-Moalla, who were waiting for a glimpse of the *huzoor purnoor* who would come to the *zer-e-jharokha*[13] at the Musamman Burj. When Huzoor appeared, there would be a great uproar and I would go along with the *hawadar* with my *qalamdaan* tied to my waist. I would write down all the verses that I could hear being recited in the noise.

After we had walked for a while, the royal order would be given for everyone to mount their horses.

There were two elephants behind the *sawari-e-mubarak* (or the blessed conveyance of the emperor) and I would ride on one of them, alternating between the horse and elephant. In brief, I would return to my house after nine o'clock in the morning.

I had a separate room in which I would sit and meet people. My younger brother, Umrao Mirza Anwar, and my cousin, Amir Mirza Khursheed, would also join me here. My friends would come to this sitting room after 9 a.m. A few students would come to us for guidance. For two hours, we would give discourses and discuss various issues. We would talk of the couplets we had written. We would discuss Persian books on poetry and commentary. This gathering would disperse at 11 a.m.

I would go inside the house and have my lunch and then I would rest for two hours. My friends from the locality would gather and we would play *ganjifa* and *chausar*.[14]

At 5 p.m. I would mount my horse and set off to roam about the market. I would return after the evening prayers. My friends would come over again, and we would entertain ourselves in various ways. Sometimes, those who came over were proficient in playing the sitar and tabla, and this would be a great source of joy for us. Sometimes, a few friends would go away, but most of us would stay together till 11 p.m., enjoying ourselves.

We had no worries in the world. Our days were festive like perpetual Eid, and the nights would pass as if each was *Shab-e-Baraat*.[15] All we did was laugh and be merry. There was no fair or spectacle we did not attend.

This group of friends included the rich, noble and gentle youth of the city. There were none who were not courteous, refined or cultured. From amongst the gentry of the city, those who excelled in various arts would visit us and be part of our gatherings. If any talented person came to Delhi, he would definitely visit my house at least once.

We lived in this happy state until the mutiny.

I got married four months before the mutiny, when I was about twenty-two years of age.

The mutiny let loose such a series of calamities on our heads that my friends were scattered and all our comforts and luxuries disappeared.

Employment

My father used to lavish every kind of attention on me and I never wanted for anything. Personally, I got a stipend of Rs 50 a month. The uncle of the Raja of Patiala, Ajit Singh, was very gracious and generous to me because of my skills in poetry. I would also make money from buying and selling horses. In all, I was never hard up for money.

Raja Ajit Singh of Patiala had rewarded me Rs 1000 for one of the ghazals I had written in his praise. His gift had also included a very expensive shawl embroidered with gold thread, a turban and other expensive items.

When I was thirteen years old, my mother's uncle, Mirza Khan sahib, passed away. He was childless and had held the post of Darogha-e-Mahi-Maratib, an official of the Order of the Fish—an honorary title of the highest rank. This post fell vacant on his death and many aspirants applied for it. I had already been presented to the emperor and had been a frequent visitor to the *mahal*[16] since I was eight years old. I had also become a disciple of the emperor and would go to him for the correction of my poems. My father decided to take advantage of this occasion and put forward my claim to the post. He requested that I be given a chance to prove my mettle and have the opportunity to serve the emperor's exalted self.

The emperor graciously agreed, and I was appointed Darogha-e-Mahi-Maratib with the title Raqimuddaula Syed Zahiruddin Hussain Khan, Darogha-e-Qauzbegi, and given the *khilat* of Khwaja Qutbuddin. When the emperor presented

himself in the blessed precincts of the dargah of Khwaja
Qutbuddin Bakhtiyar Kaki (in Mehrauli), it was my job to
accompany him and stay in attendance so long as he was there.
During this period, my food would come from the palace. I was
not deprived of this pleasure for even a single day. From the age
of thirteen to twenty-two, I executed my duties with diligence.

When the services of all the employees of the emperor
were terminated after the mutiny, I lost my job as well.

Marriage

When I was thirteen years old, I got engaged. Three years
later, my *nikah* ceremony was performed. But ceremonies
such as *sanchak*, *mehndi*, *baraat*, *chauthi*[17] and so on, which
accompany wedding festivities, had not been performed, and
neither had my bride left for her marital home, while her
trousseau, which had arrived, was kept in trust for her in one
of the rooms of our house.

I was young and hesitant to bring my wife home at that
age. I would just idle away my days, and this so angered my
father that I was deprived of the right to even present my
salaam to him.

However, my mother[18] took me to him and flung me
at his feet and had me pardoned. I agreed to complete the
ceremonies and get married.

My wedding ceremonies were celebrated with great pomp
and show, with all the accompanying rituals and festivities.
My wife was ceremoniously sent off to her husband's house
as per custom. A trousseau of Rs 5000 had been given to her.
Everything concluded happily and to the satisfaction of all.

After the ceremonies, her trousseau was locked away, and
we used the articles already present in the house.

A Herald of Imminent Destruction

The Great Mutiny descended on our heads four months later, and the British took away all our possessions. Not even a ring remained. Apart from the items which had been inherited from my ancestors, the British forces plundered articles from the house that were worth more than Rs 40,000. This was done as they were withdrawing from Shahjahanabad. They looted priceless things which can no longer be found. They also looted twenty copies of the *Quran-e-Majeed*, which had been handwritten by my ancestors, and seven which had been written by my father. All the invaluable books in our house were looted and destroyed. These included the *Tareekh-i-Rawzat al-Safa, Tareekh-e-Ferishta* and *Shahnameh* that my father had procured for me at the cost of Rs 300.

A month after my wedding, the dates for my younger sister's marriage were fixed. She was getting married to my wife's cousin. A month was spent in making the arrangements and buying the articles required for the wedding.

I was not able to enjoy myself after my wedding as Ramzan had started. On the seventh day of Ramzan, my younger brother and I left our house for Jama Masjid to while away the hours before the breaking of the fast. When we were returning, we realized that we didn't have enough time to reach our home for the iftar. I suggested that my brother and I break our fast in Matia Mahal. I went to my in-laws' house and had my arrival announced. One of the maids came out and invited me, saying, 'Miyan, why don't you come in? There is no one who does purdah with you. Your mother-in-law is the only lady in the house. The rest of the family has gone to attend Bakshi ji's wedding with Badi Begum Sahiba. Only Nawab Sahib and my Bhabho[19] are there.'

I replied, 'My younger brother is also with me. Please make arrangements for purdah.'

The maid went inside and curtains were drawn and arrangements made for purdah. Outside the house, there was a platform made of wooden beds. This was where my father-in-law was seated. My brother and I paid our respects to him by presenting our salutations.

He responded, 'Come, my children, sit down.'

We had just sat down when the cannon, which was shot to announce the breaking of the fast, was heard. We broke our fast and read our namaz. The table was laid and we sat down for dinner. After a few morsels, my father-in-law said, 'Nawab Mirza, it seems that there is going to be violence and bloodshed in the city.'

I replied, 'Sir, you are my elder, but what signs are there of any violence taking place in the city?'

Nawab Sahib said, 'Son, do you know anything which contradicts what I am saying? I swear by God that such an incident is about to take place.'

I was convinced that he was never wrong and asked, 'Will an army come from Russia?'

'Only Allah knows all,' he said.

I asked him, 'Sir, when do you think these events will take place?'

Nawab Sahib said, 'People say that whatever will happen will take place in this month of Ramzan. And let me tell you, I will also be martyred.'

I exclaimed, 'For God's sake! Do not say this. May God keep you safe. You are our elder.'

'No one can go against the will of God.'

We finished our dinner, had paan and left for home.

2

The State of the Mughal Dynasty

> Wherever you dig, the foundation stones are laid bare
> Though people are thriving, their houses are bare

The state of the Mughal dynasty was such that wherever you looked, you would see that the foundation was exposed and in a state of disrepair. The surfeit of ruined houses in populated areas deepened the impression of disintegration.

> Therefore, take heed, you who can see
> (Quran: Surah Al-Hashr: 2)[20]

The glorious dynasty of the Timurids had, for all practical purposes, departed from this world 150 years ago. The descendants were just deceiving themselves by saying:

> This is the parting of ways between me and thee
> (Quran: Surah Al-Kahf: 78)

The emperor reigned only in name, and he didn't have the powers of even the king of the smallest kingdom in Hindustan. As the poet Sauda said,

> There is a man who is in charge of twenty-two provinces
> Yet, he doesn't have the income to feed a morsel to
> the soldier

The East India Company gave the emperor a small amount of Rs 1 lakh per month. Apart from that, he had his rental income from the Crown lands, and ground rent from houses and tenements in Shahjahanabad. His total income per month would have been around Rs 1.25 lakh.[21] It was only because of the grandeur of the emperor, his pomp and show, dignity and magnificence, customs and traditions, and the arrangement of the court, that one could guess that this family must once have held magnificent sovereign authority over Hindustan. *Jalla Jalaluhu!* (May his glory be glorified!)

However, despite the emperor's fall in status and authority, the shortage of money and loss of wealth, there were two things that shocked and astonished me so much that even now I am awestruck by them.

First, by the grace of God, the emperor managed to use the Rs 1 lakh so well that one would be hard-pressed to find such magnificence in a court where crores were freely spent. Both the soldier who earned only Rs 4 and the man with unlimited resources were equally happy. No one lamented the change of fortune, and this was the result of good will and disposition and strength of mind.

Second, the royal majesty and grandeur of the emperor's darbar could not be seen in any other state.

If one were to glance at the income and expenditure of the court, one would be astonished, wondering how they could ever match each other. How was the revenue so blessed that there was never any shortage in meeting the royal expenses? These included expenses for royal workshops, personal bodyguards of the emperor, water department, dispensary, department of the royal wardrobe, department of the royal jewellery, artillery, camel shed, wagon house, workshop in charge of the umbrella and standards taken out in ceremonial procession of the Dignity of the Fish Emblem, office of the quartermaster, library, pigeon house, salary to the official in charge of collecting/tabulating the tributes paid to the emperor by guests, the official in charge of the carpets/furnishings, the official in charge of carriages, the official in charge of the porters who carried the carriage, office of the royal bodyguards, the official in charge of the eunuchs, the official in charge of executions and department of household expenses.

It is impossible to write about them in detail, as it would become too long.

Administration of the Qila

The emperor's army included the reserves, a force raised by Bahadur Shah II, which comprised of the youth of Delhi, the young princes and royal boys, royal attendants and the cavalry regiment.

The dignitaries of the exalted court comprised the ministers, spiritual masters, teachers, priests, physicians, princes living in the Qila, the steward, the paymaster of the army, the dignitaries of high and low ranks, the superintendent of the workshops and artists, etc., and those who collected the petitions.

There was a department for distributing the salaries of those working in the palace as well as of the princes and the quartermaster, the department of salaries for the estate, the department of old revenues, the department of salaries of the court dignitaries and the department for the distribution of salaries of army officers.

The Rules of the Exalted Court

The arrangement of the darbar, as well as the rules and regulations that were prevalent in the court of the Delhi Sultanate and Mughal dynasty, were inspired by the Persian courts and not found anywhere in Europe.

The *Takht-e-Taoos*[22] was kept in the centre of the Diwan-e-Khaas. Above the throne was a golden canopy with a silver mace, or *Chauba-e-Niqra*, fixed in gilded holders.

Gilded and enamelled peacocks were affixed on all four sides of the Takht-e-Taoos. These were inlaid with huge precious stones such as rubies.

Cushions would be arranged on the throne. When the emperor graced the court, there would be two rows of courtiers, standing according to rank, on either side of the throne. They would have their gaze lowered. No one could move, smile, talk or even look at anyone else. The courtiers couldn't even scratch themselves.

Two rows of attendants would stand on both sides of the darbar, red sticks in their hands. If anyone transgressed even slightly, these sticks would be hooked on to their necks and the offender would be ejected from the darbar. There was no darbar in the country that could be compared to this.

Next to the Diwan-e-Khaas was the door to the Lal Purdah.[23] Anyone who entered the Diwan-e-Khaas had to first present himself at the Lal Purdah, and stand on the *salaamgah* to pay obeisance to the emperor. This was done by performing three salaams called *kornish*, respectfully bending from the waist thrice with the hand on the forehead. The herald would announce:

'*Mulaihza adab hai. Adab baja lao. Jahanpanah, Badshah Salamat, Alampanah!*' ('Attention! Greetings, present your salutations to the Refuge of the World, long live the Emperor, the Refuge of the Universe!')

The nobles would enter from the side of the *hammam* and emerge on the stairs leading up to the terrace of the Diwan-e-Khaas. Here, they would take off their footwear and then go to the next salaamgah of the Diwan-e-Khaas, where they would pay respects again. The herald would announce the visitor's name once more.

If the courtier had come to pay nazr, he would go straight up to the throne and offer his tribute. The emperor would pick it up and hand it over to the darogha in charge of collecting the tributes paid to the emperor by guests, who would be standing by the side of the throne.

There was also a scribe who would note down the amount/type of tribute given. Once the tribute was handed over, the person would walk backwards (he had to face the emperor at all times) to the salaamgah and once again present his respects before taking his place in the rows of nobles standing inside the darbar.

Nobles would stand near the throne according to their rank, with the highest dignitaries closest to it. They would whisk away flies with *baal-e-huma*.[24] There would be several officers, called *arz beg*, whose job was to collect petitions. They would stand at the sides of the darbar, and petitioners would hand over any requests they might have of the emperor to them. They would take the petition, or *arzi*, up to the emperor and open and present it to him. After the emperor had glanced over the petition, another attendant would present a special pen and ink stand made of glass with a variety of pens in it. The emperor would sign the petition with a pencil. This meant that the petition had been granted and it would be implemented at once.

Men of Letters and Arts

The men of letters and arts employed by the emperor were all perfect in their chosen field and had been chosen for their mastery over their subjects. They had no competitors in their fields; anyone who was comparable to them was employed by the court. If they were employed by another court, even then they would receive a small stipend from the Mughal darbar, and come every year, or once in six months, to pay their respects to the emperor.

After the ruin of the Qila-e-Moalla, these artistes were in distress. They left for the regions around Delhi and tried to find patronage or employment there.

The Wedding of Mirza Jawan Bakht

Although many ceremonies have taken place in various kingdoms of India, the magnificence and elegance of Mirza Jawan Bakht's wedding cannot be matched. I have never witnessed a wedding as grand and rich as that of the late prince.

I find myself incapable of describing the ceremonies, rituals, the sanchak, mehndi, baraat, the decoration of the city, the lighting, the decoration of the *naqqarkhana*—so I am not even going to try. However, there are two points that are worthy of mention.

First, the magnificence of the gathering was unique. Various types of *mehfil*s were arranged in the *baradari* of the Diwan.[25] Each arch housed a courtesan dancing in a different style. There were separate mehfils for the princes, dignitaries and employees of the palace. The squadron of troops had a different gathering altogether. The menial servants had a separate mehfil too. In this way, every section of society had a separate mehfil.

There was a general order given stating that all the citizens of Shahjahanabad were to come and enjoy the dance and music of the event. For ten to twelve days, the assemblies were adorned and entertained by fairy-like dancers and beautiful women displaying their skills. All the royal employees and nobles of Shahjahanabad were presented with a tray or dish of various meats, called *tora*. People could either take the tora or Rs 50 cash instead. All the employees who were listed in the court were given a tora by name. For instance, my father, my younger brother, my mother (who also received a fixed salary from the court) and I were each given separate trays. I told the manager who was in charge of distributing the tora to send another one to the house, but only after eight days.

The food was distributed very generously and lavishly. The day a tora came, we would send it to the houses of various friends and relatives. There were so many items in one tray that an entire gathering could eat to their heart's content. These trays would fill up the hallway of my house. Each tray had food weighing 5 ser: there were four or five different kinds of *pulao*, many types of sweet rice coloured red, yellow and purple, 5 ser of sweets, salted *baqarkhwani* (a type of flat bread) and different types of naan. Every kind of food was present on these trays.

In brief, I have never come across such a ceremony in any other kingdom, even though I saw this particular court in its decline.

Apart from this, the poets who wrote the *sehra* and *tahniyat*[26] were given rewards and khilat, even though the court employed them all. The menial servants were also presented with clothes.

Royal Conveyance

Sixteen horses were used to pull the carriage of the emperor and eight horses employed to pull the carriage of Nawab Zinat Mahal Begum Sahiba.

Oh! Where is that great Khusrau Bahadur Shah?
Oh! Where is that master of the good-natured ones
Bahadur Shah?
Oh! Where is that compassionate ruler Bahadur Shah?
Oh! Where is that famous for his justice Bahadur Shah?
From where did these faithless rebels emerge
Who wiped out the names of these greats from the world!
What kind of fire have these tyrants inflamed
They brought the day of resurrection before it
was ordained
In fact, the righteous reign they erased
They wiped out everyone even before their time could end
No one was as devastated by their cruelty
As the house of Taimur which bore the brunt of
their tyranny

The exalted court[27] of Hazrat Badshah[28] was a place where excellence in knowledge and justice was exercised. He was the emperor of splendour and glory. Apart from his qualities as a ruler, he was a very spiritual man, well versed in religion and mysticism. He was often heard expressing his views through his poetry and poetic utterances. One of his oft-repeated phrases was:

> My children have unjust dreams of kingship
> This order can't last for long
> It will end with me
> From Taimur to Zafar

It happened exactly as he predicted.

Hazrat had taken an oath of allegiance to Hazrat Kale sahib, grandson of Maulana Fakhruddin Alaihir Rahma. He had many disciples. He was also very well versed in arts and science.

Calligraphic Skills

Hazrat Badshah was a student of my grandfather, the late Mir Imam Ali Shah sahib. From him, he learnt calligraphy in the Naskh script. My grandfather taught both the emperor and my father this fine art. They were incomparable calligraphers. All the calligraphers in Delhi were students of either the emperor or my father.

There was a panegyric written in praise of the king of *Rum* (Turkey) on behalf of the khedive of Egypt. It was sent to Britain, and from there it made its way to Delhi. Thomas Sahib,[29] the Resident in Delhi, asked my father to write it in the calligraphic style. My father responded saying that he couldn't do so without the emperor's permission; if Thomas Sahib were to obtain the permission, he would gladly do as he asked. Thomas presented himself before the emperor and made his request. The emperor then summoned my father and told him, 'Khalifa, you write this.' When my father had done so, Thomas Sahib had it framed and decorated with gold. It was then sent to Britain.

Poetic Skills

Hazrat Badshah was a peerless poet and an accomplished linguist. There was no idiom which he did not know or use. His poems had been compiled in five diwans. He was a disciple of the late Shah Naseer and Sheikh Ibrahim Zauq *Khaqaani-e-Hind*.[30]

Military Skills

The emperor was a crack shot and never missed his target, even if it was as fine as a hair. He could bring down a flying bird. If the emperor ever happened to see a fish or crocodile with its head sticking out of the water, he would shoot at its nostril and finish it off.

Archery Skills

The emperor was a disciple of Aapa Singh Sikh in archery. I have heard stories of his skills in this art from my father. When he was the heir apparent, he would fasten iron chains to his bow and shoot arrows through unyielding targets. Such was his strength and hand-to-eye coordination that even the strongest of bows became supple in his hands.

One day, the sawari-e-mubarak was returning from Salimgarh to the Qila. The garden of Mirza Fath-ul-Mulk, the second heir apparent,[31] lay along the route. There were sounds of shouting emerging from within, so Hazrat asked that his carriage be taken there. He was told that the princes were practising their archery skills. Everyone there greeted him with respect. The emperor asked for the bows to be strung and called for one for his own use. A selection of bows was presented to him; he chose one and drew three arrows. He stood on the raised spot the princes were shooting from, and took aim. The arrow went straight into the mark that had been put up and embedded itself there—only a few inches remained outside. Everyone praised him and asked for an encore. He shot another arrow which embedded itself even further into the mark. The third was completely hidden in the mark, only the tip showing. There were cries of praise all around.

I witnessed this myself.

Unarmed Combat

The emperor was a disciple of Mir Hamid Ali in the art of unarmed combat. Mir Hamid Ali and Mir Ashraf Ali were brothers, experts in the art, and had disciples hailing from the richest families in Hindustan. *Ali mad ki kasrat*,[32] an exercise that had been invented by Hazrat Ali Murtaza, Sher-e-Khuda, was part of their inheritance.

I have heard from my father that the emperor would exercise by taking on eight people, all by himself. The emperor had taken his practice to such a height that not only could he defend himself against the blows of those eight people, but he could also inflict marks on them.

Horsemanship

It is famously said that there were only two-and-a-half horsemen in Hindustan, one of them the emperor himself.

The other was his brother Mirza Jahangir, who had jumped across the moat surrounding the fort of Allahabad in his bid to escape the British when they imprisoned him there. The half a horseman was some Maratha. The emperor had crossed eighty years of age, but still he would display his horsemanship whenever he rode a horse. He would seem to be one with the horse.

One day, he emerged from the *tasbihkhana*[33] with the intention of visiting the dargah of Hazrat Nizamuddin Auliya. When he came out, he saw a row of high nobles and horse breakers and trainers in front of him. He looked towards Maju Beg, a royal employee, who presented himself immediately. The emperor asked if the new horse he had bought had been broken in for riding. Maju Beg folded his hands and said that the horse was ready by the felicity of the emperor.

The horse was brought forward and the emperor mounted it. He set off in the company of all the other horsemen. He rode comfortably, conversing with the others. They came out of the *deorhi* of the naqqarkhana and reached the parapets of Tripolia. All this while, the horse had kept his head lowered and shown a good temperament. Once near Tripolia, Maju Beg furtively slapped the horse's flank, which made the horse rear and buck. There had been a trained man holding the reins of the horse, but when it reared the emperor looked towards him and asked, 'What are you doing? I can control the horse myself and I was riding it slowly.'

At this, the horse began galloping, and for some time it looked as though a bird was flying or a deer springing. Later, the emperor calmed the horse down and ordered everyone to mount their horses. The emperor continued to ride the horse. Though it was a little playful, it was under his control. They rode all the way up to the dargah, which is 3 *kos* away from the city. Here, the emperor dismounted and entered the dargah. He returned on the elephant Maula Baksh.

Much as he was a great horseman, the emperor was also a renowned connoisseur of horses. He was well acquainted with the traits and habits of each breed of horse. When a trader brought a valuable horse to the city, he would present it to the emperor first, and only after that would the nobles and rich get a chance to look at it. The emperor would select the horses of good breeds, those that he liked. He had once said, 'In every breed of horse, in every colour, the empire stays for 100 years. The horse of this colour is the emperor's and the other colour the minister's. The horses of the emperor's colour are not vicious, and are very faithful. They are born in large numbers. The horses of the minister's colour have habits similar to those of the emperor's, though a couple of them may be vicious. They are not born in such large numbers. This age is the sultanate of the reddish horse and ministership of the tawny steed. After this, the colours will be interchanged.'[34]

There is a breed of horses called Peeriya. Its special characteristic is that it fasts on Thursday and does not let any man who is unclean or dirty ride it. If such a man were to mount the horse, it would rear and throw him off.

I was present at the darbar once, when some foreign traders brought along ten or twelve horses. They were lined up in front of the Lal Purdah, while the emperor was seated in the Diwan-e-Khaas. From that distance, he declared that one particular horse was good, so long as its temperament was also good.

The selected horse was brought forward and it was found that he was indeed much better than the other horses in the group. The emperor said, 'Let me see how he rides.' A horse trainer mounted the horse. He tried to ride the horse into the garden, but the horse began rearing and standing up straight, trying all the tricks to dismount the rider. The horse breaker was inexperienced and got scared, so he was helped to dismount.

Another man mounted the horse, but he also found it difficult to control it. The horse bolted to the hall of the *farashkhana*, destroying the things kept there. The rider hit the horse and made him jump into the water house. However, he could not control the horse and it ran out of there and into the Qila menagerie. Somehow, with the use of a whip, the rider brought him out of there too.

The rider and horse fought for nearly two hours, trying to establish who would come out on top. The horse was sweating profusely, trembling hard and bleeding in places. It was so exhausted by now that it was amenable to going in whichever direction the rider wanted. The rider brought it before the emperor and after paying his respects with a salaam, he dismounted. The emperor rewarded him with a shawl.

An Elephant Named Maula Baksh

Maula Baksh was an old elephant who had carried many emperors. His habits were almost human, and he had no parallel in his beauty or height and stature in Hindustan—not in the past, and not now. When he sat, his height was equal to that of many standing elephants. He would remain *mast*[35] for all twelve months, and he would not let anyone near him, except the one man who looked after him.

The day before the emperor planned to ride him, a *choubdar* would go and relay the news to the elephant: 'Miyan

Maula Baksh, tomorrow you have to go to work. Please bathe and be ready.'

The elephant would indicate his readiness. The *fil-baan* would unshackle him from his stump and take him to the Jamuna river, where he would get a thorough scrubbing.

The painter would then decorate his forehead with beautiful designs. The fil-baan would open his *gadeela* (the thick bedding on his back) and take him to the workshop, where he would be made to wear all his jewellery and strap the *amaari*, or litter, on his back. This was unlike the howdah. Maula Baksh would then be brought to the entrance of the naqqarkhana and made to stand there with the other elephants. As soon as the emperor appeared from the door of the naqqarkhana, Maula Baksh would let out a trumpet and present three salaams,[36] and then he would automatically sit down. He would remain seated until the emperor and those accompanying him mounted. Once the emperor was comfortably seated, he would get up at a sign from the *faujdar*.

Another unique fact about Maula Baksh was that while the emperor was riding him, two bows and two quivers full of short spears or javelins would be hung from his ears. A huge iron shield would be fixed to his trunk and a big silver *huqqa* along with its chillum and silver cover would be kept on his head. The *pechwan satak*, or the huqqa's pipe, would be kept on the shoulder of the faujdar. The emperor would smoke a huqqa and Maula Baksh would keep moving forward with such measured and trained steps that it was unthinkable that the huqqa or the chillum could fall down.

The beauty of Maula Baksh's temperament was that once he was free of his duties of carrying the emperor, he would be just as mast as he had been earlier.

Another of his special qualities was that young children could be seen sitting around him every day. He would play with them and feed them sugarcane. The children would call out to him: 'Maula Baksh! *Nakki aave!*' and he would respond by raising his front foot and keep waving it in the air till the children said, *'Tek do!'* (Put it down!), no matter how long that took.

Then he would grunt and the children would stand on one foot. If the children asked to put their feet down in less than a minute, he would shake his head. When a minute had passed, he would grunt again and put the children back at ease.

If the children did not come to play with him, he would trumpet loudly and call them.

When the British took control of the royal elephant house and the stables, Maula Baksh and Hamdam, the emperor's horse, stopped eating.

Hamdam was a magnificent, attractive horse. He was always ahead of the other horses when he was being ridden. He had been the emperor's mount since the emperor had been the heir apparent. Hamdam was forty years old at the time I am describing. His whole body was beautifully decorated with small red roses.

When these two animals stopped eating, the fil-baan intimated Saunders[37] of it: 'Sahib, the elephant has stopped eating. If something happens to him tomorrow, I will be hanged.'

Saunders refused to believe him and said, 'I will come and feed him myself.'

Saunders brought laddus and kachoris worth Rs 5 and kept the basket in front of the elephant. In anger and irritation, Maula Baksh hit the basket with such force that it flew far away and all the sweets were scattered. Had this basket hit anyone, the elephant would have been done for then and there.

Saunders exclaimed, 'This elephant is a rebel! Auction him.'

That very day, Maula Baksh was taken to Sadar Bazaar and the auction began. However, no buyer came forward. Finally, a one-eyed grocer, Bansi, who had a shop in Khari Baoli, made a bid of Rs 250, and the auction ended.

The fil-baan told Maula Baksh, 'We have spent our whole lives serving the emperor, but now our wretched destiny has something else in store. We will now have to go to the house of a grocer who sells turmeric.'

As soon as Maula Baksh heard these words, he fell straight down from his standing position with a huge thump and died.

That same day, Hamdam also left this world.

SubhanAllah! How rare it is to see such faithful friends lay down their lives for you. Such an animal is a thousand times better than cultured humans. May God grant the same ability to humans too.

Exemplary Conduct/Disposition

Hazrat Badshah was the emperor of a court,[38] resplendent with awe-inspiring majesty, magnificence, grandeur, dignity, pomp and show. He himself was so accomplished, blessed by the grace of God, possessing so many skills, yet his conduct was exemplary and he was extremely modest, humble, pious and clement.

Modesty and humility were so ingrained in the royal temperament that he called himself the equal of an insignificant servant employed in the court. The royal tongue never uttered a single word which reeked of majesty or authority. The smell of haughtiness and arrogance had not even passed by him. He met every person with the same attitude, not differentiating between high and low status.

Since he had been a prince, he had been extremely pious, devout and inclined towards prayer and asceticism. He safeguarded himself from sin. Even in the flush of youth, he had never been swayed by the pleasures of the flesh and had remained devout.

He was so eloquent that when he started speaking, one wanted to keep listening to him, and hundreds of stories, jokes, anecdotes and strange and unusual tales were always at the tip of his tongue.

He would often describe the days of his late father, Akbar Shah Bahadur, when he himself had been a prince.

It is a warning to us all—an indication that this transient world is faithless and time disloyal, betraying everyone. Time is not to be trusted; that is why an ancient and majestic sultanate is now seeing these days of decay. This kingdom once was witness to emperors of awe-inspiring majesty, whose territorial conquests were legendary, whose standards flew over the heads of the *Qaiser-e-Rum* (Qaiser of Turkey),[39] Khaqan of China and the Tsar of Russia. By the power of their sword, these men conquered territories from the west to the east and established the majesty of their kingdom in the world.

Amir Timur's conquests and victories were famous throughout the world. He brought down the biggest of rebels and all those who opposed him.

Look at the valour of Babur, who left his home and established his rule from the borders of Kabul to Hindustan.

With his sagacity and wisdom, Akbar Badshah's writ ran over the whole of India.

True to his name, Aurangzeb Alamgir was a conqueror of the world, and after spending fifty-two years in a cloth tent, he gained control over the whole of India.

This ancient kingdom was annihilated at the hands of faithless time, in such a manner that there remained nothing which could be entered into history.

> Therefore, take heed, you who can see
> (Quran: Surah Al-Hashr: 2)

Raja Ajit Singh

The anecdotes of Raja Ajit Singh are very interesting. Raja Sahib was the uncle of the Maharaja of Patiala. He came to live in Delhi in the days of his youth. He became so engrossed in the pleasures and luxuries of Delhi that he never returned to his native land.

His *jagir* yielded an income of Rs 1.5–2 lakh, and whenever money would come in from his lands, he would redo everything in his home and behave like a king. The decoration of his house, chandeliers, carriage, clothes and so on would all be bought anew. In any gathering where money was being showered on poets and artistes, he would give everything away, and thus, in a few days, would become a pauper again. He would keep a sackcloth and blanket to sleep on and would say, 'I am a mendicant.'

Within a year, he would be in debt to the tune of Rs 2 lakh. When the debt amount would cross Rs 4–5 lakh in three years, there would be complaints and public proclamations. When this news would reach Patiala, the *Rais-e-Patiala*, or the ruler, would send the money to prevent further notoriety and disrepute. Every year, they would send for his conveyance five or six priceless horses, one or two elephants, and gold and silver jewellery for the animals, which Ajit Singh would gift away to people. One year, he gifted a female elephant, along with her gold jewellery and silver howdah, and Rs 1000 for her food, to poet Momin Khan sahib, and some elephant jewellery to poet Dagh sahib.

Raja Sahib was extremely fond of two things: poetry and the flute. Dancers and singers were always present in his court, all year round.

The moment he heard of any poet, he would have him come over, and would shower him with praise and patronage.

When he had finished with his essential tasks in the morning (around 9), he would hold a court, where courtiers, friends and poets would appear. A dance soiree would be set up to entertain everyone till 10 p.m., and he and his friends would keep themselves busy in various ways.

He was fond of dressing and took care to appear very refined and attractive. He would ensure his companions were also attractively dressed.

His fondness for poetry and his generous nature ensured that no poet left his house empty-handed. Any poet who read a few verses to him would be rewarded with robes of honour and such things.

During the monsoon, there would be twenty to twenty-five tailors whose job was to stitch and provide the constant supply of bales of cloth with gold and silver lace edging. Raja Ajit Singh would buy Banarasi shawls and turbans and also distribute them to his friends. I have seen him distributing up to Rs 20,000 in one gathering alone.

The Raja would give away all his worldly possessions every year, starting with distributing cash and gold. After that, he would distribute clothes, followed by horses and then household articles. When everything had been given away, he would sit on a sackcloth.

I have never seen a person so generous and munificent anywhere else. This was the limit of generosity. It is not strange for a wealthy landowner to be so generous, but it is commendable in a person who has such little capital himself.

The Rais-e-Patiala once sent the Raja a horse worth Rs 3000. He wrote to him asking him to promise that he would not gift it away as it was priceless. He also warned the stable boys and servants that it would not auger well for them if the horse were given away. The servants tried to protect it as best they could. However, when the Raja was riding near the Khooni Darwaza[40] one day, a faqir came up to him and said, 'Raja Ajit Singh, I have heard a lot about you. I have come from very far. If you fulfil my wishes, then I will know that what I've heard is true.'

Raja Sahib asked, 'What do you want?'

'Give me this horse,' the faqir said.

Raja Sahib dismounted from the horse and handed the reins to the faqir, saying, 'I thought you would have a greater desire. This is nothing.'

The faqir took the horse and went away.

Raja Sahib reached his house on foot. When the servants heard that he had given the horse away, they searched all over the city and found the faqir. They asked him, 'Will you sell the horse?'

The faqir replied, 'Yes.'

The servants asked, 'What do you want for it?'

'Rs 1000,' the faqir said.

The servants immediately opened their purse and paid him Rs 1000, thus 'saving' the horse.

Six months later, Raja Ajit Singh gave the horse away to someone else.

Celebrations in the City of Delhi

In Delhi, Eid, Barawafat[41] and various other festivals such as the *urs*[42] of Hazrat Nizamuddin were celebrated on a grand scale. The population of the entire city would come out to celebrate.

However, the *Sair-e-Gul Faroshan* (procession of flower sellers) was a unique and colourful festival. I have never seen anything that beautiful, even though I have attended the fairs in Haridwar, Bateshwar and Mukhteshwar. Nothing can compare to the observance of etiquette of this fair. Villagers would come to the city to attend the festival, and there would be a wonderful, matchless connection between them and the Delhi residents on the occasion.

The procession itself was so pleasing to watch, and so entertaining, that though I have seen a thousand wildernesses, verdant lawns, mountains and places abounding in springs, I have never seen anything to compare with this.

The fair is held every year at the dargah of Hazrat Qutbuddin Bakhtiyar Kaki, situated at a distance of 7 kos to the south of Delhi, in Mehrauli. This district was the capital of the Delhi sultans and was also the seat of Raja Prithviraj. The foundations, forts, palaces, mosques and inscriptions of Mehrauli are still present.

There is also a mosque here, which was built by Qutbuddin, though it is in a dilapidated condition. This mosque was built from the remains of temples. It had only been half done when the *Badshah-e-Islam*[43] died, and was thus left incomplete.[44] *Kaar-e-duniya kas-e-tamam na karad* (The business of the world was left incomplete).

There is no doubt that had this mosque been completed, it would have had no peer on the face of this earth. But only one minar had been built; the other was left undone. It only reached up to one storey. The arches in the courtyard of the mosque were also left incomplete.

The minar's elevation is 80 yards. It has seven storeys. Two of the storeys are made of red sandstone, octagonal in shape with beautiful flutings with Quranic verses inscribed on them. The words are raised and written by such an accomplished calligrapher that one wants to pay respect to them by touching one's forehead to the stone. The arches and niches of the mosque have been decorated with the same calligraphy.

In the courtyard of this mosque is the broken temple, which is absolutely different and unique. It's just an arrangement of stones piled one on top of the other, but they have been put together in such a manner that they are intact even today.

The iron pillar which people call *killi*, or nail, has been installed in this courtyard. It has inscriptions in *khat-e-shastri*.[45]

The legend of this pillar is that Prithviraj was informed by a sage that Raja Basik, the serpent king, also the king of the earth, had entered the land of the palaces and forts of Prithviraj. If one drove a nail into his head, he would never be able to leave from the land, and Prithviraj's rule would last forever. Then he and his descendants would rule till doomsday.

The sage had knowledge of the sky and the earth, but he was ignorant of the ways of God.

Glory and power give rise to wondrous things in an instant,
Such things that are not in our imagination,
they make apparent!

Hence, two nails were obtained and preparations begun to install the pillar. Under the guidance of the sage, the nails were driven into the ground. However, even after the nails had been driven into the ground, the Raja remained doubtful of the sage's advice and ordered that the pillar be uprooted so that he could satisfy himself. The Brahmin priests did their best to dissuade him, but as the famous Hindi saying goes, '*Raj hat, tiriya hat*' (Obstinacy of a king and a woman—in the face of which all are helpless).[46]

The Raja didn't listen to any of them and remained adamant. He got the pillar dug up and found that, for a hand's span of its length, the nail was wet with blood. He ordered the pillar be installed in the same place, even though the sages said that it was no longer of any use, the serpent king would have moved on by then.

'He is the king of the underground. Do you think he is still sitting here? He must have moved quite a distance by now,' they said.

This killi is still present in the same place today.

The neighbourhood of Mehrauli starts at this place and extends all the way to the Jharna and Auliya Masjid,[47] where it ends.

Only the flat surfaces of Mehrauli's hilly areas are inhabited, even though the hills are not too high.

To the north-east of the incomplete mosque is a red sandstone enclosure, which is the tomb of Badshah Alauddin. Ahead of the mosque is the blessed dargah of Hazrat Qutbuddin Bakhtiyar Kaki. The platform of the shrine is a 4x4-yard square with a height of less than a hand's span. There is also a boundary wall.

There are marks of mud baskets and various other unique things still intact on the shrine. It is due to the blessings and presence of the Hazrat that, in spite of so many seasons of rain, these marks have not been obliterated. In his final will to his disciples, made just before his passing away from this world, Hazrat had ordered that his grave be of mud and remain open to the skies. Hence, no dome or structure has been built over it.

The emperor's palace is near the dargah, and towards the west are the houses of the nobles, the shops and the houses of the local populace and caravanserais. There are mansions, houses and shops on both sides, all the way up to the *jharna*. To the south and west of the residential area is a magnificent reservoir with a concrete platform in the middle, covered with a dome. The platform is open from all sides. This reservoir is famous as *Hauz-e-Shamsi*, and was built by Badshah Shamsuddin Altamash.

According to a famous legend, the Prophet (peace be upon him) once appeared in a dream of Badshah Shamsuddin Altamash, riding a horse, in that very place.

He said, 'Shamsuddin, build a hauz here.'

When the Badshah woke and went to this spot, he saw the hoof prints of a horse. He immediately gave orders for the platform and a pavilion to be constructed there and dug the tank around them.

The rainwater from the mountains flows into the hauz and keeps it full. To the east, there is an embankment upon which are mansions, buildings and shops. Near the shops, there is a hollow, and to the south of the hauz is the famous *Amriyo'n ka Andheri Bagh*, or the mango orchard.

There is another hollow at the end of the bazaar. Its elevation is about 10 yards. It is here that the jharna has been built.

The jharna is below the road that runs past the hauz. A wall has been built where the water falls into the jharna.

Joined to it is a small hall of red sandstone with steps leading up to it on both sides. At the front of the hall is a big tank with a depth greater than a man's height.

The courtyard of the jharna is a broad platform, and a water channel comes out of the tank. There are waterfalls flowing out of the canal, falling down from the platform. In front of the platform, there is a sloping stone which was earlier part of a hill. There is a staircase next to it. Men climb up this hill and have fun sliding down it. This hill is called *phisalna pathhar*, or the sliding stone. The stone is so slippery that everyone slides down.

On both sides of the jharna's hall, to the north and south, there are two halls with arches. There are shady mango trees on the sides of these buildings.

The water from the hauz keeps the jharna's tank overflowing. From here the water flows as a chute into the canal and presents an attractive picture.

There is a wonderful atmosphere during the Sair-e-Gul Faroshan, which is well worth seeing. Thousands of people dive into the tank from the top of the hall and swim out. They keep repeating this action. There is usually a continuous stream of people diving in. There are some body builders who jump in holding as many as five people! Thousands slide down the sliding stone.

The flower sellers keep sitting in the jharna buildings and make fans from the flowers, called *pankha*s. There is a huge tumult here, and the noise is deafening. It's difficult to find space to walk.

The fair is held in the month of *sawan*, or the monsoons. The pankha is offered to the dargah and the fair goes on for four days. The city's population, Hindu and Muslim, rich and poor, high and lowly, all leave the city (Shahjahanabad) and just a shop or two may be left open. All the sweetmeat sellers, bread makers and kabab sellers come and set up shop in the area around the dargah.

There is a huge crowd around the sweet shops, which are set up in a square area of 16 yards with big *kadhai*s, or woks, full of ghee heating on the fire, in which sweet and savoury snacks are prepared. Vendors sell their wares along the roads leading to the market.

The rent for houses at this time goes up thousand-fold, and many tents and camps are set up in various places. The city's population is entertained day and night by dancing, singing and other festivities that take place here. Swings are put up in Andheri Bagh and everyone comes and enjoys him or herself. There are songs of *malhar* (a raga associated with rain) in the air, the hills and forests are green and there are clouds in the sky. There is a light drizzle, and it's an unforgettable experience.

The pankha procession starts at 2 p.m. from the jharna, with the pankhas belonging to the general people and craftsmen leading the procession. The pankhas of the flower sellers bring up the rear. The crowd is unbelievable and if someone falls down, he or she will be dragged for quite a distance. In front of each fan, there is a *roshan chowki* (a musical instrument). The bearers keep stopping at short intervals, making slow progress. The *nafiri-wala*s sing malhar in very sweet voices, so every person gets engrossed in the music and forgets him or herself and keeps cheering and waving.

Thousands of rupees are showered from the houses and mansions along the road. The nafiri-wala is able to earn enough at this time for the whole year. They stand and sing below every room and it's only at 9 p.m. that the pankha reaches the dargah. The nafiri-walas then stop and blow the trumpet under the emperor's palace, and gold coins, purses and money rain down from the windows. After that, they take the pankha and offer it at the dargah.

The next day, the people are still in the area and usually busy with the entertainment offered by the fair, the jharna and in buying and selling.

A new market is set up in front of the dargah gate, where every kind of ware, especially simple gold and silver jewellery, is sold.

There are many small shops set up by vendors, and goods worth lakhs are sold and bought. For a few days, not a single man can be seen in the Shahjahanabad markets, and the ladies who observe purdah come out to enjoy the area and the visit Jama Masjid.

On Saturday, the populace finally takes its leave from Khwaja Sahib (dargah of Hazrat Nizamuddin) and returns home. The distance of 7 kos is lined by those returning. There are shops set up on the sides of the road, with toy sellers selling different varieties of toys. Those returning buy different items for the family members they left behind at home.

Hazrat Badshah stayed in this place for four full months during the monsoon.

How Mughal Emperors Cherished Their Subjects

This order also ended with the house of Timurids. The Mughals valued their subjects, and this *raiyyat navazi* has no parallel. It cannot be found in any other kingdom in history. The subjects of the Mughal emperors were considered their progeny.

Once, some Hindus, along with officers of the British government, hatched a plot to throw all the butchers slaughtering cows out of the city. The British government gave orders stating that these butchers should take their shops out of the city. They had all the shops within the city closed.

When the butchers realized that they had no choice but to obey and lose their means of livelihood, they banded together, took their wives, children and possessions, and came and camped on the riverbank under the jharokha. From there, they appealed to the king, asking 'How can we leave our city and go away?'

The cherisher of subjects, the emperor, heard their petition and gave the order that his tent be pitched alongside theirs on the riverbank.

'Whatever is the state of my subjects is my state,' he said.

As per the decree of their emperor, the servants immediately took the imperial paraphernalia and installed it on the bank of the river.

As soon as the British Resident heard the news, he came running to the emperor and respectfully asked, 'Huzoor, what are you doing? All the people of the city will come and stand here with you.'

Badshah Salamat replied, 'I am wherever my subjects are. My subjects are my children and I can't be separated from them. Has flesh ever been separated from the fingernail? Today, the butchers have been given orders to leave the city; tomorrow, it will be some other community; the day after, it will be another one, and these orders will continue. Slowly, the entire city will be emptied. If the intention of the British government is to empty the city, then tell me so in plain words. I will take all my people and go and live in Khwaja Sahib. Since you have control over the city (Shahjahanabad), you can do whatever you will.'

The Resident was taken aback. 'Huzoor, don't even think of such an action. I will redress the complaints of these people immediately and settle them in the city. Huzoor, please have your camp removed from here.'

The Resident gave orders for the butchers to go back to their houses and ply their trade within the city as before. The tent of the emperor was removed.

At another instance, the British government gave orders to the herdsmen to take their family and cattle and leave the city. They were told to go and settle outside the city. There was tumult in the city and once again, the herdsmen/milkmen brought their families and cattle and came and camped on the riverbank.

Once again, the emperor, the *Raiyyat Panah*, was so distraught by the cries of the children and the distress of the cattle that he gave orders for his tent to be pitched alongside theirs so that he could share their sorrow. Once again, the Resident came and pleaded with the emperor, and gave orders revoking the previous ones so that the herdsmen could go back to their quarters in the city.

This time, the emperor told the Resident, 'Look, do not exile my subjects from their houses in my presence. After me, you will be in control and can devastate the city.'

That was what was done.

From Kabuli Darwaza to the Qila, from Dariba to the Fort, from Jama Masjid to the Dilli Darwaza, from Kucha Bulaqi Begum to Khanum ka Bazaar, from Khan Dauran Khan's *haveli* to Daryaganj, thousands of houses were razed and destroyed. Delhi was turned into a desolate land that looked like a flat platform.[48]

3

The Start of Ramzan before the Mutiny

The revolution of the world showed us such sorcery
That whenever we bring speech to our tongue, we tell a
new tale

Uff! The heat is unbearable and we are all getting roasted. May God save us from the heat of the sun! It seems that the sky is raining fire and the sun is a ball of fire which has descended on the earth.

Tongues are hanging out with thirst, and throats feel as though there are thorns in them. The earth feels as though it has become a piece of hell.

O Lord, protect us from the punishment of the fire
(Quran: Surah Al-Baqarah: 201)

It is difficult to even utter a word. From 9 a.m., water starts being sprinkled on the cooling vetiver screens, and fans are pulled, but we are still drenched in perspiration.

Every day is doomsday, and it is difficult to get through
it. It seems as though life were ebbing out. The humidity of
the night!

Oh Allah! Protect us from all the afflictions of this
world[49]

Despite the water constantly being sprinkled on the ground,
fans being pulled by coolies, beds being wetted, we keep
tossing and turning the whole night till morn and sleep seems
far away.

To hell with such days and nights!

Three days of the month of *jeth*[50] have passed in peace,
and these fifteen rozas can be imagined to be fifteen years.

With God's help, we have been able to reach the
evening of the sixteenth day of Ramzan. It is 2 a.m., and
preparations are on for the next stage. There is a slight
coolness in the breeze. As morning approaches, the
night becomes pleasant. Those fasting are waking up for
the morning *sehri* (the meal taken before sunrise during
Ramzan), and are busy eating.

This is the best part of the day, when the drums of
Jama Masjid are rolling to wake people up for sehri. They
are waking up those who are fast asleep and dreaming. The
sentries are calling out to people to wake up. The moon of
the sixteenth night is about to disappear from the sky, and
the hectic preparations going on in the houses of those who
are fasting make it seem as though no one went to sleep.
The time approaches for people to declare their intent to
fast during the day and stop eating and drinking from that
moment till sunset. They just have time to rest for a few

moments. They are now busy chewing the paan tucked away in their cheeks and enjoying its taste. Some young men are busy enjoying their huqqa, their eyes full of sleep, nodding drowsily in their places.

The sun is changing colour and signs of the morning are appearing. The morning star has appeared, though the moonlight is still showing off. But now it is dissembling in preparation to unite with the morning.

Everyone is happily engrossed in reciting praises of Allah and moving rosary beads in prayer when suddenly the sound of a cannon is heard.

For three minutes, there is silence. All the people quickly spit out their paan and rinse their mouths, brush their teeth and read the prayer for the start of the fast.

After wishing everyone Ramzan Mubarak, we go to lie down in our beds. No one knows that the morning will bring devastation akin to doomsday.

Don't leave today's task for tomorrow, for who knows
what tomorrow has in store
What is the hope of morn for someone who is
at death's door

Now the whiteness is spreading in the sky from the east. The sun is becoming brighter while the moon is fading out and looks like an unpolished tray of brass. The light from the chandeliers is twinkling and the lamp of morning is flickering like a sick man. The gates of *Shahr Panah* are guarding the city like vigilant eyes. But the dawn is beautiful—with the call of *azaan* (call to prayer) coming from the mosques, the bells calling from the temples and the soft, enticing sounds of

Raga Bhairavi being played from the naqqarkhana, all combining to make the heart restless.

The cool breeze of the early morn acts as a lullaby for those who are awake. The gusts of wind blowing from Begum Bagh are getting entangled with the smells of flowers, herbs and grass and emitting sweet fragrance. The sentries and those who stayed awake all night are now sleeping the sleep of the dead on the terraces of the shops.

> When at daybreak the wolf lets out a howl
> From their sleep are awoken the guard and his dog
> And the rooster that was asleep now flaps its wings
> The town crier beats upon the leather drum

From the Lahori Darwaza to the Nigambodh Ghat, the waves of the river are enhancing its beauty. Chandni Chowk is twinkling like the Milky Way galaxy, thousands of pieces of the moon (people) moving around like planets in the sky. Everyone seems to be a daredevil, each better than the next. It seems as if 100 fairies from fairyland, with chiselled features, moon-like faces, slim and delicate figures, black eyes, black hair, slim-waisted like the cheetah, doe-eyed, covered with gold and silver from top to toe, are strolling in Chandni Chowk. One can see the glow of their bodies through the elegant and graceful double dupatta of silver work (*kaamdani*).

> What a delicate body, which is envied even by the soul
> What a colour of the body that vestments cannot match

Mauve and grey lehengas, their broad borders stamped with designs, fingers adorned with delicate gold rings and hands decorated with henna.

Why do they need the fingertip naked
They may dip it in any stranger's blood
This city which was a bouquet of beautiful people
This city which was the foundation of many a fresh
sapling
This city which was a gathering of the moon-like beauties
This city which was a quarter of the possessors of charm
This is the very ground that would throw up gold
This is the very dust wherefrom we find elixir.

The Jamuna has become a garden with so many graceful and beautiful girls, as if there's one more luminous river within it. The moon is swinging in the waves of the river and the stars of the sky are visible in the water. The waves of the river are rushing forward as if to become one with the shore. The bubbles in the water are eyes looking at every face, at the thousands of women dressed in delicate saris plunging in the water up to their waist, and the young girls splashing water on each other.

It is amusing, the makeup of youth
Coquetry is a jewel for this age

Some fairy-like girls are drying their hair after their bath in the Jamuna. Someone is drying her wet sari after having draped a dry one.

Handfuls of coral and pearls rain down from clouds
The moon emerges from the pocket of the tearful night

A rotund priest with a *choti* on his head, wearing a loincloth, with his paunch hanging out, is sitting cross-legged there.

With one hand he is rubbing sandalwood on a small stone. On one side is the idol of Mahadev, and next to it is an idol of Parvati and a marble bull. Some shells, conches and items for puja are kept near the priest. Mahadev is covered with milk and water and some flower petals are scattered around. On one side, coins are being collected, and on the other side, there is a heap of grain which is growing higher. The beautiful ladies who have just finished their baths wear their clothes and come to pay their respects to the priest, and he in turn blesses them. They leave after he puts a sandalwood paste *tika* on their foreheads with one of the rings on his fingers, and one leaf of tulsi in their mouths.

The Start of the Mutiny in Meerut

As the day broke the alarm sounded and the rooster crowed
And in every garden the birds chirped away their lovely songs
And from the mosque and the monastery sounds of the
benedictions emerged
And the Brahmins went to the temple to invoke the Lord
'Hari, Hari!'

Birds with sweet voices are chirping praises of God on the treetops. The parterre gardens are so full of the chirping that one can't hear oneself speak. The birds are all swaying as if in a state of ecstasy induced by their thoughts of God—it is a strange atmosphere. The redness of dawn is spreading and the moon is disappearing from the horizon while the colour blue unfurls itself across the sky.

The Ganga Jamuni (gold and silver) rays of the sun are falling on the domes and pinnacles of the Qila-e-Moalla, showing off their bright gold. The golden *burj* of the Baithak is gleaming in the sun. This is Saman Burj, the exclusive sitting room of the Timurid emperor. It has a roof, and steps leading down from it. From the Diwan-e-Khaas, a pathway leads down to the river which gives way to a track of concrete, or *patri*. Over there is an orchard, called *Pai'n Bagh* Diwan-e-Khaas. Its width is approximately 20–25 yards and it is 4–5 yards above the river.

From the east, the Saman Burj looks like a sun itself when the sun is rising. This burj is octagonal in shape and quite spacious from inside. That's why it is called Musamman Burj, popularly known as Saman Burj. Badshah Shah Jahan would sit in this jharokha after the dawn prayers and give darshan in this place—that tradition continues till today. On its northern, southern and eastern sides are beautiful, elegant windows which are called jharokhas. Below this, on the right is a toll gate, and Mir Fateh Ali Darogha[51] has his residence behind it. Next to it is another apartment in which Hamid Khan Rampuri *Jamadar Khaas Biradaran* (head of the royal bodyguards) lives, while next to it is a small thatched roof in which Siddi Qamar, jamadar of the *Habshi* (Abyssinian troops) resides. This patri runs along the length of the fort. There are houses of the sentries and guards along it.

Hazrat Zill-e-Subhani Khalifah ur Rahmani[52] Abu Zafar Sirajuddin Mohammad Bahadur Shah II had finished his morning prayers and was sitting in the jharokha. His elephant was being readied for him. A golden howdah, with beautifully decorated cushions and pillows and covered in Kashani velvet, stood in the courtyard of the tasbihkhana. There was a broad curtain on the deorhi,[53] and a few *khwaja-sara*, some of the emperor's special soldiers and a few notable nobles were standing in the courtyard of the tasbihkhana. They were awaiting the arrival of Huzoor. Below the tasbihkhana terrace were fifty to sixty porters in red uniform and red turbans, ready for duty.

Below the Saman Burj, there were some 200 special forces in grey robes and turbans, their swords at their sides. On one side, thirty young Abyssinians in red brocade uniforms and red turbans were waiting respectfully with folded hands, while below the patri, a platoon of cavalrymen stood ready.

Mir Fateh Ali, Hamid Khan and Siddi Qamar were in armour themselves. Everyone was looking at the jharokha when suddenly a shout came from the top. Mir Fateh Ali moved in front with folded hands, a forefinger pointed towards the bridge over the river. When the crowd's gaze was turned in that direction, they saw that across the river, where Mir Bahri's toll gate was situated, a fire was raging and sparks were flying into the sky. The riverside was full of smoke, ashes and dust. Mir Fateh Ali ordered the *risaldar*: 'Send the riders out immediately and find out what where this smoke is coming from.'

Two horsemen left the platoon, their horses flying forward. They had just about reached the bridge of boats[54] under Salimgarh when they saw a huge crowd comprised of boatmen and the sentries of the bridge running towards them.

'Is everything all right?' one rider asked. 'What has happened that you are all running in such a distracted state, as though bereft of your senses?'

An attendant spoke up. 'Oh sir, it is not good news! The army has come down and they have murdered Mir Bahri and set the toll gate on fire! They have looted the strongbox! We ran away to save our lives.'

As soon as the royal rider heard this, he turned his horse around and returned to his post. He informed his officer, 'Some enemy has entered Dilli. His army is hell-bent on assault and plunder. They have set the toll gate on fire and killed Mir Bahri.'

From his portico in the Saman Burj, the emperor gave orders to Mir Fateh Ali and Hamid Khan. 'Take your armies and destroy the bridge. Pull back the boats; don't let the army come down. Lock the city gates and send out riders to bring *Bade Sahib*.[55] All royal employees and courtiers are ordered to present themselves immediately in the royal court. The *kotwal* should be told that the gates must be guarded, and that he should himself man the Calcutta Darwaza. Tell the *qiledar* to ensure the safety of the qila. Send off riders and give commands to secure the Rajghat Darwaza.'

The emperor's commands were carried out immediately. Riders were sent off in every direction, but the group who had been sent to destroy the bridge were unsuccessful in their mission. They were still under Salimgarh when they saw sawars coming towards them from the bridge of boats, like the angel of death, cutting off their access. They returned to the deorhi of the jharokha before the baghi sawar[56] could reach, and entering the Chatta Chowk, they locked the door and presented themselves in the Diwan-e-Khaas and the tasbihkhana.

Hazrat Qadr-e-Qudrat Zil-ul-laahu Badshah Raiyyat Panah[57] showed great courage and presence of mind, staying unruffled and sitting calmly as was his norm. He didn't move an inch. But a tumult rose among the women of the harem and the camps. The emperor himself had to calm and pacify everyone else.

The baghi sawar[58] came down from the bridge of boats and riding below Salimgarh, reached the *zer-e-jharokha*. All the men rushed to the Calcutta Darwaza, calling out to the emperor. They ordered the sentries posted there to lock up the gate.

Meanwhile, the sentries of the Nigambodh Darwaza had received the news. Those who had gone there for ritual bathing ran and somehow entered the city, and that Gate was also locked. In this interval, Mehboob Ali Khan khwaja-sara and Hakim Ahsanullah Khan presented themselves before the emperor. Huzoor Anwar had just called them when these ungrateful sawar came like a pestilence from the sky and gathered at the zer-e-jharokha and took position there. As per protocol, they paid their respects by bending down in salaam. Huzoor ordered Hakim Ahsanullah Khan to find out who the rebels were and where they had come from, whose employees they were and finally, why they had come to Delhi.

Hakim Ahsanullah Khan went into the tasbihkhana and started questioning them. A few rebel officers dismounted and stood on the track. With folded hands, they started pleading, looking towards the zer-e-jharokha.

The Speech of the Rebel Soldiers

'Huzoor Jahanpanah! May you have a long life! You are the emperor of faith and the world, and God Almighty has given you suzerainty over twenty-two provinces. The whole of India is under you and subservient to you. The people of Hindustan are counted as your subjects. This is what has been announced in proclamations till today—*Khilqat Khuda ki, Mulk Badshah ka, Hukm Company ka* (The Lord's creation, the emperor's country, the company's command).

'But now, the British have been empowered to rule us on your orders. So we have come to you as petitioners, hopeful of justice.

'We are employees of the British. We have helped establish British rule from Calcutta to Kabul by sacrificing our lives, since they did not bring an army with them from England. All their conquests are due to the Indian army. We can present our medals and badges as witness.

'And now that the British have established their rule over every part of Hindustan and there is no one left to accept their suzerainty, there is a discordant note in the company's intentions. They want to destroy our faith and religion and convert the whole of Hindustan to Christianity. They want this conversion to start with the army. Therefore, after much counsel, they invented a new type of rifle that uses cartridges which have to be bitten off with the teeth. These are enclosed in the cartilage of animals, but we don't know which animal's cartilage has been used. The rifles were given to us and we were ordered to use them as directed. We, Hindus and Muslims alike, refused to obey this order and told them that under no circumstance would we do it, whether they kept us in employment or fired us. The Hindus suspected that the casing was made of cow's cartilage and the Muslims thought it to be of the pig. The Hindus said that most of them are Brahmin, Kshatriya or upper-caste people and they would not touch any animal flesh to their lips. The Muslims said that they wouldn't let any meat, except that which is *halal*, touch their lips. Since we did not know whether the meat was halal or *haram*, we could not use the cartridges.

'We will not obey the British orders. At this refusal, the sarkar felt that the army had flouted a direct command, and if they didn't punish us severely, the government would be considered weak.

'This matter has become prolonged and has been going on for four months. The authorities are now setting up committees, but in the cantonments of the infantry and cavalry there are letters being exchanged amongst us saying that the entire army should refuse and relinquish their duties, and if there is too much oppression, on a fixed day we should revolt all over Hindustan. Let us see if they can do anything then! Now the time for revolt has come and the entire army has risen and refused to obey orders.

'The seed of the revolt was sown when the British committee decided that the suppression of this rebellion should start at Meerut as it is a central place and there is a huge and old cantonment there. Once those soldiers bit the cartridge, no other soldier would dare to refuse, they thought. They decided to hold a parade on a specific date and time. The artillery was set up and the Third Cavalry was called and made to stand on the parade ground. The officers of the squadron were given rifles and cartridges and told to bite them and load the rifles.

'The officers expressed their inability to do the same. "Your Lordships, please excuse us, we cannot give up our faith even if the government were to blow us up with cannons," they said.

'Even then, they were ordered once again to bite the cartridges. Then, as per design, everyone declined once more. Yet again the orders were given and met with the same refusal.

'The next order was to drop our weapons.

'We dropped their weapons and were told, "Dismount from your horses."

'We dismounted, and were told, "All the officers must stand separately from the soldiers."

'There were eighty-four officers who stood away from their squadrons. Then orders were given, "Handcuff them."

We donned their handcuffs happily, presenting no quarrel. Then the order came, "You are being punished for rebellion. You will all go to the jailhouse." We saluted the commanders and went off to the jailhouse.'

> The revolving sky of destiny is a fraudster and cheat
> It creates many excuses for the oppression of men

'When we entered the jailhouse, a commotion rose up in the cantonment. There were conspiracies being hatched in every house with group discussions and debates everywhere, especially amongst the womenfolk who have less power of reasoning and don't think of long-term consequences. There were many women whose inheritance had been confiscated,[59] and they fanned the flames of mutiny with their taunts and sarcastic remarks. Their words were like oil in the fire of rebellion.

'"You are men and you claim to be soldiers," they said, "yet you are cowards, shameless and disreputable. We women are better than you. Aren't you ashamed that you stood and watched helplessly while your officers were handcuffed and you could do nothing? Here, take these bangles and wear them and give your weapons to us. We will free the officers and bring them back."

'These fiery words created an even greater anguish in the soldiers' hearts and the entire army was energized with the flame of heroism, bravery and manliness, ready to kill or be killed. After much discussion, it was decided that in the evening they would break into the jailhouse and free the officers.

'Thus, in the evening, the soldiers of the infantry and cavalry together attacked the jailhouse and freed the eighty-four officers who had been imprisoned. They cut the handcuffs and shackles of the officers and also freed all the thieves, convicts, dacoits, murderers and thugs who had been imprisoned in the jail. There was tumult in the city and fighting and killing began. The government instructed their officers to be armed and on alert at all times and brought out the cannons, and now there was cannon fire in every direction. But from the side of the Indian soldiers, a stream of gunfire had also begun.

'That whole night, we fought with the *gora*, and in the morning we left for Dilli. We covered a distance of 30 kos and have now reached the city.

'Badshah Salamat, please keep your hand on our heads and give us justice. *Hum deen par bigad kar aaye hain.* (Our faith has been corrupted.)'

The Badshah Replies

> Fate cannot be erased by human plans
> And our ill fortune cannot be altered

'*Suno bhai* (listen to me),' the emperor began. 'Who calls me Badshah? I am but a mendicant who is somehow living a Sufi's life in the fort with my progeny. The empire went away with the emperors. My ancestors were emperors, those who had Hindustan under their control. But the monarchy left my house 100 years ago.

'Those who were employees of my ancestors are now, thanks to their largesse and patronage, independent masters themselves. My house became indigent, starting from when my ancestor Hazrat Shah Alam Badshah Ghazi was imprisoned and blinded by the ingrate Abdul Qadir. Then the Marathas were called and they punished him for his wicked deed and freed Hazrat Badshah from imprisonment. For a few years, the Marathas ruled on behalf of the emperor, but they couldn't even make provision for the proper running of his household. My helpless grandfather then turned towards the kingdom of Britain. He called on the British and put them in charge of his house, entrusted Hindustan to them. They arranged for royal expenditure as desired by the emperor and brought peace to the country. From that day to this, we have been living in comfort and luxury, we have no worries or problems and we lead comfortable lives. We have nothing to do with fighting. The British make arrangements to prevent and quell any fighting themselves.

'I am a recluse. Why have you come to trouble me now? I have no treasure that I can use to pay your salary. I have no army that can help you. I have no estate from which I can collect revenue and employ you. I can do nothing. Don't entertain any hopes of help from me. It's between you and the British. Yes, there is one thing in my power. It may be possible for me to broker peace between both parties. You can wait here. I have summoned the Resident Sahib.[60] He is about to reach. Let me talk to him and see what he knows about the troubles, and God willing, I will sort out your differences.'

This discussion was still going on when Frazer Sahib, the Resident, entered with the qiledar.[62] The khwaja-sara paid respects with the kornish salaam. An order came from within, telling both the officers to present themselves in the palace. And so the Resident Bahadur, Qiledar Sahib, Hakim Ahsanullah Khan and Mehboob Ali Khan entered the royal quarters into the presence of the emperor.

The emperor asked, 'What is all this trouble that has erupted? How has a religious fight reared its head? This is a case of faith and principles. Religious persecution and bigotry is a very bad thing. Many kingdoms have been destroyed by it, and innumerable people have been killed by it. It's essential that this be sorted out immediately.

'God forbid that the sedition and riots spread all over the country and innumerable people are killed and there is a loss in revenue. The prevailing peace and prosperity will suffer. As far as possible, we should work with a cool mind and use a gentle approach. These people are illiterate. One should cajole them and insist that they desist from this. I am surprised that you didn't know of this problem already.'

The Resident spoke, 'Huzoor, your slave received a letter at eleven in the night. But because I was very sleepy at that time, I didn't pay heed to it, thinking it to be an ordinary letter. I put it in my pocket and went back to sleep. When your royal riders reached me this morning, I read the letter and learned of the state of affairs.

'Huzoor, don't worry, set your mind at ease. These are rioters. What can they do? By your auspices, all will be sorted out soon. Your slave will just go out and ask them to desist. If God wishes, this quarrel will not be prolonged.'

Saying this, the Resident came out of the palace and into the courtyard of the tasbihkhana near the enclosure where all the courtiers were standing in rows facing the darbar. Hakim Ahsanullah Khan's son and the qiledar were also standing there.

The Resident Faces the Rebels

'*Kyun* [why] *baba log?*[62] What is this seditious mischief that you have created?' the Resident asked. 'We have trained you with great care. We were confident that if ever Russia were to advance towards the borders of Hindustan we would destroy them, and if Iran ever put a foot forward we would annihilate them. If any kingdom were to ever threaten Hindustan, we would give a fitting answer. But we never thought that our army would be ready to stand against us. Kyun baba log? Does loyalty mean that today you are ready to fight us? Have we spent crores of money to train you for this moment?'

The sawaraan-e-fauj baghiya[63] spoke, 'Huzoor, you are right, there is no doubt that the government has nourished and sustained us in this manner. We will never forget the favours done for us by the *sarkar*, but till today, we have never been disloyal to you. Wherever we were sent by the sarkar, we jumped into fire or water with closed eyes. We never cared for our lives; we never stepped back when we had to give up our lives.

'It is we who marched to Kabul. We even conquered Lahore for you. We fought for you from Calcutta to Kabul, gave you our lives, had our heads cut and proved our loyalty. Now when the sarkar has gained control of all of Hindustan, you are eyeing our faith and principles. You want to convert us to Christianity. We were asked to bite the cartridge. How can we give up our faith? We are ready to give up our lives, but we will not give up our religion. Now the sarkar can do what they want with us. We are ready to die and we thought of ourselves as dead when we freed the officers after breaking into the jailhouse.'

The Resident said, '*Suno, suno, Baba log!* Please give up this line of thought and stop killing us, and then no one will kill you. I am now your mediator and give you guarantee, with God as my witness. I vow in the name of God that we will not betray you and will give you justice, and punish those who have created this trouble. They will be put straight. Just give up this murder and mayhem and stop all this looting.'

'The emperor orders you to do the same. Your faith has been harmed, and we will help you amend that. The emperor himself will be your mediator.'

The sawar addressing the Resident said, 'O protector of the poor! We do not trust the word of the government. It has often betrayed us to conquer and annex. What if we agree to all the conditions and yet the sarkar hangs us tomorrow? In such a case we would rather die by the sword than be hanged by a low-caste man.'

The Resident immediately reassured them, 'No, no, please don't think like this! I swear on the Bible that we will never betray you and the emperor also says the same.'

Many of the wise sawars said, 'Yes, the Sahib Resident Bahadur is telling the truth. We should agree to their conditions.'

However, some ignorant, unwise sawar who had got carried away by their murdering and looting said, 'We have no faith in the promises of the angrez. They go back on their word. They are Christians.'

Arguments began between these two groups as half wanted to obey the Resident ('After all,' they said, 'they are the present rulers and the owners of Delhi. They won't trick us.') and the rest were adamant that they would not acquiesce under any condition.

Finally, one unworthy sepoy said, 'Wait, I will settle it here and now,' and he took out his gun and fired at the Resident. But the Resident's time hadn't come and the bullet went past, between the Resident and Hakim Ahsanullah Khan, and lodged itself in a pillar of the tasbihkhana. A piece of marble fell. You can see that chipped pillar standing there even today.

Hakim Ahsanullah Khan pulled the Resident behind himself and said, 'These people will not listen to us so easily.

We have done our duty by talking to them. Now we should think of other ways to allay this.'

The Resident Organizes His Forces

The Resident sought permission to enter the palace, and once inside, told the emperor, 'I have fulfilled my duty by trying to appeal to them but these people are not willing to obey me. They have come determined to die. I will go and make arrangements for them. They will be blown away. The 1800 *najib* of the Kotwali platoon are enough to dispose of them.'

Badshah Salamat said, 'All right. Take my men who are here with you for your security.'

The Resident smiled and said, 'These men are here to see to the security of the court. Let them stay here to keep the deorhi safe. Your Honour's eminence is enough for me. Don't worry. All arrangements will be made.'

Sahib Resident Bahadur left the emperor's palace along with the qiledar, went out through the Lal Purdah, and via the Bakshigiri chowk, came to the screen door. From there he crossed the Diwan-e-Aam, went through the naqqarkhana and got into his carriage. Orders were given for the gate to be shut and for the soldiers posted at Ajmeri Gate to stay alert.

'Be ready with fully loaded rifles, patrol the walls, and if the rebels come up to the gate, blow them up. Stock the armoury with cartridges. We are going to secure the Calcutta Darwaza. Stay alert. Keep the gate of the barbican closed, and only the wicket gate[64] should be left open.'

After giving these orders, the Resident and the qiledar went out of the gate and reached the Calcutta Darwaza. They found it secured and locked, with the kotwal, *thanedar* and jamadar present along with policemen. On the parapet of Shahr Panah, from the Calcutta Gate to the Moat Darwaza, the najib were standing to order. Near the Nigambodh Darwaza and Calcutta Darwaza, a loaded cannon was installed on the small burj of Shahr Panah and pointed towards the bridge. It was estimated that the rebel forces would have to come from this direction as they would come via the Jamuna. The entire najib force was standing there, preparing to keep them from the city.

Arrangements were being made, everything was in order, the force was battle-ready, but no one knew what fate had in store for them.

Five Sawars

The Resident Bahadur left to head towards the Qila, and fate threw a fresh set of dice. The rebel horsemen did not go to the Calcutta Darwaza and instead turned towards the Rajghat Darwaza. I have heard a couple of stories about what happened there.

Some say that the darwaza was closed and manned by the najib. A number of people were waiting there for the gate to open so that they could complete their ritual morning bath in the Jamuna and then eat. They were arguing with the soldiers and demanding that they open it for this purpose.

The gatekeepers said that it could not be opened without orders from the sarkar. Finally, the people waiting to bathe flared up and started pelting stones at the gate and thus finally managed to open it.

Or maybe the gate was already open? This possibility seems faint since the gates of the city were all locked up, and the Calcutta Gate was so heavily guarded. So how could this one be open?

I cannot say for sure how this gate was opened.

To make it brief, the baghi sawar entered the city from the Rajghat Darwaza. The road from the gate ran along the ditch, which runs down the width of Daryaganj and ends in front of Sunehri Masjid. Below the Sunehri Masjid is a crossroad from which one road goes to Lal Diggi from below the Lal Qila, one road goes to the bazaar, and it is from here that the ground below the Qila starts. There are two roads to the south that go towards the Dilli Darwaza. From the canal, another road goes towards the south-east to Daryaganj. At the top of this road is the house of the Padri Sahib. This padri was a Hindu who had converted to Christianity. He was the first victim of the riot.

The sawar came and stood on the veranda of his bungalow.

Sawar: 'Who are you?'

Padri Sahib: 'Padri.'

Sawar: 'Muslim or Hindu?'

Padri Sahib: 'Christian.'

As soon as he said this, one of the sawars pressed the trigger and as the sound of the shot rang through the veranda, the priest's soul left for its eternal abode. Padri Sahib fell down in a heap on the veranda and a chain of destruction was set loose. The sawar set fire to the bungalow and moved ahead.

They reached the Lal Diggi and entered the hospital where they interrogated the doctor.

Dr Chiman Lal was a *kayastha* by birth, but a while ago, he and Master Ram Chandra had converted to Christianity. The sawars entered the hospital as angels of death for Dr Chiman Lal. They started questioning him.

'Which religion do you follow?'

'That of Jesus Christ,' Dr Chiman Lal said.

The sawar dispatched him to join the priest with one bullet. They then vandalized the hospital and destroyed it completely.

The news of the death of these two eminent personalities spread through the city like wildfire. All the undesirable elements of the city—rascals, thieves, pickpockets, shoplifters, pilferers, impounders, swindlers and embezzlers who were always on the lookout for such opportunities—came out of their houses and joined the rebels in large numbers. Now for every sawar there were at least fifty of these undesirable elements running alongside them.

While the sawars tyrannized, these rascals indulged in loot and theft and left a trail of destruction behind. They were running away with whatever they could lay their hands on all across the city till the Lahori Darwaza. Once they reached this point, the rebels inquired, 'Where are the Englishmen?'

Someone said that all the Englishmen, the thanedar and *kotwal-e-najibaa'n* were gathered at the Calcutta Darwaza.

On hearing this, five sawars turned their horses towards Calcutta Darwaza and took off in that direction. The rest of the sawars kept standing near the wall of the moat at the edge of the fort on the Lal Diggi road.

The five sawars thundered their way down to Calcutta Darwaza, and as soon as the sound of the horses' hooves reached the ears of those guarding it, a wave of fear paralysed them. No one could move an inch to take action against the sawars.

One of the defenders said, 'Oh, they have come!'

All those gathered fled at once. There was an atmosphere of fear and cowardice and no one dared attack the five riders. The five sawars made such an impression that those guarding the gate jumped down from the parapets and ran off towards the Nigambodh Darwaza.

If these men had even thrown a handful of dust at these riders, their numbers alone would have seen to it that the rebels were buried, but *Astaghfirullah!* (I seek forgiveness from Allah!) Who amongst them had the courage to face the sawars? The scene was reminiscent of a lion descending upon a herd of goats, and their only course was to flee.

Now the field was clear. Only the poor Resident Bahadur and Qiledar Bahadur were left behind. Else, not even a bird flapped its feathers there.

The five sawars surrounded the carriage of the Sahib Resident Bahadur—but such was the courage and nerve of the Resident that he didn't let fear control him and bravely turned the carriage towards the Qila instead. He whipped the horse to make it run faster.

The sawars were running alongside, naked swords in their hands and murder on their minds, when one of them moved ahead to attack the Resident. The Resident took out his pistol and fired. The bullet hit the sawar in the chest and he died on the spot.

The other four said, 'Now that you have killed one of our companions, we will never let you live.'

Somehow, the Resident reached the gate of the fort. He jumped down from the carriage and entered via the wicket gate and got that locked behind him.

He yelled at the soldiers standing there. 'What are you staring at? Why don't you open fire on these rebels?'

Then he and the qiledar entered the chatta in the Lahori Gate and started climbing the steps. The qiledar reached his house, which was on top of the gate. The Resident, who was corpulent, was still labouring behind him.

The sawars came up to the guards at the gate and asked, 'Are you all followers of the faith or of these people?'

The guard said, 'Of the faith.'

'Then why have you locked the gate?'

The guards immediately threw the gate wide open.

'Where have the sahibs gone?' the sawars asked.

'To the top of the gate.'

The sawars jumped down from their horses and handed the reins over to the guards. They took off in the direction of the chatta and caught up with the Resident as he toiled upwards.

The Murder of the Resident

Alas! More's the pity! The sawars, who had been drawing salaries from the British government until now, did not give a thought to the debt of loyalty they owed them, and behaved outrageously with this high-ranking and powerful officer. Drawing their swords, they finished him off and went off in the direction of the qiledar's residence, where they murdered him, his wife and his children, cutting them into pieces.[65]

This world in truth is a place of warning of the hereafter. That's why those on whom God has bestowed foresight and prudence, and who are worried about the outcome of their actions, would never even think of committing such dastardly acts.

There should be no dependence on the outward trappings of power in this world. Thousands of powerful and majestic emperors have come and gone without leaving a trace.

We should ponder the majesty and awe-inspiring authority of the British government. No one had the courage to look them in the eye, but now the tables had turned drastically, allowing some illiterate rebels to grind them into the dust.

> Say: 'O Allah! Lord of power (and rule) Thou givest
> power to whom Thou pleasest and Thou strippest off
> power from whom Thou pleasest Thou enduest with
> honour whom Thou pleasest and Thou bringest low
> whom Thou pleasest; in Thy hand is all good. Verily over
> all things Thou hast power.'
> (Quran: Surah Ali 'Imran: 26)

News of the Ghadar Spreads through Shahr Panah

> All the tricksters, drunkards of this world
> Hoodlums, drunkards, mutinous backbiting ill-gotten men
> They became a part of a wicked army
> And sullied the name of all those with a reputation

In my room, the clock showed 7.25 a.m. I had gone to sleep in my canopy bed sleeping the sleep of youth after declaring my intent of keeping roza. I was twenty-two years old and newly married; only four months had passed since my wedding.

When the sun rose high above the lofty houses and came down from the roof to the arches in the veranda, trickling into the room through the net and on to my body, it disturbed my sleep.

When I woke up, I could see the wide courtyard in front of my room. My room faced the east. Towards the south was a high wall, and towards the east also there was a tall wall with a staircase. There were two exits from the staircase: one went towards the roof of the *diwankhana* and the other into the courtyard in front of my room. The bedstead was towards the front of the room, and beyond it was a sitting arrangement of wooden settees covered with rugs and pristine white sheets. There were beautifully decorated bolsters placed on them.

After finishing my morning ablutions, I was sitting on a stool. The maidservant was still holding the ewer. I had just finished washing my face and hands and, looking at a mirror that had been kept on a chair in front of me, I was trying to do my hair. Suddenly, another maidservant came running in, gasping for breath, frantic and disturbed, white-faced, dripping with perspiration. She flopped down on to the floor with a loud sound.

'Oh, Mubarak, is everything all right? Why are you looking so perturbed? Is everything fine at home? Mubarak, from where have you come in such a state?'

Mubarak indicated with a wave of her hand that she was waiting for her breath to return to normal before she told me anything. She sat with her head in her hands for four minutes, and when she regained her composure she said, 'Miyan, I have been sent by Nawab Sahib and your mother-in-law, and they have inquired after your welfare and whether you are at home or in the Qila.'

'I am absolutely all right by the grace of God. I go to the Qila only every third or fourth day during Ramzan. My wife is also very well and is sleeping, as you can see.'

'Who is sleeping here on the wooden settee, covered by the sheet?' she asked.

'Fahim-un-Nisa Maani [the maid] is sleeping there.'

'Bi Maani, why haven't you got up yet? Do you know? There is a ghadar taking place in the city! And here you are, sleeping!'

Maani spoke, 'Oh, go away, you unfortunate one. Why would there be a mutiny in the city? You have a habit of saying such calamitous things. Why have you come here so early in the morning? I stayed up the whole night, so let me sleep.'

I asked, 'Mubarak, what is this talk of a ghadar?'

'The shops of the city are closed,' she said. 'Sawars are roaming the streets and the dust of destruction is blowing all over the city. That's why Nawab Sahib wanted to know if you were safe or not.'

'Mubarak, what are you talking about? What sawars? From whose cavalry?'

'Miyan, I am a mere woman. How would I know whose cavalry they are from? If I had been a man I could have questioned them, asked them where they had come from and who they were.'

'Mubarak, did you see these sawars yourself or are you repeating hearsay?'

'*Haan Miyan*, I have seen with my own eyes. There were five or seven sawars roaming under the Jama Masjid. In fact, they followed me till the Shah Bola Road. I went into Roshanpura and they went towards Qazi ka Hauz.'

'What type of sawars were they? What were they wearing? What did their horses look like?'

'They were wearing white clothes, but the trappings of their horses were English.'

I was very shocked when I heard this and sat silently with my head bowed for a few minutes. Various thoughts kept turning in my mind, and then suddenly it struck me: Aha! This was the manifestation of the prophecy made by the elderly saint!

About four to five months ago, I had been in the Paiwala'n Bazaar at a bookshop. Suddenly, an elderly gentleman came inside. He was very well built, tall, statuesque, with long black hair and a flowing beard. He must be around sixty years of age. He was wearing a loose *angarkha*, pyjamas and a round topi, holding a staff, with a rosary around his neck.

He said, '*Salam Aleik*,[66] brothers.'

Maulvi Isa, the shop owner, and I replied respectfully.

Maulvi Isa said, 'Welcome, Hafiz Sahib.'

Hafiz Sahib came and sat next to me and said, 'Brother, is there a *Kalam-e-Majeed* amongst these books?'

'Hazrat, yes, there is,' I said.

I took down a Quran which had been printed in Lucknow, and handed it over to him. Hafiz Sahib started reciting Quranic verses. When he had finished a section, his demeanour began changing—his eyes turned red, his face shone, the veins on his neck swelled up. In a state of anger and fury, hands raised towards the market, he said:

'Here you go! He has been killed, he has been killed, he has been hanged, he has been hanged! Waah! Waah! What a grand spectacle it is! He is killing them one by one. He is hanging all of them one by one! He is hanging someone now and no one dare say anything. Barburton[67] Sahib is enjoying the scene.'

After saying this, Hafiz Sahib said to himself, 'Just stay quiet. Who has given you permission to announce the divine secret?'

Then Hafiz Sahib lowered his head and went back to reciting the Quran.

After reading another section, he went back to the earlier state and started repeating his words. He repeated this sequence of events three times, and after that, Hafiz Sahib kissed the Quran, placed it on his head and handed it back to me. I put it back in the cupboard.

Then Hafiz Sahib addressed me again and said, 'What are you doing, sitting in the city? Go out and see the vicinity. A worldly person should not be sitting at home all the time.'

I kept sitting quietly, too awestruck to utter a word.

He said, 'Your father is a famous calligrapher in the Naskh script. Please ask him to write a Quran for me where the whole chapter finishes in one page and the entire *Quran-e-Majeed* can be written in thirty pages.'

'Yes, sir,' I said. 'I will convey your request.'

'Please get some parathas and *methi ka saag* cooked for me,' he said.

'As you wish. Where will I find you?'

'In the nearby baker's shop.'

Saying this, he wished us again and went away.

I was just thinking of all this when Amir Khan, a male attendant, called out to one of the maids and asked, 'Is Miyan sleeping or is he awake? If he is sleeping, wake him up. The choubdar has brought some orders from the deorhi.'

I heard these words, and immediately came down to the diwankhana.

The choubdar relayed the orders: 'Huzoor has sent orders via Mehboob Ali Khan that all the employees of the sarkar should present themselves at the deorhi. Please hurry up and go there. I have to deliver these orders to many other places too.'

I paid my salutations to him and told the choubdar, 'I will dress and leave at once. Please tell Govardhan to keep my horse ready.'

I told Amir Khan to get ready and entered the house. My respected father, may Allah keep him safe, was sitting on the settee in the courtyard, leaning against the bolster and writing the *Quran-e-Majeed*. I went up to him and, presenting my salutations, sat down next to him.

My father looked at me and asked, 'Is all well?'

I told him of the morning's events. He kept aside the *Quran-e-Majeed* that he had been writing and sat in silence for a few minutes. Then, raising his head, he said, 'I can't understand what this is all about! Tell the porters to bring my carriage. I will leave immediately.'

I implored him with folded hands. 'Sire, please stay here. Your servant is going into the emperor's service and the choubdar has not mentioned your name. He has only given the order for me. The emperor himself has released you from active duty. Please take care of the house. I am leaving some men here. I am only taking Amir Khan and Govardhan with me, and the other five servants are at your service.'

I came upstairs to my room, changed my clothes and tied my turban. As I was leaving, everyone in the house was looking at me with tears in their eyes. I pacified them and came down. I decided that it would be prudent to take some weapons, and started inspecting the swords and daggers that had been lying unused for years.

My respected father called out, 'Careful, don't do such a thing! The British are governing us and we don't know the real state of affairs. Just go straight to the deorhi. When orders are given and Huzoor gives permission, only then should you touch your weapons.'

I mounted my horse and left, and as I came out of the gate of the Chota Dariba, I saw that a few sawars wearing kurtas and dhoti with a small cloth tied around their heads were standing in the shade of a peepal tree next to the wall of the canal. They had only a dagger in their hands. Some Hindus were looking after them. Someone had brought *puri*s for them, someone had brought sweets and someone had brought water in a brass pot. I didn't pay attention to them and rode off in the direction of the Qila. My horse had just moved a few steps ahead when I saw the rogue, Gami Nahrwala, the local bodybuilder, dressed in a kurta and his trademark loincloth, and with a cap on his head, holding a stick and leading a group of fifty profligates in similar loincloths and with cudgels in their hands, going in the same direction. On reaching Ashraf Beg's apartment, he hit his stick on the lantern hanging there, and when it shattered he said, 'I have killed one more infidel.'

Saying this, the group started breaking the lock of a draper's shop. I just urged my horse forward and left. As I moved ahead, I saw a few more sawars moving around, but I didn't say anything to them and they didn't pay attention to me. I went via the Kotwali to the Khooni Darwaza and saw that there was a huge crowd of scoundrels looting the shops of bankers and moneylenders. Amir Khan was hesitant to go with me. When I reached the walls of the Qila, I saw some fifty sawars near the moat, and pages of English books flying in the air. There was a strong wind blowing and the pages were drifting towards the Qila door.

A little way away from the Qila Darwaza, there was a completely nude, drunken man, holding an old English shoe. Pages of the book were flying towards him, and he was hitting at them with the shoe and abusing them in anger.

Arrangements for the Funeral

I took my horse to the naqqarkhana, and dismounting, entered the Diwan-e-Khaas. Mehboob Ali Khan was leaning against a pillar in one of the arches, and Hakim Ahsanullah Khan was sitting in front of him, leaning against another pillar.

The courtiers were sitting in two rows on both sides. I went forward, presented my salutations and sat in one of the rows.

I saw a Punjabi Muslim cloth merchant whose shop was at the edge of the Qila.[68] He used to supply clothes to the princes and the queens and princesses in the harem. In front of him were bales of white Nainsook[69] cotton and black cloth. A tailor and a steward were sitting next to them. Hakim Ahsanullah Khan was enumerating the bales and cutting cloth for a shroud. I was astonished at what was happening. Whose funeral shrouds were being cut! Who had been killed to warrant these elaborate arrangements?

Mir Fateh Ali and Mirza Ahmed Beg, superintendent of the water department, were on either side of me. I asked them quietly about the chain of events, but they had only been able to tell me a little bit when the sound of our conversation reached the ears of Hakim Ahsanullah Khan.

He called out loudly, 'Why don't you tell him clearly that Sahib Resident Bahadur has been killed? Also that it is the order of the emperor that all his employees ensure he is given a proper funeral. He has given instructions that the Resident be buried in the qiledar's estate. Huzoor is extremely anguished by their murders. Seven men have been killed so far. Their corpses are lying at the gate of the Qila.'

I lost my senses when I heard this, but after a while I regained some semblance of order. I heard an account of the morning's events from those present in the court.

The shroud had still not been readied when suddenly we saw the angel of death appear in front of us. The sawars were coming from the Lal Purdah!

Hakim Ahsanullah Khan exclaimed, 'Everyone recite prayers for your own safety—death is on our heads!'

Truly, to Allah we belong and truly, to Him we shall
return
(Quran: Surah Al-Baqarah: 156)

Everyone started reciting the verses from the Quran as
the sawars reached under the hall of the Diwan-e-Khaas,
dismounted and hung the reins of their horses on the enclosure
rails. They came and sat down with us. There were around
thirty men and most of them were officers. They were dressed
in European style and we could not distinguish between the
officers and the soldiers since they were all wearing cotton
shirts, loose pyjamas and small scarves tied on their heads
with their pates showing. Some had muskets and others
carbines, pistols or swords.

Seeing the yards of white cloth spread around they asked
Ahsanullah Khan, 'What are these things?'

Hakim Ahsanullah Khan replied, 'We are trying to make
amends for your actions. You started the fire; we are dousing
it.'

The sawars said, 'Arrey! You are all dishonest Christians.
Arrey! You are all infidels. You have eaten the leftovers of the
British.'

They looted all the cloth being cut for the shroud, and
tearing it to pieces, tied it around their own heads. One of
the sawars moved forward and kept his pistol on the paunch
of Mehboob Ali Khan khwaja-sara. Mehboob Ali Khan was
suffering from dropsy and had swelling all over his body. But
even though he was a eunuch, he was a man at heart.

'Give us provisions,' the sawar said.

'From where would we receive provisions?' Mehboob
Ali Khan asked. 'Do we have an army? Do we have a force
for which provisions are available? We have no provisions or

anything else. If you want to take our lives, you are welcome to do so. I am sitting here, ready to die. It would be excellent if I died at somebody's hands.'

Sharif Ali Khan Darogha, who was much attached to Mehboob Ali Khan, caught the hand of the sawar and said, 'Why are you asking him? Ask me! I will give you what you want.'

Hakim Ahsanullah Khan said, 'Our Huzoor has already told you himself that we don't have any money—no riches, no country, no treasure. We are sitting here like mendicants in a convent. From where can we give you provisions? Yes, we have some gram, which comes once a month for the horses of the royal stables. That is available. Apart from that we don't have a grain. The emperor's horses will die of hunger, but you fill your stomachs! How long will the gram last? It won't last you even a day. Sharif Khan, go and open the stores and distribute 3 ser of gram each to these men.'

Somehow, this calamity was averted.

The sawars went and tied their horses in the Mehtab Bagh. Many more came and gathered. Around another fifty to sixty men also came looking for food and water. They were also sent off with the same excuse. Now another sixty men arrived looking for food, and very soon about 250–300 sawars had gathered in the Mehtab Bagh. All those coming now were making a beeline for the Mehtab Bagh.

It was 11 a.m. by the time these events unfolded, and many of the infantrymen were also coming in now. Around 300–400 infantrymen had entered Delhi and the city was in a state of uproar. The resident scoundrels were looting the city.

Some of the rebels came into the Diwan-e-Khaas and told Mehboob Ali Khan and Ahsanullah Khan to arrange for provisions and food and water for them.

A royal employee said, 'What arrangements can we make? You have already killed those who used to make arrangements for the city. You have created an uproar in the city and the city is being looted, shops are shut. So what arrangements can we make for your food now? Make your own arrangements from wherever you can. Because of you, even we don't have any means of getting food for ourselves.'

The sawaraan-e-fauj baghiya said, 'Please request the Badshah Salamat to get the bazaar reopened. We will take whatever we can get to eat.'

The royal employee yelled, 'You have already looted the shops! What is left in them that you want them reopened? And why should shopkeepers open their shops? You have created an atmosphere of strife in the city. The shops can only be opened if there is peace.'

The sawaraan-e-fauj baghiya spoke, 'We will make arrangements to stop the plunder and we won't let anyone use force or oppress another. We will set up guards at regular intervals. Please send the emperor's herald to announce this in the city and get the shops reopened.'

The royal employee said, 'First, promise that you will not kill anyone, of whatever faith, neither will you loot and plunder the markets. We will send out the Royal Proclamation, and you set up guard posts at all points.'

Arrangements for a Peaceful Stay

The rebels agreed to restore peace and asked the Mughal officers to send soldiers with them. They would station these soldiers at regular intervals, along with their men, to ensure the safety of the shops and to prevent plunder. They would shut the roads and put up roadblocks. Anyone caught stealing or looting would be arrested. A few noblemen and royal officers went with the rebels, and the kotwal called the town crier and told him to announce the Royal Proclamation throughout the city:

'*Khalq Khuda ki, Mulk Badshah ka, Hukm Badshah ka*, no one should oppress another. Anyone found looting, plundering or appropriating another's goods will be punished by the emperor.'

The messenger went to the houses of the *halwai*s and grocers and had their shops opened. Purbias[70] were put on guard here and a few other shops were also opened. The halwais once again put their huge woks on fire and started frying puris. The grocery shops were opened and those who were fasting began buying the food items required to open their roza.

At this time, Ahsanullah Khan gave orders to yours truly and Sufi Mazharullah Beg, the royal risaldar: 'Go and inspect the state of affairs in the city. Has the looting and plundering stopped?'

As per orders, the two of us mounted our horses and went into the bazaar. We went towards the Fatehpuri Masjid. We found peace and calm prevailing in the city. There was no looting and plundering anywhere and some shops were open. There were guards set at the open shops and there was buying and selling going on. The soldiers were paying the required price and getting the selected merchandise weighed.

We were going back when we saw a crowd gathering in front of the kotwali. There were many purbias there under a tree. Many local goons were gathered there as well. The goons told the rebels in one voice that the kotwal of the city was sympathetic to the British. As soon as the rebels heard this, they pointed their guns at the veranda of the kotwali and fired. The door of the kotwali fell, whereupon a few people ran out and jumped over the wall at the back and ran away.

At this time, we saw another crowd emerge from the side of the Koriya Pul.[71] As we stood there, we saw two young and beautiful European women[72] being pulled along by the crowd as prisoners.

As soon as I saw this, my companion turned towards the men who had promised to maintain law and order. These men were standing in front of the kotwali under the neem tree. Moving his horse forward, he said, 'You had just promised to eschew high-handedness and now you are indulging in it once again. What kind of false promises are these?'

The rebels who had been addressed took the two women from the purbias and handed them over to us. I asked them, 'You are handing them over to us here, but what if the rebels snatch them away from us further down the road and kill them?'

Two sawars were sent with us as escorts. When we reached the gate of the Qila we saw that a large group of purbias, accompanied by Hindus and Muslims (approximately 5000 people altogether) were coming towards us.

'What is this huge mob?' I asked, startled at the sight.

'They are the helpers and assistants who were with us in Meerut,' the sawars said.

We reached the deorhi safely, but neither Mehboob Ali Khan nor Ahsanullah Khan was present there. I sent the two women into the palace with the khwaja-sara. After leading them in, the khwaja-sara returned and said, 'Huzoor Anwar was very pleased with this act. Keep an eye on the general welfare of the people as long as possible. No one should be killed.'

Later, we learned that the group of goons who had imprisoned the women had also included convicts who had been released from the jail.

I was observing the fast at this time, and so was very thirsty. I sat under the shade of the tasbihkhana.

Not much time had passed when another uproar began. As a young European man came striding up the steps of the tasbihkhana, he was held up by the purbias. The European held a small brass water container and the hilt of a sword—but the sword itself had been broken in two and was red with blood all the way up to the hilt. He held the hand of a very beautiful, delicate Miss.[73] This young maiden was around sixteen or seventeen years old and was tall with an oval face and a slim waist. There were spots of blood on her and she was pale. She looked extremely frightened.

As soon as I saw this, I rushed towards them. A thought crossed my mind: This man held a bloodstained, naked sword in his hand and no doubt had murder on his mind. God forbid, what if he attacked me?

If he let go of the girl's hand, he would have been finished. I decided to disarm him first and take the sword from him, then make him let go of her hand. As soon as I reached him, I caught his wrist in a powerful grip with my right hand and put my left hand on his sword. I said, 'You disrespectful man, don't you know that this is the emperor's deorhi and you cannot enter here with your weapon?'

Hearing this, the rest of the men crowded around him. When the young girl saw a sympathizer and protector in me, she came to my side and caught my waist. When her body touched mine I realized that she was shivering and trembling in fear, and her heart was pounding. I snatched the sword from the man's hand and asked, 'What do you want? Please tell me.'

'Brother,' he said, 'I swear on God, we have not looted anything. Even though the world has looted property worth lakhs, we did not touch a single thing. I have only taken this one thing, and if I get this, I don't need anything else.'

Giving the sword back to the European I said, 'You cannot take her just now. If I tell this woman to go with you now, you will lose your life, and this poor, helpless girl will also lose hers. Your attempts and sacrifice will be wasted when these soldiers murder both of you. The best course is for you to stay patient for a few days. Once this tumult has died down and the mutiny has been suppressed, your charge that we have kept in trust for you will be returned to you. Until then, she will be with the emperor.'

The khwaja-sara and others who were present in the deorhi joined in with me. We somehow pacified the European and sent him away.

The young girl heaved a sigh of relief and moved away from me. I asked her about the events that had transpired and how she had come to be with the young man.

The young Miss put her hand to her mouth and made a sign asking for water. I got some from the water room and gave it to her.

When she had regained her composure she said, 'This man murdered my sahib and grabbed my hand and walked away with me. On the way, the sawars tried to snatch me away from him, but he wouldn't let go. He was ready to kill and be killed, and fought his way here. The world has taken all my possessions. Now will you give me back to that man?'

I spoke sympathetically, 'Absolutely not! That cannot happen. You have come into the protection of the emperor and whatever the emperor orders will be done. You will enjoy all the comforts while you are under his protection. No one will touch you. Once the mutiny is over, you will have the right to decide where you want to live. You will be in charge of your own destiny. It was your destiny to reach this place safely, and now no one can kill you.'

The young Miss took a long breath. 'Let us see.'

I told the khwaja-sara to take her inside the palace. The latter lifted the curtain of the deorhi and called out to the servant, '*Bi baridar*, Memsahiba is coming. Take her into the presence of Huzoor.'

The curtain of the deorhi was lifted and the young lady disappeared within.

Looting the Bank

It was now 2 p.m. The clock hands were moving on to 3 p.m.

When the goons and scoundrels of the city saw that a prohibition had been placed on loot and plunder, and realized that they could no longer get their way, they decided to hijack the movement.

There is a famous saying: *Ek toh karela upar se neem chadha* (an already bitter gourd with a coating of the bitter neem). The goons began instigating and exciting the undesirable elements amongst the rebels, those who were already inclined towards wrongdoing. The rebels joined forces with them and the local scoundrels planted their new allies on the doorstep of the bank.

The government bank was situated in the garden and mansion of Begum Samru, opposite the Khooni Darwaza.[74] Its southern part joined the beginning of the road to Urdu Bazaar.

As soon as the plunderers and looters set foot in the garden, they came up against the British officers[75] who were guarding the treasury. A few women and children had also taken shelter here. The officers refused to give up the money in the bank. They went inside and brought out their weapons and faced the rebels and scoundrels sternly, determined. The rebels on their part faced up to them and the battle started. There were guns firing on both sides, and a great tumult prevailed for some time.

After a while, a few of the scoundrels jumped over the garden wall and set the roof of the mansion on fire. The huge beams on the ceiling of the mansion were burnt and began to fall down. The flames rose high and the billows of smoke from the mansion darkened the sky. Soon, the front of the mansion was destroyed and all the brave men defending it were burnt to cinders.

The purbias entered the mansion and mercilessly murdered the European women and children sheltering within. The inner rooms which housed the treasury and vaults were safe from the flames. The men entered the bank from the back and broke all the locks on the chests. They started looting them.

Amongst these shameless looters were the sepoys who had rebelled in Meerut and come to Delhi with their platoons. They had also been joined by the local weavers, shoemakers, washermen, water carriers, grocers, butchers and paper sellers from Kaghazi Mohalla and sundry other rascals from the city. Bodybuilders, musclemen, cudgellers, petty thieves, pickpockets and many others were also present. There were no men from decent families there. All those who lived good and honest lives were locked inside their houses, totally unaware of what was happening in their city.

The rebels looted as much as they could carry away. Each shoemaker took approximately three bags of cash. The residents of the Kaghazi Mohalla, who had been economically backward, were now flush with money. There is a famous saying: *Maal-e-muft, dil-e-beraham* (freely got, lavishly spent). How much can anyone loot? There were Rs 14 lakh in the bank, but who would leave something like money behind? Within an hour, the thieves had looted everything. They even took away the strongboxes. This pandemonium lasted for two hours.

Blowing up the Magazine

> Delhi, the heart of the age, is now in ruins
> It didn't realize that the Tilangani were cruel at heart
> They are plundering the heart that is God's residence
> They have spoilt God's house, woe to them
> There is no refuge from such oppression anywhere
> Only God may save us from revenge for this

It was 5 p.m., and even though the sun was setting, the day of reckoning was still underway.

The heat of the riot was on the rise, and for the citizens of Shahjahanabad it was every man for himself. The waves of trouble and turmoil were causing the ground to swell up. While the river of blood and carnage was boiling, loot and plunder raged. Fearless and pitiless tyrants had created pandemonium in the city, and no one knew what was happening to anyone else. Everyone was concerned with saving themselves.

Messengers were sorting out the mail, and news of complaints and petitions for mercy were pouring in from every direction. The scoundrels of Satan were inflicting violence all around.

The royal employees were sitting with Hakim Ahsanullah Khan in the *khan-samaani* hall, reciting *Ya badee ul ajaib bilkhairi* (Oh unique originator of goodness) on the rosary. A prayer for peace was on everyone's lips when suddenly there was a tremendous noise. Even if 1000 cannons had been fired, their noise would not have been so loud.

The khan-samaani building is from Shah Jahan's period and its walls are 4 feet wide. It is made of lime and mortar. The ceiling of the hall is very solidly constructed of red sandstone and salmon-coloured stone. After this noise, dirt and mud started falling from the walls and everyone was covered in dust. The earth shook as if there had been an earthquake.

It was almost as though the building were going to fall down on us. Everyone rushed out into the courtyard in panic. It seemed as if the Quranic verse, 'When the earth is shaken with its [final] earthquake' (Quran: Surah Az-Zalzalah: 1), was coming true.

When we turned our eyes to the west, we saw a column of smoke rising from the ground to the sky and corpses of men flying around in the air like crows and kites. Three minutes later, it seemed as though pieces of the mountains were raining on earth.

And the mountains will be like wool, fluffed up
(Quran: Surah Al-Qari'ah: 5)

We ran back to the hall, shocked by what was happening.

A pair of messengers came running and told us that the magazine and arsenal had been blown up. The incident had taken place more than a mile away from the khan-samaani building. The details of the chain of events were described thus:

When the rebels went to besiege the magazine, they found a few Europeans present and guarding it. There were also a few women and children who had taken shelter there.

At first, the besieged faced the rebels squarely and kept firing at them, but when the crowd of rebel forces overwhelmed their capacity to hold them off, they had no option but to give up their lives and take the rebels with them. They went to the cellar where the ammunition was placed and set it on fire.[76] Thus, they died themselves and took around 1000 of their enemies with them.

There were men standing on the city wall near the river and a crowd on the other three sides when the magazine blew up taking them all with it. 50 yards of the city wall of Shahr Panah were also destroyed, along with all the men standing near or on it. Many were blown up in the explosion and the ensuing rain of stones killed others. European women, children and four or five old men who had been hiding in the other rooms and the few young men left inside were all injured. The purbias arrested them.

The Attempt to Free the Prisoners

In the meantime, the royal employees, including Hakim Ahsanullah Khan, came to the Diwan-e-Khaas from the building of the khan-samaani. It might have been a few minutes to six, or even past, and it was nearly time to break the fast. Extreme thirst was sapping our energy and making us impatient even as the sun was about to set.

There were only faint rays of sunlight remaining on the pinnacles of lofty houses when suddenly a huge crowd appeared in front of the Lal Purdah door. When the crowd reached the courtyard of the Diwan-e-Khaas, we saw that fifty to fifty-five women and children and four or five injured men were coming along, surrounded by a huge crowd of purbias and others. The purbias made their captives sit on the steps of the tasbihkhana.

We got up to see them and found that they were covered in dust and blood. They were in a state of fear and panic. When they saw us standing near the tasbihkhana, they started pleading for water. We called two water carriers from the water house who brought two waterskins and helped them wash their faces and hands and drink water by cupping their palms to hold it. Some infants couldn't drink from the cupped palms and I felt sorry for them. I got two paper cups from the water room and gave them to their mothers to help the children drink. When they had washed themselves and drunk water, they said, 'Brother Muslims, *Lā 'ilāha 'illā-llāh, Muḥammadur Rasūlu-llāh!*[77] We all are converting to Islam. Don't take our lives!'

When I heard them say this, I started crying. The others also became teary-eyed. This news reached the Huzoor, who sent orders from inside, telling us to control the rebel forces and take these people into our custody.

I remember two people present there: one was Gulab Khan Risaldar of the Third Cavalry and the other was Qadir Baksh, *subedar* of Safar Meena Paltan, a platoon that came from Meena.[78] These two were blessed with old age; they would have been between fifty and sixty years of age. In comparison to the other soldiers, they seemed more merciful and tender-hearted, so we caught their hands and started a conversation with them in the first hall of the Diwan-e-Khaas.

'Listen, O Muslims!' a royal employee said to the rebels, 'You say that the foundation of this dispute is your faith, and that you have come here after your religion was endangered.

Therefore, it is obligatory and compulsory for you to listen to the elders of your religion and follow the rules of Islam and Islamic law. If you behave of your own accord and allow bigotry to creep in, then you will be no longer be worthy of being called a Muslim. In the age of the Prophet (peace be upon him) or in the age of his Caliphs, when wars were fought against the Jewish and Christian sects on the basis of religion, they were presented with three conditions which, when accepted, were enforced.

'The first condition was: If you follow Islam and read the kalima and accept the oneness of Allah and the prophethood of Mohammad, then you are brothers. You are what we are. And there's no difference between us. We have nothing to do with your property, possessions, wife and family.

'The second condition was: If you don't accept Islam but agree to pay *jeziya* (the tax on non-believers), then you are under our protection and we will never break our promise to you.

'The third condition was: If you refuse to agree to either of the two stated, then the sword hangs between us.

'If these people had decided to fight and it reached the stage of do or die, they would be punished, but no one has ever lifted a finger against women and children. Women and children were exempted from the punishment and those who came into the community as *zimmi*[79] were not harmed by anyone.

'It is astonishing that these people are reciting the kalima and accepting Islam, yet you want to murder them. What faith is this and which religion are you advocating? No religion condones the murder of women and children.'

One of the rebels responded, 'All right. So what should we do then?'

'You should hand them over into the custody of the Badshah-e-Islam and he will convert them and get them suitably married as per their choice,' the employee said.

Thus, after this long conversation, they agreed to hand the prisoners over to us and said, 'Keep them in safe custody.'

This request was sent to the presence of Huzoor, and he sent orders that they be kept safely and proper arrangements made for their food and rest. Employees were also instructed to give first aid to the injured.

I stood on the terrace of the tasbihkhana and invited all those who were sitting under its steps on the ground in the courtyard of the Diwan-e-Khaas to come inside. There were a few men, and the rest were women and children. In my estimate, there were around sixty of them. They all got up and were coming via the tasbihkhana into the Diwan-e-Khaas when some man told them, 'This person has saved your life with a lot of effort.' Then the people started blessing me. In this interval, the curtain of the deorhi was lifted and the beautiful Miss whom I had saved from the European and the purbias came out, followed by the other two women. All three asked me, 'Where should we go now?'

I replied, 'There are other people from your community in the Diwan-e-Khaas. You may all go and join them.'

The Miss knew that I had saved her and she was a God-fearing lady. In such a state of despair, one clutches at straws. She asked me, 'Where will you go now?'

I replied, 'I will go home and present myself in the emperor's service tomorrow.'

She said, 'Take me to your house. My life will be saved.'

I said, 'Now no one will kill you. You are under the emperor's protection.'

'That has to be seen,' she said. 'You must take me with you.'

I asked, 'How can I take you with me? As soon as we step out of the Diwan-e-Khaas, these people will kill us both.'

Hearing this, she went towards the Diwan-e-Khaas with tears in her eyes.

I left for my house, going through the Diwan-e-Aam and naqqarkhana and coming out of the Qila's Lahori Darwaza. When I reached the road in the Urdu Bazaar, there was total silence in the city—not even a bird was flying. A strange kind of desolation seemed to have spread. Shops had been looted and the doors of the houses were shut tight. There was total darkness and lanterns were lying about with their glass broken. Passing through the Khooni Darwaza in front of the kotwali, I reached the gate of Chota Dariba. Here I found that the shops of sweet sellers and cloth merchants had all been broken. There was an injured, opium-eating Brahmin faqir lying outside the moneylender's shop, groaning and crying. He had three shallow sword wounds on his back. I came to my house via Maliwaara.

It was dusk and I had still not broken my fast. My tongue was thick and hanging out with thirst. As soon as my father saw me, he offered thanks to the Almighty for my safe return. I broke my fast and drank sherbet and ate my dinner. My father asked me to give an account of what had transpired and I described the day's events to him, telling him of how I had saved the lives of many people. My father blessed me for my good deeds and prayed that God would reward me. I was very happy as we are Saiyyeds,[80] and Allah's Prophet (peace be upon him) and his progeny have always been merciful. Indeed, Janab Ali Murtaza Karam Allah *Wajhahu* (May Allah bless his countenance) had given a bowl of milk to his assassin.

A little while had passed before we heard cannon fire coming from the direction of the Qila. I thought the British army had arrived, so I sent a man to find out what was happening. The man returned and said that the platoons from the cantonment had come inside the city and were now firing warning shots.

I was dead beat from the events of the day and went off to sleep as soon as I laid my head on my pillow.

After my ablutions the next morning, I left for the Qila, and spent the day following the various orders that I had been given. On this day, the city's administration was carried out on behalf of and on orders from the emperor and a kotwal was appointed to see to them.

I was ordered to take a few water carriers and douse the fire raging in the magazine; if the gunpowder caught fire, the whole city would be blown apart. The kotwal sent a few water carriers to me and we doused the fire that was raging in some of the houses in the city. The city wall in the direction of the river had fallen down and there was a mountain of cannonballs there, along with around 200 cannons. There were innumerable guns and pistols there and the whole magazine was full of weapons of war. I left it thus, but a few days later, I heard that ruffians had looted the magazine and taken the weapons away, leaving some of the cannonballs behind.

The atmosphere of the city was such that the ruffians and goons were looting houses with the help of the purbias. They would put the latter on guard outside the houses of the wealthy, since they felt there were treasures hidden inside. Then they would enter and plunder the mansions.

Death was on the heads of the royal employees at all times, and people with pointed guns could surround us at any moment. One day, twenty or twenty-five of us were sitting in the khan-samaani with Hakim Ahsanullah Khan when purbias came and surrounded us. They pointed guns at us and accused us saying, 'You are all without faith. Arrey, you are all Christians! You write letters to the British.'

We were confounded and distressed and said, 'Kill us once and for all. That will be better than daily harassment.'

A few sensible officers pacified the sawars and took them away, but we were fed up with their constant harassment and oppression.

The state of the army was such that every day 200–400 soldiers who had deserted their regiments would come and gather in Delhi. Four companies had come from Koli Jaiser and 500 more soldiers had come from the Safar Meena platoon. Now, there were 7000–8000 purbias in the city.

> They destroyed half the pillars of honour's edifice
> They blew out the lamp in the gathering of justice

The Murder of the Prisoners

One early morning, I left my house for the Qila, and entering through the naqqarkhana reached the Diwan-e-Aam. From there I decided to go to the khan-samaani and meet Hakim Ahsanullah Khan to find out if Huzoor had given any orders. With this in mind, I avoided the lattice door and entered the khan-samaani door. When I had walked a little beyond the Mehtab Darwaza, I saw the purbias bringing the prisoners out of the Bagh.[81]

'Where are you taking them?' I asked.

'We will take them out of the Qila and keep them elsewhere,' one of them said.

'This is part of our agreement,' I protested. 'Please don't take them away.'

But they refused to listen to me. I was worried that they might play foul and so rushed to Ahsanullah Khan sahib, who was lying in the upper storey of the khan-samaani. I told him, 'Khan Sahib, are you aware of what is happening?'

'What?' he asked.

'Those ruffians are taking the prisoners away. I am afraid that they will murder them. Please make arrangements for their safety.'

Ahsanullah Khan retorted, 'What can I do?'

'Khan Sahib,' I said, 'this is a test of our loyalty. If you want to save the emperor, please reason with the rebels and save the prisoners. Or remember that the British will raze Dilli to the ground.'

Ahsanullah Khan replied, 'Miyan, you are very young. How would you know that man does not listen to reason when caught up in circumstances such as these? He does not think of the result of his actions. If we remonstrate with them now, they will kill us first, and then murder the prisoners.'

'It is better that a few of us are killed,' I said. 'At least the Badshah's empire will be saved.'[82] Saying this, I left from there and came back to the deorhi.

I sent a message to the emperor through the khwaja-sara stating that the purbias had taken the prisoners whom Huzoor had kept in his special protection. The emperor gave immediate orders to call Hakim Ahsanullah Khan so that he could make arrangements to save the prisoners.

The khwaja-sara came outside the palace and sent a messenger to get Hakim Ahsanullah Khan post-haste. Two more messengers were sent one after the other, but though time was passing, Hakim ji did not move from his place. After some time, Hakim Ahsanullah Khan came to the tasbihkhana and entered the presence of Huzoor.

The emperor gave orders: 'Call the officers and reason with them and save the prisoners.'

Hakim Ahsanullah Khan said, 'All right. As you wish.' He came out to the Diwan-e-Khaas and sat down against the arch in the middle enclosure. Perhaps he sent a few people to call the rebel officers.

Suddenly we saw that two companies of purbias, bearing loaded guns on their shoulders, were coming from the door of the Lal Purdah. As soon as they came into the Diwan-e-Khaas, they surrounded us and stood in front of us with guns pointed at us. All of us were praying to God and reciting the kalima. There were ten or twelve of us and we thought that they would blow us up at any moment. For a few moments, they kept standing there like that. After that, two sawars lofted a red flag outside the Lal Purdah, which was an indication to the other sawars to put their guns back on their shoulders and leave.

A messenger came after a few minutes and gave us the news: 'The prisoners have been murdered.'

I cannot describe my distress at hearing those words. I was just as sorrowful at the killing of these children as I was at the death of my own son. I am astonished at how stone-hearted these villains could be to lift their hands to kill those innocent children and helpless women.

I left for my house to mourn in peace. When I reached the darwaza of the naqqarkhana, I saw that the hacked corpses of the prisoners had been strewn to the right of the darwaza. I could not bear to see this scene of death and destruction, and covering my face with my handkerchief, I came away from there. My servant was standing near the hauz with my horse. I mounted my horse and came home in a distraught state of mind. Seeing that I was beside myself with grief, my father asked, 'Is everything all right? Why are you so distressed today?'

I described the horrific events of the day. My father was very affected by them as well and said, 'It has been listed in your register of deeds as a reward for you, but death was ordained for these innocents. Thus was the will of the Almighty.'

Even now when I think about that event, I cannot stop my tears from flowing. For many days, I was in a state of mourning.

After this event, the purbias began to rule the city and their writ ran large: *Andher nagri chaupat raja* (Knaves rule in the kingdom of fools).

The residents of the city were miserable as they had no recourse to justice. They prayed to God to help them get rid of this unforeseen, unexpected evil. We would find peace and the city would go back to normal only if the oppressors left it and went away.

By now, the rebels had become very wealthy from the loot they had plundered from the British, the city's markets and the local populace. They didn't have space to keep their cash and had converted it into gold coins which they tied to their waists. The price of gold coins had fallen so low that one was being sold for Rs 30. Meanwhile, the populace was dying of hunger and all workshops had been shut down, with craftsmen and writers sitting idle.

4

The Advent of the British Army

What meaning does the assault hold?

The British forces had arrived on this side of the Hindon River, near Ghaziabad, and the sound of the bugles could be heard everywhere.

The army was getting ready for battle in a hurry. The *topkhana* was ready and the wooden carts were standing loaded with cannons in the magazine.

The platoons were standing at attention and the regiments were standing on the other side when the call was given to attack. The army immediately left through the bridge door, below Salimgarh, passing over the bridge over the Jamuna along the road to Shahdara.

It was 10 a.m.

The First Battle

It was noon when we heard the sound of a cannon being fired. Initially we thought it was the shot announcing the time, but then suddenly another shot was fired and we realized it was announcing the start of a battle. There was now a volley of shots from the cannons as well as guns. This continued for two hours and was then replaced by intermittent fire. The battlefield must have been 12–13 miles from the Qila.[83]

It was now 3 p.m. It seemed that the British army had not only reached the city at double speed, but had also engaged the rebels within two hours of getting there.

Within three hours, the outcome had been decided. But inside the city we were still waiting to learn who the victor was and who the loser.

At around 5 p.m., as I left the Qila, I saw the Indian forces returning to the chatta of the Lahori Darwaza, their wooden carts bearing artillery leading the way. A young man was sitting propped up against a wooden box holding the cannonballs on the cart, but he was unconscious. I thought he was wounded and asked the front rider, 'Where has he been hurt?'

The rider said, 'He isn't injured. He was hit by a *thanda gola* [spent cannonball] and fainted from the impact.'

I saw that the cavalry and infantry were all joyously trooping along, blowing trumpets.

I asked one of the sawars, 'Why did you return so quickly?'

The sawar said, 'We were victorious and the goras ran away from the field, hence, we returned.'

I questioned him further. 'What kind of battle did you fight?'

He said, 'We were on this side of the embankment and they were on the other. There was artillery fire from both sides, and we prevailed. We fired shot after shot but the gora could not tolerate the heat of the day. We could see from afar that they were standing up to their knees in water, and when our cavalry attacked them they ran away in panic. They took their artillery guns with them.'

The Second Battle

The second battle was very fierce.[84] After the first battle in Ghaziabad, there were no more instances of any battle or fighting. The purbias were enjoying themselves but were no longer disturbing the populace. They were drinking lots of *bhang* and eating *laddu peda*. As they had stopped cooking for themselves, they ate puri kachori and sweets for both their meals and slept well at night.

Aid was pouring in from all sides: the regiment from Lucknow had come and the platoon from Jullandhar had also deserted and joined the rebels. There were now 12,000–15,000 infantrymen on their side. Apart from this, the ruffians in the Meerut jail who had been released by the rebels initially and had come with them to Delhi were also still with them. The petty thieves, pickpockets and such folk who had been released from the Delhi jails were with the Indian army as well.

A month and a half had passed since the sixteenth day of Ramzan, the day the rebels had come to Delhi from Meerut. It was around 5 p.m. that I was coming home from the Qila when I met two cavalrymen in blue uniforms. They had blue flags in their hands and it seemed from their appearance that they were officers of some regiment. They were Muslim, and we wished each other. Since I had never seen anyone in that uniform, I suspected that they were new entrants in the Indian ranks.

'Which regiment are you from?' I asked.

'The Fourth Regiment,' they replied.

I was surprised. 'There is no Fourth Regiment here!'

'The Fourth Regiment has come with the British forces,' they said.

'Where are the British forces?'

'In Alipur.'

'Why have you come from Alipur?' I asked in surprise.

'We have come secretly to tell our Indian brothers that at the time of battle we will desert the British and join them instead. They shouldn't fire at us by mistake and must remain careful.'

The cavalrymen asked me where the officers of the Indian army were and I directed them: 'Go to the left side from the chatta, through the Tripolia and the canal. When you reach the Qila Darwaza, you will see the old bridge over the river and the Salimgarh Darwaza. Enter that and you will find all the officers there.'[85]

The sawars left for Salimgarh and I went to my house. A little time had passed and it was 6 p.m. when the bugle sounded. At the sound, the Indian forces got ready and left with their artillery from the magazine. I could see their preparations from the rooftop of a friend's house, and watched as they left, the bullocks pulling the wooden magazine carts.

It was a moonlit night. This force went out of the Qila a little later. They had mounted the big guns and artillery on a hill, a force of 2000 on that front; the rest of the forces reached Alipur and took up positions. I have heard that there was 1 mile or so between the armies. The night passed in this entrenchment. The purbias had kept three big guns on their left and the rest mounted on horses in the heart of the army. The big guns were now firing. I have heard that these were

instrumental in inflicting heavy losses on the British. The
British forces launched an attack on the big guns before the
morning namaz. These soldiers were wearing blue uniforms
and waving blue flags, so the Indian soldiers thought they were
the soldiers of the Fourth Regiment that the two cavalrymen
had told them about earlier. The Indian soldiers didn't fire on
them as they had discussed.

Alas! The Indian soldiers had fallen for the British ploy.

The battle raged on. Once the sawars realized that these
were British soldiers, they loaded their guns. By now, the
British soldiers had come close to them.

When the firing began, a witness said, the scene was
similar to one where cotton is being carded by the cotton-
dresser, the fibres of cotton flying in the air. Similarly, pieces
of the soldiers and their horses were flying in the air.

Nonetheless, the commander called out to his soldiers
with such passion and courage that the whole battlefield
echoed with his voice. The soldiers responded by jumping
their horses over the corpses and reaching the big guns.

The rest of the battle was fought with spears and bayonets.
The British soldiers eventually captured the guns of the rebels
and used them to fire on them. The infantrymen began
fighting each other and there was a volley of firing from both
sides, which was deafening.

> With the hooves of quadruped animals, on that broad plain
> The heavens and earth added another realm

The smoke from the gunpowder blackened the sky, and the
dust raised by the riders was similar to that of the day of
resurrection. It is impossible to determine how many soldiers
died on either side.

This continued for some time. For two hours, I heard the volley of fire continuously, and even after that, there was sound of sporadic fire.

At 8 a.m., when I was going to the Qila on duty, I passed by Jauhri Bazaar and saw the wounded soldiers returning to the city. Every injured man was being supported by three or four purbias. The streets were discoloured by the blood flowing from their wounds. It reminded me of Holi, when the streets would be coloured like this.

Two sawars passed by me. I saw that they had bullet wounds on their chests and a multitude of open wounds on their backs. Their entrails were in pieces, clotted with blood. In their right hands they held their pistols, and in their left the reins of their horses. There were no signs of affliction or panic on their faces. Indeed, they were in their senses and talking to each other as they came along. To this date, I am surprised as to how they stayed alive for so long and how they survived the journey of 5 kos from the battlefield to the city.

I saw three riders galloping behind them, holding blue flags. People asked them where they got those flags.

'They are the flags of the British cavalrymen. The horses also belong to them.'

For proof, they said that the hooves of those horses bore British numbers, which I bent down and saw for myself. They said those horses belonged to the cavalrymen they had killed, and their forces had won. However, they were lying. The case was, in fact, the opposite, which I will describe later.

There was a sawar galloping behind them. His horse had bayonet wounds, and blood was flowing from them like water from a tap. Its head was red with blood. There was another injured man behind him. He had lost his arm below the elbow and blood was flowing from it, yet he was walking on his own.

He was accompanied by a couple of purbias who kept telling him that they would carry him to the camp, but he refused their help and told them to stay away.

I met many such wounded and injured men on my way.

I found Hakim Ahsanullah Khan and Mehboob Ali khwaja-sara and a few other royal employees sitting together when I reached the Qila. They were discussing the battle but no one knew the true state of affairs or its outcome. By now it was 11 a.m., and Mehboob Ali Khan and Ahsanullah Khan got up and went to their houses to eat their meal. I too left for my house for lunch. When I reached the gate of the naqqarkhana, I saw that a few purbias were bringing in a man they had captured. An officer of the arsenal walked alongside me, coming from the Diwan-e-Aam. When they met each other at the gate, the purbias said, 'This prisoner is a cavalryman from the Fourth Regiment. He was surrounded by our sawars at the time of battle. We have captured him.'

The officer didn't question the captive. Instead, he pulled the captive's Isfahani sword and immediately began attacking him with it. As I was next to the captive, I was rattled and quickly climbed on to the platform made for the soldiers to sit on. The officer gave the captive's face three blows, but strangely there was not a single mark on his body. One of the purbias said, 'Chase him away,' and he was released. He ran towards the Dilli Darwaza's Tripolia. A purbia shot him from behind and he fell down, face forward.

I left from the Qila Darwaza, and going via Urdu Bazaar, I passed the Khooni Darwaza in front of the kotwali and reached Ashraf Beg's apartment. There I saw around 200–250 sawars in a bad state. They had muddied faces and uniforms, and their sweaty horses were coated with mud, standing under the trees near the strip of concrete in the river. They gave every appearance of a routed army. The risaldar from the Third Regiment, with whom I had spoken regarding freeing the British captives on the first day, was standing before them.

As I was already acquainted with him, I greeted him and asked about the battle. He told me the whole sequence of events, from the beginning to the end. He said, 'We were fooled by two cavalrymen from the Fourth Regiment. We were misled and the British captured our artillery. The platoons from both sides kept fighting each other and there was firing for one and a half hours. Our forces were losing. We were retreating and firing at our enemies. While our riders were firing from the big guns, the Lucknow regiment, which had recently come to our aid, asked us to retreat. They asked us to let them attack the cavalry that was suppressing us. We let them have the field and the Lucknow regiment came down fiercely on the British. A fierce battle ensued with pistols being fired constantly on each side. This raged for an hour and some sawars were wounded and some killed.

'A few sawars returned safely and the cannons were mounted in the Tripolia near Mahaldar Khan.[86] The sawars hid on both sides near them. The cannons were mounted in all the three arches of the Tripolia and they blocked the way for the British army. Finally, the British cannons came and faced us. One of the British cannonballs hit the front of our cannon and completely destroyed it. It was sent off to the city. The second cannon was hit on the wheels and became useless. The wheel was replaced and it was sent off to the city. A cannonball stuck in the mouth of the third cannon, and thus, all three cannons were rendered useless. When our cannons stopped firing, the British army attacked us and forced the artillery to retreat. They were unaware that our forces were hiding at the sides and came forward fearlessly. When the rebels saw that the British forces were now in the middle of the road, they fired a volley of bullets from both sides. Many British soldiers were killed and the scene was reminiscent of a cat among pigeons. The British retreated toward the cantonment and the rebel forces came inside the city and locked the gates.

'When our forces on the ridge saw that the army had entered the city, they left everything and came back to the city as well. They left the cannons and tents behind, along with the magazine.

'When the British entered the cantonment and saw that the ridge was completely deserted, they captured the ready-made front and set fire to the tents. They turned the cannons towards Delhi and strengthened their defences.

'The purbias who had returned took the cannons from the magazine and mounted them on the towers.'

The Rebels Are Shut inside the Fort

Now there was no more fighting on the open battlefield. Instead, there was entrenchment and fortification. Guns were being fired day and night. The British were entrenched on the ridge, from Frazer Sahib's kothi to the Flagstaff tower. On the other side, their encampment stretched from the Kashmiri Gate Burj to the Siyah Burj[87] of the Kabuli Darwaza. From the Lahori Darwaza Burj till the burj of the Farashkhana wicket gate, artillery was mounted. There was firing all day on the city.

May God keep us safe from cannonballs. When one bursts and its pieces fly in the air, it can destroy entire buildings, however high they may be. If it falls on the ground, it can make a 10-yard crater and blow all the houses of the area in its wake. It is the wrath of God.

The bugle would sound as soon as it was morning, and fauj-e-baghiya would get ready and station themselves outside the Lahori Darwaza. There, they would begin firing. This would continue till evening when the soldiers would return to their camps.

Now the baghis were pouring in from every side and *kampu* would join them every day.

First, the Nasirabad kampu came, and then the army from Nimuch and Mirar.[88]

Now there was a kampu of Sidhari Singh and one led by General Ghaus Mohammad Khan Tunde, so called because he had lost both his arms in battle. Many other regiments and artillery came and joined them and crowds of people from the cantonments nearby collected in Delhi.

The Nasirabad force taunted the rebels as soon as they had arrived. 'You haven't gained victory over one hill so far! Tomorrow, we will go fight. You wait and watch what we do. You keep fighting here and we will go and attack the British army from the rear.'

The Third Battle

The Nasirabad forces got ready by 8 a.m., and taking a lot of ammunition with them, set off towards the cantonment via Teli Wada and Dheeraj Pahari. They crossed over the bridge and circuited the Mughalpura gardens.[89] The battle with the British forces began at noon. There was fierce fighting, the sound of cannon fire echoing everywhere. The cannon fire reminded me of two fencers facing each other with their foils, crying out when hit.

The firing was continuous, and once in a while gunshots could be heard too. It was a unique battle, the likes of which no one had seen or heard. The reality was that both armies facing each other belonged to the same government and had been trained by the same British officers. It was a fight between master and pupil, the only difference being that the government's star was dominant and the ungrateful rebels were overpowered. If this fauj baghiya had been facing some other enemy, they would have torn them to pieces.

The narrators, who swear that any errors are on their head, said that the government army had set up camp in Alipur and the camp followers and baggage had set off for the same. Only God knows what is true or false. I can only relate hearsay since no one had gone there to verify these claims.

In brief, the fighting and bloodshed continued from 12 p.m. to 9 p.m. We could hear the sounds of battle. After a while, the sounds stopped.

The army came back the next day at noon and described what I have already outlined above. There is no need to repeat it.

'What could we do? Our ammunition ran out. Had we got some more we would have fought the whole night, since the government's army was on the run. We sent sawars to get more ammunition, but the people at the darwaza stopped them from taking it out and said, 'It's night and God forbid the British army snatch it away from you.' They argued with us the whole night. The British army attacked us three times and we managed to contain them. We only had three cartridges left.'

The Arrival of General Bakht Khan

General Bakht Khan[90] arrived from Bareilly after this battle with a kampu of 14,000, some cannons and two or three cavalry regiments. He also brought a few lakh rupees. Another general came with a kampu from Mirar. He brought 500 soldiers in the blue British uniform. Riffraff entered the city as well, coming in large groups of 300–400 men.

The state of Delhi was such that when the sawars went to attack their enemies, the mischief-makers would also go with them and collect money, weapons and horses from the injured and dead. No Hindu or Muslim from the city ever accompanied the fauj baghiya—not at the beginning of the fighting, nor at the end. From the very first day, it was these ignoble people who looted the city, along with the purbias.

They looted houses, the bank and even the *bakshikhana*, and now they had purchased horses and entered into the service of the rebels. Most of them were from Kaghazi Mohalla and from the area around Kashmiri Darwaza. They consisted of butchers, paper sellers, shoemakers, local musclemen such as Gami, cudgellers and sundry ruffians—there was no genteel person among them. In fact, the decent people had stopped coming out of their homes as they were busy trying to overcome their own troubles.

The royal employees had been living hand to mouth ever since these rogues entered the city, since they were not being paid salaries. In fact, even the Badshah's stipend had been stopped; how could he pay salaries, then? The Badshah got a stipend of Rs 1 lakh from the British treasury. When the British were uprooted and their treasury looted, there was no one to make the payment to the Badshah.

This was a scene of strife, trouble and destruction. Those who had some valuables at home were selling them and making ends meet while soldiers with salaries of Rs 4 were starving. Since factories had shut down, the people who earned a bit of money via their skills and craftsmanship had no means of livelihood left.

The poor Badshah was always in a state of worry and anxiety and had stopped coming out of his Mahal. He was always sad and teary-eyed. Sometimes, he would come out in the evening and sit in the tasbihkhana alone and curse the ingrates.

We were instructed to take turns and be present in the deorhi in the evenings.

The Emotions of the Emperor

It was the third quarter of one of my nights in the deorhi when the baridar called, 'At attention.'

We quickly put on our turbans, adjusted our clothes and got ready. There were only a few of us there: Shahzada Mirza Qaiser, Hameed Khan *jamadar khaas biradaran*, Mir Fateh Ali *jamadar kaharaan*, and Hussain Baksh, the *arz begi*, when the Badshah came out of the palace.

We made our salutations and the Badshah sat on the marble throne in front of the tasbihkhana. Hameed Khan stood against one column while Mir Fateh Ali leaned against another. Mirza Qaiser was to the right of the throne. I stood next to him while Hussain Baksh stood beside me.

Huzoor addressed us. 'Do you know what the outcome of the events unfolding before us will be?'

Hameed Khan replied with folded hands. 'Huzoor, your glory has been revived after 150 years. The empire which had been taken away has been returned.'

Badshah Salamat replied, 'You are all ignorant of the facts that I know. Hear me out. I had nothing to lose. The foundation of strife is wealth, treasures, land and kingdoms, and I had none of them. I was already living the life of a mendicant. Why would anyone have any enmity with me?

Why would anyone be envious of a faqir? I was spending my life like a faqir living in his *takiya*[91] along with a few of my close people, and I had nothing to lose.

'Now a fire was started in Meerut by God's will, and is raging in Delhi at present. Trouble has begun and I have realized that the rebellious sky and wicked world (*falak e ghadar aur zamana e na-hanjar*) want to see my family destroyed. The family of Chaghtai Sultans had been reigning thus far, but now no traces of this name will be left.

'These ingrates who have rebelled against their masters and appeared here—they will go off soon. When they couldn't stay loyal to their masters, how can I expect any loyalty from them? These rogues came to ruin my dynasty, and now they have destroyed it. After they leave, the British are going to cut my head off, along with that of my children, and hang it on the Qila merlons. None of you will escape their wrath.

'If any of you are still alive, then mark my words: You will never be able to eat in peace, and the nobles of Hind will fall lower than village peasants.'

After these painful words, he went back into the Qila.

Four or five days after this, the emperor came out of the palace again at around 8 a.m. After getting on to his sedan chair, he went towards Salimgarh. On his return, he stopped in the garden of the late Wali Ahad Bahadur Mirza Fakhru,[92] his second son, who had died a year before. I was holding one of the legs of the emperor's sedan and he told me, 'I have heard that Agha Begum is very fretful and worried. She cries a lot. You must go to her and try to carry out her orders to the letter. I am sending you because you have grown up in the palace, since the age of four. No one is a stranger to you. You can go and talk to her through the curtain.'

I folded my hands and accepted the work given to me.

The emperor continued. 'You must tell them that Huzoor has said that the family of the prophets and saints of Allah have borne countless miseries and hardships, but these ended along with Prophet Mohammad (peace be upon him) and his progeny. Think of the calamities that befell them. In spite of them, they stayed calm and patient. Your honour is not more than that of the ladies of the Prophet's family, the *Rasool Zadiya'n*.[93] Find solace in recalling their misfortunes, and stay calm and bear your troubles with fortitude.'

When I heard these words from the lips of the Badshah, I started crying. Once his sedan reached the palace, I left for the palace of Nawab Agha Begum Sahiba, the emperor's daughter.

I sent word via the khwaja-sara, telling her that her humble slave had come with a message from huzoor purnoor.

The princess made arrangements for purdah inside the palace and invited me in. She told me to give her the emperor's message on my oath of honour.

After saluting her, I relayed the emperor's message verbatim. The princess asked me to take her answer to him. She said that though she had been very anxious about the destruction, loss of reputation and honour before, she was at peace now. 'Insha'Allah, now with Huzoor's guidance such a transgression will not occur.'

I came back and relayed the message to the emperor through the khwaja-sara.

Earlier that same day, Hakim Ahsanullah Khan had joined the people walking with the sedan on the emperor's return. He had joined us when the sedan was passing under the apartments of Mahboob Ali Khan. Four or five purbias came and said something to Hakim Ahsanullah Khan. God knows what he said, but one of them pointed his loaded gun at Hakim's chest and wanted to shoot him. However, one of the emperor's bodyguards moved the gun's muzzle towards the sky. The emperor stretched his hand out from his sedan and caught the Hakim's head and brought him in front. He began abusing the ungrateful purbias. All the purbia officers who were standing in the Diwan-e-Aam came running out and began apologizing with folded hands. Things were sorted out.

There was always a conflict between these uncouth purbias and us, the royal employees.

One morning, around 7 a.m., the Badshah came out of his palace and sat on a chair in the central arch of the Diwan-e-Khaas. A few people were present. Two royal attendants were standing behind the chair and flapping the baal-e-huma. My brother-in-law, Agha Sultan, was standing next to the chair and I stood beside him with a few other men.

Suddenly, I saw a well-built, short, middle-aged purbia, clad in a coarse kurta and dhoti. He had a cloth tied on his head in such a way that the pate was visible, and an officer's sword hanging from his neck. He came from behind the hammam, walking up to the emperor and saluting him.

My brother-in-law stopped him. 'Hey, you! Where do you think you are going?'

He didn't listen to him.

The purbia came close to the emperor and caught hold of Huzoor's hand. He said, 'Listen, you old man, we have made you the emperor.'[94]

I could not control myself and started trembling with anger. I pushed him hard. 'Oh disrespectful, uncouth man!' I said, 'Is this the way to behave in an emperor's court?'

He managed to save himself from falling, and standing upright, put his hand on his sword. I started pulling out my

own sword. When he had caught the sword's hilt, a son of a
Saiyyed from Najafgarh (who was my own age, an officer in
the British regiment) moved forward and caught his neck in
such a strong grasp that it seemed his eyes would pop out. My
sword was only halfway out when those around me caught my
hand and said, 'Let him go.'

With a wave of his hand, the Badshah indicated that
I come behind his chair. The purbia was pushed out of the
Diwan-e-Khaas by the people gathered there.

The Badshah started giving the choicest of Mughal abuses
and ordered that his sawari be called. He wanted to leave the
Qila and go and live in Khwaja Sahib. He had only reached
the latticed door when all the officers got together and came
running and stopped the emperor's sedan. They pleaded with
him and pushed the erring purbia at his feet. The Badshah
wanted to leave the Qila,[95] but the officers didn't let him leave.
Instead, the sedan chair was reversed towards the tasbihkhana.

I didn't know that this unfortunate and uncouth man was
actually General Bakht Khan. We learned later that he was
the general from Bareilly. Since he was dressed like a soldier,
I thought he was one of them.

Ever since Bakht Khan had arrived with his forces, there
had no longer been daily battles. He stopped the Indian forces
from going to fight the British every morning. He had other
strategies in mind.

For twenty days, there were no battles, though the
bombardment of the city continued as usual.

I must describe one more thing here. The 500 men from
the British regiments who had come to join the rebel forces
were very impatient. They would incite the soldiers to fight
and take them to the places where the conflict was fiercest.
Then they would remove themselves from the scene.

There was one old woman who would wear a headband and tie a dupatta around her waist and be right in front during the fighting, instigating the soldiers: 'Come on, sons, let's go for Jihad!' We didn't know who she was. She would gather people from the market every day and take them to fight. Though she led them, she always returned safe and sound, while hundreds were slain because of her.

When the army entered the city, no one could find her. She simply disappeared.

The Fourth Battle[96]

The soldiers gathered in the city were getting restless and criticizing their inactivity, as there had been no action since the arrival of Bakht Khan. 'You have put the war in abeyance! What is the reason for that?'

The generals decided that they would lead the soldiers behind the ridge and besiege the British army, cutting off their supplies. This met with everyone's approval.

One day, Bakht Khan took his kampu and encamped at a distance of 4–5 kos from the city on this side of the river, near the bridge. The next day, Sidhari Singh and Ghaus Mohammad Khan left with their kampu. When they reached Bakht Khan's camp, they remonstrated with him and asked him why he had not camped on the other side of the river.

'If the British blow up this bridge, we will be cut off and stranded,' they said. They both crossed the bridge and set up camp on the other side.

The camp had not yet been set up when it started raining and the jungle was flooded. Sidhari Singh had set his camp up near a hollow and a lake. The Najafgarh Lake is famous and the water of the Sahibi River[97] flows into it. The cannons and big guns were drowned in the water, which rose to waist height. The magazine boxes that held the ammunition got stuck in the mud and slush.

The British forces began firing continuously from their cannons and artillery. They blew up barrels of gunpowder in the river, which in turn blew up the bridge and cut off the escape of the encamped forces.

Bakht Khan's army opened fire on the British forces from the other side. Sidhari Singh and Ghaus Mohammad Khan were caught in the crossfire and had no place to run.

Somehow, Sidhari Singh and Ghaus Mohammad Khan managed to take the few men that they had left and bring them to Shahjahanabad in the morning. The camp was abandoned and the tents, magazine and artillery left there. Thousands of lives were lost in this episode.

The next day, Bakht Khan returned to the city with his kampu.

The Rebels' Arsenal Is Blown Up

After the battle at Najafgarh, the purbias started losing steam and their enthusiasm and desire to fight was greatly reduced. During this time, another unfortunate event took place on 7 August.

A magazine had been kept in Begum Samru's haveli in Chudiwala Mohalla, where gunpowder was prepared. 700 mounds of gunpowder were made and used here every day. One afternoon, around 3 p.m., there was the sound of a huge explosion. It was as though 100 cannons had gone off simultaneously. I climbed up to the second floor of my house and looked around. I saw a huge cloud of smoke and dust in the sky, rising to the south of my house. It seemed the magazine had exploded.

I sent someone to find out what had happened. My man came back and told me, 'All 700 men working in the magazine were blown up along with it. There is a heap of corpses and houses are catching fire. There's a huge crowd of spectators. There is total chaos. Those whose relatives worked in the magazine are crying and wailing inconsolably.'

We were talking when Azizuddin Khan, nephew of Ahsanullah Khan, came running to me in a state of panic. The women of his house had come along with him. I brought all the ladies into the house and asked him to tell me what had happened.

'As soon as the magazine blew up, the purbias came to Hakimji's house,' he said. 'They accused him of conspiring with the British and blowing up the magazine.[98] They have now looted his house. Fortunately, Hakimji was not at home, and was in the service of the emperor at the Qila, or else he would have been killed. The women of the house jumped into the neighbour's house. I have brought them now to your house.'[99]

The Surprise Attack

Just a few days had passed when another event took place.[100] Half a mile from Kashmiri Darwaza, there was a yellow kothi near the ridge, where the purbias had set up a front and put up big guns and cannons. They were using them to inflict considerable damage on the British forces. They had two platoons and people to man the artillery present at all times. Everyone had to stay there for two watches.

One day, as luck would have it, the soldiers departing after day duty told their replacements to be careful, just in case the enemy attacked at night. The night guards took their places.

Now let me tell you a few things about the night guard. It was these very men who had looted the bakshikhana and the bank. They were often in a state of stupor thanks to drinking bhang and eating *kalakand* and laddu peda during the day.

When they reached the kothi, they were alert at first, but when the night came and a cool breeze started blowing, they were unable to stay awake. They kept the guns at an angle and, spreading their dhotis, fell into deep sleep.

> Drink bhang in such a manner that you empty all the stores
> All your family is lying dead and you lie inebriated

These people were snoring away to glory. The spies took this news to the British. They informed them that the front was abandoned, the soldiers were all fast asleep and it was the right time to attack.

The British officers took two platoons of Gurkhas, one of Majwi[101] and one of the British themselves, and rushed barefoot down the ridge. They carried away the guns, captured the cannons and only then woke the sleeping soldiers, saying, 'Get up, people of the faith, the goras are here.'

One soldier got up, rubbing his eyes. The Gurkhas shot his head off.

They started attacking with swords and sabres. There was tumult and crying from every side and the few who were not killed ran in a state of panic towards the city.

The Nasirabad Platoon, which had changed duty with these men, had found the city gates locked when they tried to enter the city, as it wasn't safe to leave them open at night. They were resting on the patri outside Kashmiri Darwaza when the ambushed soldiers reached them. After abusing and scolding them, the Nasirabad platoon told these fleeing soldiers to lie with them and they themselves lay down silently but with loaded guns.

Meanwhile, the British force came chasing them, hoping to enter the city behind them. They were unaware of the Nasirabad platoon lying in wait. A volley of firing began and the soldiers manning the cannons on the parapet of Kashmiri Darwaza and Siyah Burj also joined in when they saw the British forces. The situation can be best described as *Khuda de bande le*—only divine intervention could help.

It was difficult to save oneself from the volleys of fire. There were heaps of corpses all over.

The British troops retreated. They rushed back and took over the yellow kothi they had attacked earlier and turned their guns towards the city. These guns were now fired incessantly at the city. This continued for the whole night.

Cannons and artillery were being fired from both sides, but the Indians lost the front they had set up in the kothi, which was now under British control. The British forces were also reinforced by troops from outside.

A senior British officer was killed in this battle and his corpse was left lying between the two forces. In the morning, both sides tried to pick up the dead body. Cannons and artillery were firing from both sides with the purbias hell-bent on acquiring the valuable weapons that were on the dead officer.

The dead body was lying a short distance before the Kashmiri Darwaza. The two sides fought a day and a half for the officer's corpse. It was a matter of prestige for both of them.

The guns fired day and night and thousands of people were killed.

At last, as the sun set, one purbia reached the body by rolling on the ground. He tied one end of his turban to the dead body and slowly pulled it behind him. He and his fellows took the officer's pistols and sword, and, after stripping the body of valuables, left it there.

In the morning, the British saw that the body had disappeared. The battle was stopped.

The purbia brought the weapons taken from the officer and showed them to everyone in the Qila. He brought it to the house of the royal steward. He showed them to Ahsanullah Khan and told him they had fought over these weapons for two days.

I saw the weapons with my own eyes. The pair of pistols was good but the sword was invaluable. There was golden carving on its hilt and the scabbard was black. Its colour was like the neck of a peacock, with something written on it in gold.

A New Front at Siyah Burj

After this battle, the British established a front on the position they had snatched from the Indian forces and slowly began spreading towards the city.

The road outside the city gate turned from Kabuli Darwaza and went towards Kashmiri Darwaza. There was a hollow and a drain a short distance from this road. The wood sellers had their outlets here. There was a pile of wooden logs and discarded girders lying about. All this was next to the Siyah Burj of the Badar-Roo Darwaza.

One night, the British forces set fire to the wood. The billowing smoke provided the perfect cover and they began setting up a front here.

The Indians at Siyah Burj were perplexed at the origin of the smoke and could not figure out how it had arisen.

Once the British had everything in readiness, they brought forty cannons, and fired at the Siyah Burj.

It was then that the forces at the Siyah Burj woke to what had happened. But there was nothing they could do! They tried their best, fired from their big guns, but they were of no use against the cannons of the other side.

The battlements and turrets of the Siyah Burj, which were being used by the Indians as cover, began falling, and it was difficult for them to stand and return fire. As a result, all the armaments began falling into the ditch.

This firing continued for eight days and nights. On the eighth day, the British saw that the Siyah Burj had been abandoned and there was no one to stop them. Then they came down from the Ridge and into the ruins of Mir Hasan's buildings. They set up their topkhana on the other side of Kabuli Darwaza. The fauj-e-baghiya brought their artillery from that side, and turned to face them. They spread out from the Lahori Darwaza to the canal at Kabuli Darwaza in the Teliwada grounds.

The canal provided the only cover between the two forces. Continuous firing could be heard from both sides, from here as well as from the artillery on the ridge.

The purbias were firing all their artillery from their positions on the Lahori Darwaza Burj. On this day, the city's houses, streets and doorways were trembling in the crossfire. It seemed as if it weren't a battle, but the advent of doomsday.

It was like:

> When the earth is shaken with its [final] earthquake
> (Quran: Surah Az-Zalzalah: 1)

Only God knows whether 300 or 400 cannons were raining fire on the people. This firing began at 5 a.m. and continued till 10 a.m.

I was going towards the Qila with five or six people around 8 a.m. when I saw that the entry gates of most of the streets were closed. There were locks on the doors, though the wicket gates were still open. I came out of the gate of the Chota Dariba and saw a few men returning from that side. One of them was the emperor's courtier.

'Where are you going?' he asked me.

'To the Qila,' I replied.

He told me not to go. The Qila gates were locked, he explained, so I returned.

At this time, all the shops in the bazaar were closed. There were just a couple of men walking about.

I thought that I would go and find out what was happening. When I neared the Darwaza,[102] I found it was closed. There was a lock on it, and a cannon mounted in front of it. There were a few men standing behind the darwaza and one *havaldar* on top of it, giving an account of the ongoing battle. The people were listening to him avidly.

During this time, one regiment of sawars came from around the side of the Qila and told the people at the darwaza to open it so that they could go out. The keepers of the darwaza refused to open the door, and the havaldar asked the sawars to exit from the Kashmiri Darwaza.

He said, 'There is a huge crowd there. Look out! Your sawars have attacked.'

The Indians were going towards the Mithai ka Pul while the British soldiers were heading towards the Kashmiri Darwaza. The sawars turned their horses towards the path that ran behind the Lahori Darwaza parapets towards the Kabuli Darwaza.

I turned towards my own house. When I reached Bhawani Shankar's Chatta, I saw that there were innumerable purbias running out of it. There were many people in the bazaar at this time. They stopped the purbias and asked, 'Where are you running after having forced the battle on us?'

The purbias threw down their weapons and said, 'Brothers, we are done fighting; now you fight yourselves.' And leaving their guns, they ran away.

When people saw this state of affairs, they all went back to their houses. I went swiftly towards Ballimaran, but found the gate was locked. I ran towards the gate of Chota Dariba and though this was also locked, the wicket gate was open.

Now I was presented with another spectacle: when I reached the wicket, a volley of firing came towards me from the front of the kotwali. The bullets began hitting the stone of the drains, as if they were hailstones. I saw that there was a party of the British standing outside the kotwali.

One of those with me complained that he had been shot. I told him, 'Let's go now. We will see to it at home,' and going quickly through the wicket gate, I pulled him after me.

Once all of us were inside, we locked the window and made haste towards our houses.

When we had reached, I asked the injured man where he had been shot. He replied, 'In my stomach.' As soon as he opened his dress the bullet fell out on to the wooden settee. It was long and empty at the ball, like the areca nut. There was a four-finger-wide leather amulet hanging from the man's neck. The bullet had burnt through it and been stopped by the actual amulet that hung inside. As a result, the man was merely bruised. The bullet had left a huge, round, red mark, but he was not seriously wounded.

I was sitting in my diwankhana, lost in thought over the situation. 'You have seen with your own eyes that the British forces have entered the city and purbias have run away. Now the British soldiers are going to enter the houses and slaughter the inhabitants. Death is at our doorsteps! Let's see what happens now.'

But I had still not told my mother about these events for fear of causing her anxiety. I was just sitting there and softly chanting prayers for deliverance to Allah.

This continued for an hour or so, until I heard the firing of a cannon. It seemed very close, as though it were in my own *mohalla*.

When I heard it again, I took a few people with me and went out to investigate. When I reached the main road of our mohalla, I found that there seemed to be a lot of people there, just like on normal days. I asked them, 'What happened? Where has the British army gone?'

They told me, 'The people have chased them away. There are riots in the city now.'

I went to Chawri Bazaar and saw that there were thousands of people roaming the streets carrying sticks, clubs, cudgels, swords and poleaxes.

When I reached the bazaar via the Jama Masjid, I was presented with a strange sight. Corpses were piled like logs. This was the same place where the dervish had made the prophecy to me four months before the ghadar, saying there would be bloodshed at this spot.

I went ahead and saw more dead bodies. When I asked the people of the bazaar how this had happened, they said, 'One party of the British army reached the steps of the Jama Masjid, and some people were looting the houses of the common folks. The British soldiers wanted to enter the Masjid. The Muslim travellers gathered inside saw this and feared that they would now kill inside God's house. They thought it would be better to go down and fight the soldiers. The Muslims came out of the Masjid Darwaza and down the steps. The British forces aimed their guns at them. The ones who survived kept moving forward and a terrible fight ensued.

'A huge uproar arose in the city. People ran out of their houses with whatever they could lay their hands on—wooden sticks, rods from their beds, swords and so on. Some of the British party were killed—they are the ones whose bodies are lying here. The rest ran off to join their army.'

I went via the Dariba Kalan through the Khooni Darwaza to the front of the kotwali. I saw dead bodies piled up, lining the street from the Jama Masjid to the kotwali. There were many corpses at the point where I had been fired at in the morning. I saw a metal bag filled with gunpowder in front of the kotwali hauz.

When I reached the Chota Dariba gate, I saw a cannon under the peepal tree, but there was no one manning it. I was convinced that the cannon shot I had heard had come from this cannon. After investigation, it was found that some men had pulled it from the Lahori Darwaza and once they had set it up here, they had fired at the British forces and harmed those standing in front of the kotwali. A few men had been injured in that attack, and some killed. When they fired a second time and more people started dying, the British fled towards Kashmiri Darwaza. It is said that the people of that area took shelter in the Kashmiri Darwaza and the courthouse.

After learning these details, I went back to my house via the Chota Dariba again.

By evening, the rioters had spread all over the city, all the way to Hamid Ali Khan's kothi. The British forces had set up cannons near the kothi, and this prevented them from moving further, since they didn't even have a gun to protect themselves. The chaos lasted all evening, after which the tired people came back to their houses.

At midnight, the British soldiers started the slaughter. They entered houses and began killing those sleeping inside, climbing on to the roofs to get at those sleeping there too.

In the morning, people living near and in Kashmiri Darwaza, Badar-Roo Darwaza and Kabuli Darwaza, as well as those in the Subhan Phatak, started running towards our side of the city.

The Emperor in Humayun's Tomb

Let me provide a brief summary of the entry of the British forces into the city. When the havaldar on the Lahori Darwaza stated that the British forces had advanced towards Kashmiri Darwaza, in reality they attacked just at that time. Finding the Siyah Burj unmanned, with no one there to stop the assault, they descended into the ditch and scaled the Burj with a ladder. After they had climbed the Siyah Burj, the purbia army standing on the nearby parapets jumped down and ran away. Thus, from the Kabuli Darwaza to the Kashmiri Darwaza to Baggapur Ghat, there was no one to man the parapets of the Shahr Panah. Even the soldiers on the parapet of the Lahori Darwaza and the bombardiers on the Burj ran away.

The Indian forces stationed outside the city remained there. The soldiers manning the city parapets ran away and joined them.

Thus, the British army entered the city. Those who were outside were left out there.

Now there were only locals left in the city, with all the purbias having fled. The British soldiers were spread throughout the city, from the Lahori Darwaza to beyond the Dilli Darwaza. They surrounded the area extending from Paharganj to the Jailhouse.[103]

The people of the city would walk around in the day, bent on killing or being killed. In the evening, the British forces would come out and force their way into houses, murdering the inhabitants.

The city was desolate, all the shops closed. There was no way to buy provisions. The people had no access to food, and there were deaths from starvation. The distressed, distraught and suffering locals began leaving the city along with their women and children, leaving all their possessions behind.

This continued for three days. On the third day, in the evening, the emperor left the Qila and went to Humayun's tomb.

By evening the populace of the city also panicked and, taking their women and children, rushed out of the city, leaving behind their possessions and houses. The tumult and turbulence of that day was akin to doomsday and cannot be described.

> The exodus of the citizens without their possessions
> The ladies who used to be veiled, now bare-headed

The misery of the populace who had nothing to sustain them, the loss of purdah for women who had never stepped out of their houses, their anguish at having to come out without veils and cover, the clamour of the hungry and wailing children, was enough to tear at one's heart. Only those who saw this scene can understand the pain.

> It was no less an agony than doomsday
> May God never show us such a turn again

The City Is Abandoned

The evening the emperor left the Qila and reached Humayun's tomb, Nawab Hamid Ali Khan's servant came to my father at midnight and gave him a message.

'Why are you waiting free of care in your house? The emperor has left the Qila and the locals are fleeing the city. For God's sake, leave your house and depart from the city with your family. Can't you see that the city is being murdered? I am going out of the city with my family. You can send the women of your family along with mine.'

Nawab Hamid Ali Khan's house was near the Kashmiri Darwaza, but a month earlier he had rented a house in our mohalla.

After this message, everyone left the house in whatever clothes he or she was wearing. My mother didn't even pick up a ring from her jewellery in her state of panic. My wife had stitched a mattress and bolster in which she had stuffed the valuable clothes she had got in her trousseau, along with her jewellery. She spread the mattress in the cart and kept the bolster beside her.

Thus, my parents, my wife, all my siblings and all the women of Nawab Hamid Ali Khan's house went to Matia Mahal to my in-laws' house.

My mother and Nawab Hamid Ali Khan's wife told my father-in-law's elder wife, *jagirdar* of Sadirpur and Raispur villages, 'Begum Sahiba, why are you sitting here? Pack up and leave with your children. This is not the time to sit in your house. We have come to take you along with us.'

She agreed to come with us. I pleaded with my father-in-law, Nawab Amir Mirza Khan, 'For God's sake, please come away with us.'

By 1 a.m., arrangements had been made for travel. My in-laws and children came to Matia Mahal Phatak. My younger brother-in-law, Kazim Mirza, was sitting in my father-in-law's lap. We reached Matia Mahal Darwaza, conversing with each other. Here, we met an unforeseen calamity. A woman named Kilo was sitting in a state of *majzuba*[104] just in front of the Darwaza. As soon as she saw my father-in-law, she called out loudly, 'Miyan Amir Mirza sahib, where are you going? God has not given permission for you to leave. Have you forgotten?'

As soon as these words left her lips, Amir Mirza Sahib's feet became glued to the ground and he told Kilo, 'Undoubtedly, I have erred.'

The carriage driver was ordered to return to the house at once. I pleaded with them for a long time, others asked them too, but my father-in-law refused to listen. We all begged him to have mercy on the family of fifty people, to come along with us.

He kept saying, 'It is not God's will.'

Another catastrophe struck us at this time. Miyan Nasiruddin sahib, my father-in-law's maternal cousin, came and said, 'Bhai Sahib, please come back. Come to my house. There are some European women hiding there. They are saying that you have nothing to fear. They will plead your case to the British and save you.'

Hearing this, my father-in-law's mind was set at ease and he told me, 'Son, you go. I can't bring myself to leave.'

There was nothing I could do but leave with the women of my house. He returned to his house with his family.

I took my family and the women of Nawab Hamid Ali Khan's house to my maternal grandmother's house near Dilli Darwaza. It was 2 a.m. Some of my other family members were also gathered there. There were 200 men and women altogether in the haveli of Hakim Momin Ali Khan.

We prepared to leave the city at dawn. My wife had not come with me and had instead gone back with her parents. I sent my younger brother, Umrao Mirza, to their house to ask whether they would send her with me. She would share my state of affairs. But if they wanted to keep her with them then, May God protect you! We would be considered separated for life.

My brother went and relayed my message to my father-in-law. He said that I could take his daughter wherever I wanted, as he had no rights over her. The women of her house kept asking her not to go, but my brother put my wife in a palanquin and brought her to me.

We all left the city and came out of the Dilli Darwaza.

The ground in front of Dilli Darwaza was like the day of resurrection.

There were thousands of *purdahnasheen* women, tiny children, young and old men pouring out of the city in a state of panic. No woman remembered to veil herself. A few pious women were walking barefoot with just a chador to cover themselves.

Wretchedness had spread on delicate ladies
A pallor was seen on moon-like faces
Woe the impropriety of the veiled women
Doomsday had come before its time
How do I describe the turn of fate?
Oh! That burning sand and barefoot helplessness

After a lot of tribulation, our caravan of 200 people reached the *barfkhana*. Nawab Hamid Ali Khan sahib had already taken the entire barfkhana on rent. We spent the evening there, sans food or water. In the morning, some efforts were made to provide food to the group.

I asked my wife if she had brought any jewellery with her. She replied, 'Except for the name of God, I have nothing with me. Whatever jewellery and clothes I brought to my grandmother's house were left there. My grandmother said, 'O foolish girl, what are you doing? Don't you know that such possessions are the enemy of life! Bandits will loot you for them. Your husband will be killed. Throw them away as a sacrifice for your life.' She kept my jewellery in a house where other noblemen had kept their costly possessions. That place can only be accessed by someone who knows about it.'

I was very troubled upon hearing this, as I didn't know how we would survive without money. After a while, I remembered something and told my family to hurry up while I went ahead to make arrangements for our journey.

I left the barfkhana and hurried to my house via Ajmeri Darwaza. The canopied bed was intact. I quickly started stripping it of the silver plating. I took whatever I could in my state of anxiety. I managed to strip around 1.5 kg or more of silver from it, which I tied in a bedsheet. In the storeroom,

I found a bundle with around four or five *do-shaala*s (double shawls, normally worn by men), angarkhas and handkerchiefs with silver and gold embroidery on them. I picked those up and left the house again.

When I was leaving, I found a blind relative, his wife and another woman standing in the portico.

'What are you doing here?' I asked them.

'We have come to seek shelter with you,' he said. 'Where are you going?'

I described my circumstances and asked them to come along.

He said, 'I am blind. How can I go? Leave me here in your house.'

I showed them into the house and told them where the food was kept. It would be enough for two or three months.

I left the house with my bundle. By the time I reached the end of my mohalla, the bundle had started to feel too heavy, and I realized that I would not be allowed to reach the barfkhana with it as someone was sure to loot it on the way. The Gujjar bandits and Mewati villagers were killing and looting anyone who set foot outside the city. They were even stealing the clothes off one's back. I thought of returning to my house and leaving the bundle there, but at that moment I spotted a friend, Jauhri Kilomal, who was also a resident of the area.

I asked him to take my bundle to his house. 'If it escapes being looted, I will come and take it; otherwise it is an alm in lieu of my life,' I said.

Kilomal made excuses and refused to take it, but I kept insisting, and we finally reached Ajmeri Darwaza. By now the populace of the city was leaving. The entire area outside the Dilli Darwaza of Paharganj and Jaisinghpura[105] was like a jungle crawling with people.

I somehow managed to reach the barfkhana with the silver. I took it to a bania's shop and asked him to give me provisions in its place.

He said, 'I will give you 12 annas (75 paise) for this.'

I gave him the silver and took back 4 annas cash. I bought some earthen vessels and rations with the rest.

I gave the vessels and provisions to my family and asked them to make a simple meal of khichri. My brother filled water from the well and we all ate the khichri.

The city gates had been open till that day. From the next day, all the gates were locked. Those outside stayed outside, and those within remained there.

We could hear sporadic firing. I began worrying about my in-laws and my sister and her family. God knew what was happening with them.

Somehow, the night and the day passed.

The Departure of the Rebel Army

The next day, the rebel forces that were stationed outside the city blew up their magazine at 9 a.m. In the resulting confusion, they picked up their tents and possessions and left.

The officers of the rebel forces went to the emperor and begged him, 'Huzoor, please come with us. We have lost the battle here. We will set up a front in some other place and fight the British.'

The emperor replied, 'I won't go with you. You came to obliterate my house and destroy my subjects. You have accomplished that. Whatever was written in my fate has happened, and whatever else is written will happen. Go wherever you can.'

The rebels kept pleading with him, but the emperor refused. Finally, they left.

The Imprisonment of the Emperor

A day later, the Dilli Darwaza was opened, and Saunders[106] Sahib told the emperor, 'By the majesty of the emperor, the ungrateful fauj baghiya has been thrown out of the city. Now they will face their punishment. The city is now empty. Huzoor, please come back so that the city can be populated once again.'

The Badshah said, 'What will I achieve by returning? What connection do I have with the city? Let me remain in my ancestor's mausoleum where I have sought refuge. Whatever you have to do with me, do it here. Why do you want to humiliate me by taking me there? I know what your intentions are.'

Maulvi Rajab Ali[107] was also present and said, 'Please do not let such thoughts enter your mind. Please come with us. Begum Sahiba Nawab Zeenat Mahal should also accompany us.'[108]

Had he refused to accompany them, the emperor might have prevailed. But the unfortunate Badshah said, 'Bismillah,' and getting into his hawadar he left the tomb.

Zeenat Mahal got into her palanquin. Perhaps the young princes Jawan Bakht and Shah Abbas were also with her, but I cannot ascertain that.

When they came close to the Dilli Darwaza, Saunders Sahib asked the men carrying the emperor's hawadar to stop. He told the crowd that was accompanying them, 'Baba log, it is not expedient for all of you to enter the city. The British army is spread out through the whole city; there is the danger of riots. You must all stay here. I will call you once we have made arrangements in the city.'

He chose eighty-four old men to look after the Badshah. He took the emperor into the city and ensconced him in the mansion of Zeenat Mahal at Lal Kuan. The other men were told to give up their arms or they would be taken as rebels. Everyone surrendered their weapons.

It was proclaimed throughout the city that whosoever was found with weapons would be considered a criminal and rebel by the sarkar.

Accordingly, the entire populace surrendered their weapons as they didn't have the courage to face the British and, in any case, they would gain nothing by doing so. They began saying that the ungrateful tormentors had to be destroyed, so that their continued tribulations might stop.

Had the British forces, which entered the city, given solace to the embattled populace as rulers, instead of looting and plundering them, there would have been no riots. The general public was, in any case, sitting quietly behind closed doors. Not even a bird flew in the bazaar.

But when the British forces reached Khanum ka Bazaar and Paiwala'n Bazaar, they started killing all those who came in front of them. They even forced their way into the houses of a few residents, thus forcing them to retaliate and riot. Had this not happened, there would have been calm in the city. The common men would have sided with the British forces and tried to defend themselves against the baghis.

The Murder of the Timurid Princes

To cut a long story short, the day after the British forces took the emperor back into the city and stripped the populace of weapons, Saunders[109] Sahib took a group of cavalrymen and went to Hazrat Nizamuddin Dargah.

With the help of Mirza Ilahi Bux, he arrested thirty Timurid princes, including the Badshah's sons, grandsons and sons-in-law, and murdered them outside the walls of Delhi. He sent their heads to the emperor.

> The young saplings of the prosperous garden were
> trampled underfoot
> The flowers of the beautiful garden of khilafat were
> drenched in blood

The Slaughter of the Peaceful Citizens

Let me narrate the state of the citizens who had stayed inside the city. These poor people had thought that the British force would be their protector as they had always been faithful to them. They had prayed morning and night for the ungrateful fauj-e-baghiya to leave the city and were well-wishers of the British government from the bottom of their hearts.

They did not expect the British to put obstacles in their way or punish them. Hence, they felt that it was better to stay inside the city and ride out the storm for a few days. They expected peace to prevail in the city after a few days.

They did not know that a conflagration was waiting to burst in the form of a punishment from a wrathful ruler. In the frenzy of punishment meted out by the mighty, what place does mercy or justice have? Fear of God's punishment was not a consideration for the punishers.

Sins committed in a state of fury and excitement are put in the same category as other sins. There was no well-wisher or protector of the people at this time, and as the saying goes, along with the wheat, the chaff also gets ground in the mill. Thus, those who stayed on in the city were caught up in this situation.

> The bearded chap committed the crime
> But the moustached one was caught

The triumphant British sepoys celebrated their victory by indulging in the wholesale ransacking of the city's houses. They entered the vacant houses and plundered and vandalized them. Whenever they found men or women inside, they put them to the sword without a thought.

I was thinking of my relatives and friends, especially my in-laws, when I saw my father-in-law's servant, Gaami, coming towards us.

'Gaami, is all well?' I asked.

Gaami said in a subdued tone, '*Ji haan*. Everything is fine.'

I immediately became alert and started praying for the safety of my family. 'Where are they?' I asked.

'They went to Nawab Najaf Khan's mausoleum in Shah-e-Mardan[110] yesterday,' Gaami said. 'I have come in search of you. They have called for you. Please come with me.'

I went inside and told my wife that her family had come to Shah-e-Mardan and had summoned me; I would go and find out how they were.

Then I left for Shah-e-Mardan with Gaami.

When I reached Shah-e-Mardan, and entered the tomb of Najaf Khan, the women saw me and set off a storm of weeping and lamentation. There were 200 women beating their heads and sobbing and wailing in loud voices. I am sure their lament was reaching the heavens! Oh! What was this catastrophe?

When I think about it now, there were only a few boys and adolescents there. Miyan Amir Mirza and Nasiruddin were missing.

When the weeping subsided, I asked the women gently to tell me what had happened.

Badi Begum Sahiba started telling me the sequence of events. 'The day after you left us, we heard that General Sahib had set up camp inside the Jama Masjid. After a while, a few goras forced their way into the house and said, "Give us money." The women went and hid in the storerooms while the men gave them some money and sent them off. After some time, more came, and they were also given money and sent off. Now there was an uninterrupted flow of these people coming and asking for money.[111]

'Miyan Nasiruddin said that he would go and talk to the General Sahib and ask him to stop it. He took two attendants with him and went to the Jama Masjid. I don't know what conversation took place between them, but one attendant came and took away the European women we had sheltered in our house during the ghadar. Those women told us that they would come back with Miyan Nasiruddin, bringing a certificate for us. They reached the Jama Masjid and entered, while the attendants remained standing on the steps outside. But alas! Neither the women nor Miyan Nasiruddin returned.

'Our attendant came back in the evening and described the series of events to us. We were in a state of unease all night. The men and women of the mohalla gathered in our house. The men were outside in the gardens while the women were in the two havelis within. There were 200 men and women gathered altogether. Munshi Agha Jaan and three of his women were with us too.

'In the morning, Munshi Agha Jaan and his son were sitting in the garden with the others. Miyan Amir Mirza had just finished his morning namaz and was busy as usual in remembrance of Allah. He was chanting the kalima on his rosary when two goras suddenly entered the garden and said, "Give us some money."

'Miyan Amir Mirza replied, "We have no money." One of the goras took out his gun and shot it. The bullet hit Munshi Agha Jaan's son in the chest. He called out to his father, and Miyan Amir Mirza said, "Son, remember Allah at this time. This is not a time to remember your father."

'He had just said "La Ilaha IllAllah . . ." when the second gora shot and hit him in the chest. Miyan Amir Mirza completed the kalima, and saying "Muhammadur Rasulullah", fell flat on the ground with the hand holding the rosary on his chest.

'These tyrants reloaded their guns and, shooting two attendants, went off on their way.

'It seemed as if doomsday had come to Matia Mahal. The noise of this clamour reached the Jama Masjid and two angrez came out to investigate.

'They asked, "What is this noise and commotion?"

'The women complained, "Just see the tyranny and oppression of your soldiers. Our men have been killed for no fault of their own. See! The corpses are still lying here." They were asking us for money to escort us out of the city. We agreed, but we asked for some time so that we could bury our dead. We dug the graves and buried them in the clothes they were wearing, as we had no means or time to arrange for shrouds. We then left with the angrez. They took us to Turkman Darwaza and sent us out of it.'

I was silent after hearing Badi Begum's narration of events, and when I reached the barfkhana. I knew that if I mentioned it, there would be a storm of weeping and crying here too.

But my family was insisting that I talk. 'Why are you so silent?'

Eventually I started crying and my wife guessed that something very untoward had happened. She made me swear to tell the truth.

I said simply, 'What we feared has come to pass.'

She knew that her father had been martyred.

All the women started crying. After a while, I told them everything that Badi Begum Sahiba had told me.

> All the young and old of the city were martyred
> Every tribe, every family was martyred
> Every eloquent, sweet-tongued was martyred
> In short, an entire world was martyred

Of all the people who stayed back in the city, the notable and prosperous men were killed. Those who were martyred were the pride of Delhi, unique in their talents. No one comparable to them has been nor ever will be born. Some of them were:

1. Miyan Mohammad Amir Panjakashti, the calligrapher.[112] No one on the face of the earth could match him.
2. Maulvi Imam Baksh Sehbai and two of his sons, Mir Niyaz Ali Waqia Khan and many people of respectable families from Kucha Chela'n.

I have heard that 1400 men from this mohalla were arrested and taken to the river from the Rajghat Darwaza.[113] There, they were bombarded by guns and the corpses were thrown in the river.

The women ran out of their houses with their children, and jumped into wells. The wells of Kucha Chela'n were full of dead bodies.

My pen is unable to move now. I don't think I have the courage to write about it any longer. I couldn't bring myself to investigate personally, and am writing what I have heard from others.

All mistakes are on the neck of the narrator

As far as the rest of the city was concerned, men and women were pushed outside the walls. The men were thrown out of the Kashmiri Darwaza and the women out of Kabuli Darwaza,[114] which resulted in everyone being separated. They ran around wildly, searching for each other.

Once men and women were thrown out of the city, the spies went into action. The same ruffians who had joined the ingrate baghis now joined the British for the lure of money. They informed the British of the whereabouts of men and money, of the treasure hidden by people, and, as a result, had it plundered. They were paid Rs 2 for every person they helped catch. They helped the British mount many men on the gallows.

5

Migration

We had spent four or five days in the barfkhana when we heard that the British had hung Mir Nawab, captain of the royal bodyguards, even though he was the son-in-law of Mir Haider Ali, the darogha of the British elephant house. Mir Haider Ali had been with the British on the ridge throughout the ghadar. He was in charge of the entire commissionerate and had been of great help to them. He pleaded with the British, but his pleas fell on deaf ears and no importance was given to his loyalty.

When we heard of this, we were all scared for our lives.

Nawab Hamid Ali Khan sahib told my mother, 'I don't think it's advisable for these boys to remain here. Please send them away. They should go wherever they think they will be safe. The British will not leave anyone alive. You and I are old, so it doesn't matter. We will look after the families, but these young men should leave at once.'

I should have done this long ago. I entered my father's presence and said, 'Nawab Sahib is correct. The need of the time is that you give permission to my brother, me, and my brother-in-law, Agha Sultan. We will go wherever God takes us. I am more concerned about Agha Sultan than myself. He was a *bakshi* in the royal army and he will be lynched if he is found. If God wills that we stay alive, we will come again and kiss your feet.'

I took a few strips of silver, and separating the sole from my shoe, stuffed them in the gap before fastening it again. My wife put one piece of a gold *pahunchi* bracelet[115] in front of me. When I asked where it had come from, she replied, 'When I took off all my jewellery and put it away for safekeeping, this bracelet remained on my arm.'

I separated its beads from one another and stuffed them inside my drawstring belt. I tied my turban, a sash around my waist, picked up a stick, and was thus ready to leave.

My brother, Umrao Mirza, and Agha Sultan were also ready to leave. The scene of our farewell was no less than a scene from doomsday. My wife could not express herself because of shyness, but was weeping uncontrollably. When I was about to leave she said softly, 'My father and uncle have been killed. You are all I have left. In whose custody are you leaving me?'

I replied, 'I leave you in God's custody. If I stay alive, I will come and unite with you again. If I am killed, please forgive me the *meher*.'[116]

With a Bismillah on my lips, I left, taking the direction of Khwaja Sahib.

We had travelled about half a mile when we saw some riders coming towards us. They surrounded us and gave orders that we be searched. We were body searched but they found nothing on us. One rider took my turban and then rode away.

I took off the sash around my waist and tied it on my head.

We had gone just a little way when we saw more riders coming. They also body searched us for money and jewellery and left after finding nothing on us.

As this seemed to be becoming a pattern, I took the gold beads out and bundled them into a ball by threading the drawstring through them. I tied my pyjama with a knot. Whenever I saw such riders coming I would throw the ball far away, intending to retrieve it later.

I would think, 'You may be dacoits, but I am your ustad. How can you loot me?'

In this manner, we reached Khwaja Sahib after facing a lot of obstacles. There, I saw a huge crowd of men and women who, like us, had come for shelter. In the evening, I sold some of the silver to a jeweller, and after buying and eating food, all three of us lay down on the floor of its Diwan-e-Khaas.

In the morning, a caravan of 15,000–20,000 people, which included Aminuddin Ahmed Khan, Ziauddin Ahmed Khan and Ahmed Quli Khan, the emperor's father-in-law and many other dignitaries, left Khwaja Sahib. They paid Rs 2000 to the Gujjars, and taking them along as bodyguards, left the venue. We joined this group and travelled along with them, braving adversities of weather, shortages of food and water, and bandits on the way.

There were thousands of veiled women and children with us, but there was no food in sight. The soles of our feet were blistered, our throats and lips parched. The women and children were crying and weeping but there was nothing anyone could do to alleviate their discomfort.

> That scorching sun, that swirling dust, that hot wind
> That army all around, everywhere the hunter's snare

Somehow, with God's name on our lips and his help, we reached the *sarai* of Sol Basant that evening. We were exhausted, and had huge blisters on our feet, but we could only be patient and grateful to have escaped. We bought some roasted gram and ate it for dinner, drank water and went to sleep on the hard floor of the sarai.

We were not sure of our destination: where the road would lead to, which cities would fall on the way, which kingdom we would land in. We were just dazed, travelling wherever the caravan went. Whichever way the caravan turned could be considered our destination.

We had never left our homes, nor faced any calamity, let alone one of this magnitude! We were unaware of where roads led, and ignorant of the cities on the way. We only knew about the British government and nothing about the other princely states in Hindustan.

I had travelled only once or twice in my life, only to Agra and Meerut. We had gone in great luxury and comfort, with servants to attend to our every need. It had been a very enjoyable journey. Now we had to walk on foot through thorns and brambles. I had heard the names of Jaipur, Alwar and Bikaner, but never visited them. God alone knew how far they were! In the evening, we just lay down in a state of fatigue. In the morning, we would set off again. We entered Farrukhnagar in the afternoon. I sold some silver and got some food for us.

Now we were faced with roads leading in different directions.

A common pot of khichri was cooked for everyone, and people began consulting and advising each other. Some wanted to go in one direction, some in the other.

We were in a dilemma. Oh God, where should we go?

Finally, someone told us that Jhajjar was close by. Finding some relief, I exclaimed, 'My *mamu*, Hakim Mirza Qasim Ali Khan, is the state bailiff there! Let us go there and abide by his advice. We should go where he guides us.'

Arrival in Jhajjar

We left for Jhajjar on the second day, after finding out the way. We reached the same day. We asked after our uncle and went to his house.

When Mamu Sahib saw our faces, he began wailing loudly. 'Oh, you poor things! What calamitous events you have been trapped in!'

He consoled us, made us wash up and took us to his diwankhana and asked us to stay there.

He also knew Agha Sultan very well. Later, he took my brother and me into the house and told his wife, my *mumani*, 'See the state my nephews have been reduced to. My sister Badshah Begum underwent such hardships to bring them up. Now they are caught in such a sorry state.'

Mumani also started crying and asked us to describe the series of events that had brought us here. We told her everything.

The next day, mumani got some bolts of cloth and told us, 'Now you are not going anywhere. You will stay with me.'

We stayed there for eight days. But even this was not acceptable to fate and we were dealt another cruel blow.

At midnight, the Nawab Sahib called my mamu. He came back in an hour, tears in his eyes.

'Mamu, is everything all right?' I asked.

'What can I say?' Mamu said. 'The same catastrophe that brought you here has descended on us too. The British army has reached us. Let's see what transpires. That's why Nawab Sahib called me. I think that it would be prudent for you all to leave. Set off for Panipat via Sonepat. I have just received news that your family has already reached Panipat. My bullock cart will take you to Sonepat. You can find some other conveyance from there. You have some maternal relatives there too. Maybe they will let you stop there.'

We left in the bullock cart for Panipat. My maternal grandfather's brothers had houses there. They asked me to stay till the ghadar was over and leave only after calm had been restored.

I said, 'My father, mother, brothers, sisters and wife are in Barsath in my aunt's house.'

I reached Barsath[117] around 11 p.m. My father was crying in the courtyard and praying loudly for our safety. 'O Khuda, you are the one who unites those who have been separated. Please unite me safely with my children. I had placed them in your custody.'

I reached the door at that exact moment, and called out to him to open it. My oldest aunt recognized my voice and ran forward.

My father was still in a state of shock and disbelief. He only believed it when my aunt swore, 'I have just heard Nawab Mirza's voice. He is calling out at the door.'

As soon as the door opened, I fell at and embraced my father's feet. He bent down to say prayers of gratitude.

We Arrive in Panipat

These times are warrior-like and I in heedlessness
Seek with the coat of mail of contemplation defence
from injury!
The catapult of the sky rains down stones of dissension
And I, O simple one, seek sanctuary in a fort of crystal![118]

After a few days, we all left for Panipat and took up residence
there. We decided to take to trading as a means of earning
livelihood and rented a small shop. We employed one man
to do the buying and selling, but I controlled the accounts. I
would go to the shop twice a day.

By the generosity of God, the shop flourished and we
were able to live well. After deducting all expenses from the
shop, we made a good profit. In a short while, we had goods
worth Rs 300–400 in our shop.

The expense of the household was Rs 2 a day. For five
months, all went well, but once again a twist of fate destroyed
our happiness. Jealous destiny decided to uproot us once again.

The sky let loose a hail of stones and the earth prepared
strife by letting loose poisonous scorpions. The scoundrel
Gami[119] descended on Panipat and punishments and hangings
began here too. They started arresting all those who had come
from Delhi.

In Barsath, Nawab Hamid Ali Khan was arrested, along
with his entire family. All hell broke loose in Panipat and it
came under siege.

The people of Panipat protected us and behaved in such a
kind manner that it rivalled that of a father with his son. They
were ready to lay down their lives and reputations for us and
hid us in the women's quarters.

They had already helped us with money and provisions and now they were ready to die for us too. I don't think anyone would have done as many favours for anyone as the *Panipatwaala*s did for the *Dilliwaala*s.

The Siege of Panipat

Panipat had been besieged from all sides, and all roads to and from the city were blocked. One by one, the Dilliwaalas were arrested.

One afternoon, I left from the back of my house for my aunt's lodgings. She was a tenant of Maulvi Ibrahim sahib. There, we discussed the ongoing arrests and I got agitated and got up to leave. My sister asked me to stay but I came out of the house. That was when I saw the thanedar, leading a number of men, coming into the alley. If I went inside, I thought, they would be alerted and force their way into the house and arrest everyone.

I walked past them nonchalantly, saying, 'Bhai, we have also got into trouble because of these Dilliwaalas.'

I walked past them without being recognized. They entered the house I had just left. Meanwhile, I had reached the end of the huge deorhi of the house and found my feet had turned to lead. I couldn't move further and hid beneath a pile of cattle fodder lying in a corner. The thanedar arrested my uncle, brother and brother-in-law and walked right past the place where I was hiding.

When they left, I started crying and moving senselessly. I kept falling down in my grief. Finally, I reached my mother-in-law's house in a state of anguish and related the whole incident. 'I think it is prudent that I leave from here, or I will be arrested too,' I said.

She called for a local named Bu Ali, whose family had worked for hers. She requested him, 'Please take both my children from here to a place of safety.'

Bu Ali said, 'As you wish, Begum Sahiba. I will take them to a safe place.'

Departure from Panipat

Before dawn broke, Bu Ali escorted Yusuf Sultan, my brother-in-law's younger brother, and me from our house. He made us jump over a broken parapet in the city wall and we thus exited Panipat. Moving quickly, we covered a distance of 8 kos and reached Garhi, a village of Sheikhzadas,[120] in the middle of the night.

Bu Ali woke up the villagers and told them our sorry tale. The villagers were very brave and generous and they looked after us well and comforted us. They said, 'Even if you stay here for the rest of your lives, we will not let anyone find out your whereabouts. There's no one who has the power to arrest you here.'

When dawn broke, they advised us, 'The two of you must take up residence in a hut in the low alluvial land near the river. Come back to the village in the night. You must also start dressing like us. Two of our people will stay with you at all times. Our cattle graze in that area, and if you are disguised as villagers, no one can find you out.'

We agreed and started living as they described.

I told Bu Ali to also rescue my father and brother. They were hiding in Peerji Mohammad Hussain's house. I asked him to bring them to Garhi. He agreed at once.

Bu Ali left and came back on the third day with my brother and Agha Sultan. I rewarded him with some money for his wonderful deed.

We spent one more day in that village. The next day, we crossed the Jamuna and reached Mustafabad, a village in which Saiyyeds lived. The Saiyyeds of Mustafabad made us feel very welcome and said, 'As long as this tumult is not over, you may stay here comfortably. No one can harm a hair on your heads.'

'This is your kindness and generosity,' I said. 'Please do us one more favour, and escort us across the Ganga through the good services of the people of Meerapur of Jansath (a village near Meerut). That area is not under the British.'

The headman said, 'Oh, this is a small matter. I will give you a letter. You can take it to Mir Talib Ali, who will help you cross the Ganga.'

We left in a rented bullock cart and reached Sambhal Heda. We put up outside the *qasba* and sent the letter to Mir Talib Ali Numbardar[121] as directed. But he refused outright to help us. However, his nephew, Mir Inayat Hussain, was very kind and came to meet us. He took us to his house and hid us there for three days. He called the Gujjar villagers and asked them if they could help us cross the river. They said, 'It's impossible during the day as the British have sentry posts on one side of the river and the Najibabad state police on the other. We will try tomorrow night.'

One night,[122] thirty Gujjar villagers armed with guns, swords and spears came to the house. They had also brought horses. We were mounted on the horses and taken along with them.

The Ganga was 7 kos from the house. We passed through more Gujjar villages on the way. The leader of our group left a message with these villagers, telling them that they should warn him if they heard any noise or commotion.

I told one of the Gujjars, 'You are very united.'

He said, 'If even one of us were to fire a shot, 3 lakh Gujjars would collect here. All these villages are ours.'

We reached the Ganga, and after leaving the horses, prepared to cross. The Gujjars put our luggage on their heads and took us across the river.

The village on the other side was called Ferozabad. It belonged to Saiyyeds. When we reached it, they gave the *numbardar* the letter from Mir Inayat Hussain and took a receipt of acknowledgement from us and sent it back to Mir Inayat Hussain.

We were cold and weary from our exertions and just plopped down on the grass, where we went to sleep. When we woke up in the afternoon, the villagers fed us and asked us to describe our plight.

We were telling them of our ordeal when a man came from the Nawab of Najibabad. 'Who crossed the Ganga at night and came to your village? Is there any British spy amongst them?'

I spoke out, 'We have come.'

He said, 'All right. One of you must come with us.'

I decided to go along with him. The army was camped at a little distance, a few respectable people sitting on chairs. He presented me to them.

The gentlemen asked me to give an account of my arrival.

'We are residents of the afflicted city Delhi,' I began. 'We are running around, trying to escape the British.'

One of the men said, 'Why don't you take up employment here and stay on?'

I replied, 'We are not qualified for employment. We want to go to Lucknow.'

I returned to my companions and spent the night in that village. We left in the morning.

Finally, after a lot of difficulty, we reached Bareilly via Moradabad. There, we stayed in the house of a friend, Agha Zaheen sahib Marsiyago. He looked after us so generously that I cannot find words to describe it. We were planning to move on when we heard that Lucknow had met the same fate as Delhi.

'O Lord, where should we go? What should we do!'

We stayed in Agha Zaheen's house for fifteen days.

One More Calamity

Because I think of you as the redeemer of the weak
Why should I not, in this weakness, call out your name?[123]

One day, another Delhi resident, Jung Baaz Khan (who had been employed in the emperor's cavalry) and I went to the Bareilly bazaar to buy shoes in the shop of a Muslim shoe seller. I picked up a shoe and asked its price. The shopkeeper replied, 'Rs 100.'

I quickly put it down. He said, 'Why have you put it down? Tell me your price.'

I said, 'Bhai, I don't have the ability to pay this price. I want a cheaper pair of shoes. I am a poor man afflicted by circumstances.'

He asked me, 'Where are you from?'

I replied, 'I belong to Delhi.'

He said, 'You are all impotent cowards! You let Delhi be captured, and after losing your homes you are now roaming around begging for help.'

I kept quiet on hearing this, but Jung Baaz Khan, who was from the Mughal bloodline, a soldier on top of that and hailing from Lal Kuan, which was famous for the bravery of its residents, could not tolerate this insult.

He retorted, 'Son, don't worry. They will also come here and you will be hiding behind your wife's skirts.'

No sooner had these words been uttered than that shop owner got up and caught my hand and Jung Baaz's hand and called out loudly, 'Friends! Come quickly! These two are British spies.'

This statement spelled catastrophe for us. Purbias ran at us from all sides. At this time, there were hordes of cavalry and infantrymen[124] in the bazaar and we couldn't find a way to escape. They came and caught us and said, 'Take them to General Sahib.'

We were chained and taken to him.

A huge crowd was now accompanying us. It was as if someone were being taken to be hanged.

The Qila was half a mile away, tents put up in front of it. We were taken and made to stand in front of a fifty-five-year-old purbia. He was wearing a gold bead in a band around his throat, and was standing in front of one of the tents.

The people who caught us said, 'These two are British spies. We have arrested them and brought them here.'

Please pay attention to General Sahib's sense of justice! Without asking any questions, he said, 'Tie them to the mouth of a cannon and blow them up.'

We were immediately tied to the two cannons stationed there.

Gunpowder was loaded into the cannons and a message was sent to Nawab Khan Bahadur Khan, governor of Bareilly, saying that two British spies had been caught and they were waiting on his orders to blow them up.

In a few minutes, the messenger returned with the order. 'Blow them up!'

Looking up into the skies, I thought, 'Oh God! What is this new misfortune that we have got caught up in? We had somehow managed to escape from Delhi and find shelter here, little knowing that our death was destined to take place here. It seems as if our death has pulled us to this place. We have no one to whom we can appeal except you.'

Jung Baaz Khan was looking at me and I was looking at him. Another messenger was sent to Khan Bahadur Khan, but he brought back the same order.

We were now reciting the kalima and preparing to die, as we had no hope for our lives.

Our captors were waiting for the third order before lighting the gunpowder. But Allah is the almighty and He can send help from unseen sources, and thus rescue us mortals from the hand of death. As they say, 'The one who rescues is much more powerful than the one who kills!'

We suddenly saw some people running out of the Qila gate, led by a man dressed in white. He wore a white turban, and was mounted on a golden horse. He was coming towards us. The retinue of sepoys he brought immediately gave orders to have the crowd dispersed.

The rider rode up to Jung Baaz and said, 'Arrey, Jung Baaz! How are you here?'

Jung Baaz said, 'Why are you looking at me? Look at the other one with me.'

As soon as the rider saw me, he jumped down from his horse and cut the ropes binding me to the cannon. He freed Jung Baaz as well, and catching us by our hands, took us to the general.

He abused the unreasonable general profusely and said, 'Ingrates! You destroyed our Badshah's house, ruined Delhi, dislocated and destroyed the Delhi populace and even now you have not learnt your lesson! Arrey, these are royal employees who are trying to escape the wrath of the British forces. They are no spies! You should at least have given them a chance to tell their story. You gave orders for their execution without any investigation. Had I not come here, you would have killed these two innocents? They were destined to live. That's why I reached in time.'

He turned to me and asked me to narrate my circumstances. Jung Baaz described the entire chain of events. The rider then told Jung Baaz to come to his house and told me to return to my own.

We should know the name of my saviour who was also a royal employee: Mir Fateh Ali, the darogha of the royal porters.

When I reached my house, my father and other relatives were waiting anxiously, worried about my safety. As soon as they saw me, they asked what had happened. Jung Baaz told them how we had escaped from the jaws of death. Everyone was naturally perturbed, but thanked Khuda that we had returned safely.

After this incident, we realized that this city was no longer safe. We had to leave before the British forces reached and cut off all avenues of escape.

We had run from Delhi and reached here. Where could we go now?

We started thinking furiously, but could come up with no option.

But we must never forget the originator of causes who can create opportunities out of nothing. It is only he who can take us out of calamity and lead us into peace and plenty.

One day, we saw another dishevelled man from Delhi in the bazaar. He was dressed as a traveller and had a stick in his hand. He was accompanied by a woman wrapped in a chador, holding a small bundle in her hands. When he came closer, we recognized each other and wished one another.

'Aha! Mir Ghulam Abbas! You are here?'

'I am coming from Lucknow,' he said.

'Where will you stay?'

'Wherever God takes us.'

I invited him to stay with us. We could all travel together to whichever new place God had willed for us.

He came with me to the house, and described his circumstances. He stayed with us that day. The next day, we all began discussing the safest place for us to go.

Ghulam Abbas said, 'The safest place to reside in, in my eyes, is Rampur. I can think of no better alternative. My unfortunate stars pulled me in the direction of Lucknow. But I faced the same situation I had seen in Delhi there.'

Everyone agreed that we should go to Rampur. But how could we go there? The roads were closed, and there were patrols and checks on the borders of Rampur and Bareilly. The army was camped there.

At this time, there was a crowd of fugitives from different places, all camped in Bareilly. Even the chiefs of the rebel forces, such as Nana Rao, Firoz Shah and people from Delhi and Lucknow, had gathered here.

As many as 30,000 people from Rampur were employed in Bareilly. These men had long, decorated turbans and flowing sashes, four pistols and a pair of swords at their sides. They were roaming the city on their horses.

Altogether, there were 50,000 cavalry stationed in Bareilly. There were rumours of the imminent arrival of the British.

To cut a long story short, the next day, seven of us left Bareilly using lesser-known roads and heading towards the south. We decided to use only the unused and unfrequented roads to enter Rampur.

We reached qasba Aonla and rested there in an old mosque. One of the men from Aonla came to us and asked why we had come. He insulted us the same way the shoe seller had. Jung Baaz was once again enraged and was about to retort when I put my hand on his mouth.

A short time had passed when we saw two horsemen coming towards us from the jungle. They came to the stairs of the mosque and, dismounting, tied their horses to a tree and entered. I recognized one of them as General Ahmed Khan of Jhajjar.

'Aha! General Sahib! You are here!' I said.

'I had put up a front on the Kach Ghat with a force of 20,000, which included cavalry and infantry and artillery,' the general said. 'When the British army started crossing the Ganga, my army ran away without putting up a fight. I tried to stop them but no one was willing to listen and they deserted us. Only my son and I remained. Helpless, we also had to run to save our lives.'

As soon as Ahmed Khan had stopped talking, Jung Baaz Khan turned towards the old men who had been calling us impotent and timid. They gathered themselves and left in some confusion.

We stayed the night in Aonla. The next day, we left with the intention of reaching Shahabad, which was in the Rampur state. It was 18 kos from Aonla.

We were dead tired by the time we had travelled 12 kos and didn't have the strength to move further. Our feet were swollen and blistered. We sat down under a tree by the side of a pond, outside a Jat village. A Muslim artisan from the village came to fill water at the pond. As soon as he saw us he said, 'Why are you all here? Go off on your way. If the villagers see you they will kill you. These people are sworn enemies of Muslim Pathans because the people who governed them under the rule of Khan Bahadur Khan oppressed them terribly. Now they are taking their revenge.'

'We are also ready for death,' I said, 'but we are such accursed men that even death doesn't come to us. We are praying to God that someone kills us and ends our daily misery.'

That artisan took his water pot and left for the village. After a while, he returned and said, 'Muqaddam ji (the village headman) is calling you.'

I replied, 'We are faqirs. What will we do in the village? Just let us be. We will leave in the morning.'

But he didn't listen and took us with him to the village square. There we saw that a huge, powerful, bearded young man was lying on a cot. A wooden stick was kept in front of him. This young man said, 'O Miyan ji, sit down.'

Next to him was another cot with higher legs. He asked us to sit on that. The woman who was with us (Ghulam Abbas's wife) went and sat down in a secluded corner.

He asked us about our circumstances.

I said, 'We are strangers, residents of Delhi who left our homes after being ruined. We are trying to save ourselves from the British wrath and want to reach Rampur.'

That merciful man sympathized with us and asked us to freshen ourselves. He put gram flour rotis smeared with ghee, dal and glasses of milk in front of us and invited us to satiate our appetites. Food was brought separately for the lady.

We spent the night in this village square. When we were preparing to leave in the morning, this generous man said, 'Your feet are swollen. How will you travel?'

He called his cart driver and asked him to take us to Shahabad. He also gave us Rs 5 to ease our travel. We kept refusing to take the money, but he would not listen to our protests. He thus ensured that we reached Shahabad safely.

We offered thanks to God for all his mercy.

Reaching the State of Rampur

We reached Shahabad, which was in the state of Rampur. Rampur was 12 kos from there and we decided to rest in this place at night and leave for Rampur the next day.[125]

Before the morning prayers, I went out of the residential area, taking my brass pot with me for my early morning needs. I had not yet finished when I saw the army coming from the east.

I went as still as a mouse. The army was setting up camp outside the city. They fired two cannons as salute.

I quickly washed up and went back to the sarai and told my companions of the incident. At the same time, a few soldiers entered the sarai and started aggravating the villagers. A few of the soldiers came to stay in the sarai too. We were staying in one room in the corner and the soldiers came and occupied other rooms.

We consulted amongst ourselves and decided it wouldn't be prudent to leave today with the British forces roaming the city. They would kill us, thinking us to be baghis. We stayed on, trusting in God to keep us safe. We decided we would leave the next morning.

That night, we stayed in the same sarai as the British army, but no one came and troubled us. In the morning, the British force left for Aonla and we set off in the direction of Rampur.

This British force mercilessly hacked down all the fugitives they met on the way to Bareilly. We were fortunate, and by God's grace and protection, we reached Rampur in the evening.

However, we couldn't enter the city via the Darwaza at night, since the guards thought we were travellers and refused to let us in. We went to the other city gate but there also the situation was the same.

'Oh God! What can we do now?'

Mir Ghulam Abbas was familiar with the city of Rampur since he had already stayed here on his way to Lucknow. He said, 'Should I take you in through another way?'

He took us in through a small gap in the city walls and thus, we finally entered the city. Now we were inside, but where were we going to stay?

Mir Ghulam Abbas told us about a Mir Ibrahim of Delhi who stayed in Rampur, and said that we should go to his house.

At around midnight, we went to his house and called out to him. He came outside and recognized us. I had been close to him in Delhi. He embraced me at once. We all went inside his house and sat down in the deorhi.

We were just telling him about our troubles and travels when a calamity descended on us. A woman who had been sleeping in the neighbouring shop heard our story and started shouting, '*Mohalla waalon!* Come quickly! Baghis have come and are hiding in this Saiyyed's house.'

Mir Ibrahim Ali pleaded with her with folded hands and swore that we were not baghis, just his unfortunate relatives who had come from Delhi, but that woman wouldn't listen.

Finally, he said, 'Please be quiet. I will take them somewhere else.'

He took us to an Irani's house and told him that we were relatives of his. Could he be kind enough to keep us in his house for the night? He said he would take us away in the morning. The Irani agreed and we stayed in his house for the night. In the morning, we left his house and asked Mir Ghulam Abbas, 'What do you suggest now?'

Mir Ghulam Abbas said, 'Let's go and stay in the sarai of Ajitpur, which is outside the city. I will take you to the house of a noble of the state. If he agrees and lets you stay in his house, then even the Nawab Sahib can't expel you.'

He sent everyone else to the Ajitpur sarai, and Ghulam Abbas and I went to the Amir's house. There I saw a huge darwaza with a diwankhana with a wooden settee. The prayer mat was spread out on it and a man with a very luminous face was seated there, reciting on his rosary.

As soon as he saw Mir Ghulam Abbas, he ran to embrace him. 'Arrey Mir Ghulam Abbas! Where had you gone? My eyes were longing for the sight of you.'

After he had greeted each of us by clasping our hands warmly, we sat down on the wooden settee. The man asked Mir Ghulam Abbas about his recent travels and the latter described all the events that had assailed him since his departure for Lucknow.

Then, looking at me, the noble man asked, 'Please introduce me to this gentleman.'

Mir Ghulam Abbas said, 'Please don't ask him to describe his troubles. You will not be able to bear it. In short, let me tell you he was a noble resident of Delhi but is now just a poor, oppressed Saiyyed.'

As soon as he heard the word Saiyyed, the elderly gentleman got up and embraced me and told Mir Ghulam Abbas, 'For God's sake, tell me everything. I am very saddened to see him in this state.'

Mir Ghulam Abbas gave him a brief introduction to our family and said that we had lost everything. We were now running around to save our own lives. Even the earth was not sheltering us, he said, but if the noble let me take shelter in his house for a few days, as a sign of hospitality to Saiyyeds, I would be very grateful to him.

That angelic man said, 'I can't believe my luck. The presence of the progeny of Fatima[126] will bless my wretched house. It is extremely good fortune for me if they stay in my house. Please remember that as long as Fasihullah Khan is alive, no one can lift an eye in their direction.'

He immediately gave orders for his bullock cart to be taken to the Ajitpur sarai and for the rest of our group to be brought here with full respect.

He had a carpet laid out for us in the diwankhana and told his servants to stay and serve us. He gave orders for food to be prepared for us in the house. In a little while, my father, brother and brother-in-law also arrived. Nawab Sahib greeted everyone very warmly.

Finally, God's bounties were showered on us. After so much danger and trouble, we came to rest in an oasis of peace and calm.

Two or three days later, this blessed man went to the late Nawab Yusuf Ali Khan sahib Bahadur.

The Nawab Sahib asked him, 'Dada[127] Sahib, why have
you troubled yourself to come here?'

Fasihullah Khan said, 'I have brought a priceless gift for
you.'

Nawab Sahib Bahadur asked, 'What gift is this?'

Fasihullah Khan replied, '*Zaad-e-Aqba!*' (Provision for
forgiveness in your afterlife.)

Nawab Sahib asked what this means of forgiveness could
be.

Fasihullah said, 'I have sheltered five people descended
from Lady Fatima in my house. I want help from you so that
you too may be included in this merciful deed. I want you
to either tell me outright that I shouldn't keep them in my
house, in which case I will send them off on their way, or you
should agree to help and then extend every possible aid to
them. I will not be able to bear it if you arrest them after a few
days and hand them over to the British. Only after beheading
me can anyone touch them.'

Nawab Sahib Bahadur said, 'Dada Sahib, do you think I
am someone who would betray a descendant of the Prophet
(peace be upon him) when they come to seek shelter in my
house? I will never do such a lowly deed. My only condition
is that they should not have taken any employment in
Bareilly.'

Fasihullah gave his word. 'These people are from Delhi.
They have nothing to do with any employment. They are royal
employees; what jobs could they find in Bareilly? Maybe you
know of these people as you have lived in Delhi for many
years.'

When Fasihullah Khan told him our names and ranks,
Nawab Sahib recognized us and said, 'I know all these people.
None of them are rebels. Please keep them in your house and

give them my assurance that they are no longer in any danger. They are my responsibility now. Once matters are settled in Bareilly, I will personally intervene on your behalf and get you a letter of amnesty. Till then, they may stay here comfortably.'

Fasihullah Khan returned to his residence and told us, '*Mubarak ho!* (Congratulations!) I have cleared all Nawab Sahib's doubts. He has promised to get you a letter of amnesty. Now you can stay wherever you want, and you won't have any trouble.'

Our minds were now completely at ease. We began living there without any fear of danger.

Dagh[128] Sahib heard that we were living there and came to meet us immediately. He graciously got my brother, Umrao Mirza Anwar, and me employment with Sahibzada[129] Mohammad Raza Khan sahib, son-in-law of the late Nawab Yusuf Ali Khan sahib.

Sahibzada would hold many a mushaira at his residence and the late Munshi Ameer Ahmed sahib Minai[130] would come and recite the Nawab's ghazals, and then his own.

Sahibzada Mohammad Raza Khan said to me, 'You also write ghazals.'

I tried to refuse. 'I am not yet in my senses. We have been struck by trouble on all sides. What ghazal will I be able to write?'

But Sahibzada was insistent and eventually I wrote ghazals and recited them in the mushaira. From that day on, my ghazals became famous in Rampur and the populace grew fond of us. Keeping his promise, the Nawab Sahib went to Bareilly and got a certificate of absolution for us.

We lived in Rampur for four years, and in this time, our extended family came from Panipat to this city.

6

The Return to My Land

Nawab Fasihullah Khan, who has been described above, was the son of the late Nawab Faizullah Khan Bahadur and related to Nawab Yusuf Ali Khan of Rampur.

A year after my family joined me in Rampur, I was blessed with a son. We named him Sajjad Mirza. Sajjad was seven months old when I saw an advertisement which said that the British government had forgiven the crimes of their subjects, and those who had land or property in Delhi could go and put in their appeal. After investigation, they would be given a certificate of succession.

I decided to leave for Delhi. At this time, Hamilton Sahib was the commissioner of Delhi and Cooper Sahib the deputy commissioner. Both these officers were merciful, just and caring of their subjects' needs. I can't praise them enough. They were the ones who resettled Delhi and called its people home. They were so merciful and generous that all the troubles of the ghadar were removed from the residents' minds and hearts.

I have written a verse in shahr ashob in praise of Cooper Sahib Bahadur and it tells the truth. There's no exaggeration. The residents of Delhi had faced tyranny and persecution based on the testimony of spies. They had been arrested and brought back to the city. There were three gallows put up in Delhi and thousands would be hung from them every day. Metcalfe Sahib had fun hunting down those he deemed rebels. Metcalfe would just shoot whomever he saw with his pistols, without conducting any investigation to find out whether they were guilty or not.

Many innocent Delhi residents, especially those of noble and reputable families, and notable men were brought to Delhi from wherever they had fled. For example, Mohammad Hussain Khan, Nawab Muzaffar-ud-Daula and Mir Mohammad Hussain, residents of Ballimaran, were arrested in Alwar and brought to Delhi. When they reached Gurgaon, the collector of the district gave orders saying that there was no need to take them to Delhi, and that the decision on their fate should be taken here. These three gentlemen were shot dead in Gurgaon itself.

In Delhi, thousands of innocents were hung to death. The emperor was imprisoned and sent to Rangoon along with Zeenat Mahal, Jawan Bakht, Shah Abbas and many others. He was placed under house arrest there.

Then came a time when Nawab Viceroy Lawrence Sahib Bahadur[131] came to Hindustan from England as the governor general. He was appointed as the just and merciful ruler and he embraced his subjects as though they were children. They were recalled from wherever they had fled and resettled in Delhi. Their properties were returned to them.

Mr Ford, the collector of Gurgaon who had given orders to shoot down the three gentlemen brought from Alwar, was now put in charge of finding and giving pardon to the baghis. He went to Kujli Ban, the forest area near Pilibhit, and pardoned all the baghis who vowed allegiance to Ismail Khan, the rebel leader. He confiscated their horses and weapons, gave them certificates of pardon and sent them off to their homes.

I was living in Rampur when Ismail Khan, general of the fauj-e-baghiya, came to the city. I learned of all these events from him. He told me of the 40,000 soldiers of fauj-e-baghiya in the Kujli Ban who had surrendered their weapons.

The Search for Employment

Once I came back to Delhi and retrieved all my property after meeting Cooper Sahib, my father also returned, bringing my family back to Delhi with him.

My younger brother, Umrao, was employed in Maulvi Rajab Ali Khan's printing press as a writer, receiving a salary of Rs 50 per month in Jigraon,[132] in the district of Ludhiana. My father accompanied him.

I was unemployed and living with my in-laws, along with my wife and mother-in-law. I was worried that even though I had returned to Delhi, I had no means of earning a living. This was also a period of famine, but Khuda is the provider. I realized that I needed to take up some trade. In those days, the railways had not come to Delhi and mail was delivered by horse cart. Since many of the horses of the post office had died, there was an urgent need for horses. I started searching for horses and found a horse in the Qila. It was owned by a British man. My friend and I bought that horse for Rs 14 and sold it to the post office for Rs 70. We gave Rs 14 to the owner and shared the profit.

We then made it a regular practice. We would leave our houses in the morning with a prayer on our lips: 'O complete Provider, only you can provide for us.'

We would spend the day hunting for horses in the city. We would normally get one or two, which we would buy cheap and sell dear at the post office. The God of the universe would ensure we got Rs 10–Rs 15 every day, after which we would happily return home.

We normally bought a horse for Rs 13 and sold it for Rs 70. God was providing for us generously. The reason why we were able to do this was that most people's circumstances had become so straitened that they found it difficult to maintain a horse. Hence, they sold them at very low rates.

One day, we were roaming around in search of a horse but found none.

In the afternoon, we were passing through the Kanchni Gali (near Kashmiri Darwaza) when a man came up to us and said, 'I have an excellent horse. If you want to buy it, I will sell.'

We went with this man and saw the horse. We found it to be good, of Turki-Bukhara[133] breed. We bought it for Rs 80 and gave Rs 5 as earnest money to the owner. We promised to give him the rest of the money in the evening.

Putting our trust in God, we took the horse. The Kabuli Darwaza was still standing, but houses of the city were being demolished. When we reached Kabuli Darwaza, we met an attendant who asked, 'Is this horse for sale?'

'Yes, it is for sale.'

The orderly said, 'Go out of the Darwaza. My sahib's platoon is camping there. He is the captain of the platoon. Ask where his tent is. He has been searching for such a horse and will buy it as soon as he sees it.'

We went out of the city and had just reached the camp when the Captain Sahib himself came out and asked, 'Are you selling this horse?'

'Yes, Sahib, it's for sale,' I said.

Captain Sahib asked, 'Is it mischievous or wicked?'

I replied, 'Sahib, he is a Turki horse and doesn't know how to be wicked.'

Captain Sahib said, 'Could I ride him?'

I said, 'Please do ride him and check him out.'

The captain had the horse saddled and mounted him. The horse was elegant and well-paced and sahib was very happy with it. He dismounted and asked us the price. We quoted Rs 400. He said, 'The price is too high. Please quote a reasonable amount.'

After a while, he asked us to take a horse in exchange, plus the difference in price. We asked to see his horse. This was also an excellent young horse, but it was a Tartari breed. We took the horse anyway, plus Rs 100 in cash. We handed our horse to him.

We were returning to the city to give the remainder of the selling price to the owner when an old gentleman called out to us from a room near the Kabuli Darwaza, 'Are you selling this horse?'

We replied in the affirmative. He came down from his room and examined the horse. He liked it. The same situation that had played out with the Captain Sahib arose here as well. The old man wanted to exchange his horse and give us the difference in cash. His was also a young and flawless horse, but it was weaker than ours. We took Rs 100 and the horse from him, and handed over the captain's steed.

By the time we had reimbursed the owner of the first, Turki horse, evening had fallen. We divided the profit and

I rode the horse to my house, buying food for it on the way. I made the horse eat its fill and put some grass in front of it. That evening, I rested. The next day, we sold the horse to the post office for Rs 75.

By God's grace, in one day we earned a profit of Rs 200. So long as the famine lasted, I was never short for anything, nor did I feel the rising prices. After a year, this buying and selling of horses stopped.

My father went to Panipat to arrange Umrao's wedding. After the wedding, he left him in Panipat and came to reside with me in Delhi.

Unfortunately, he fell sick as soon as he came. I was unwell too, and both of us were running a high fever.

Complaint by the Mahajan

While we were sick, the mahajan, Banarsi Das, filed a case against us for the money we owed him. The debt was from the pre-ghadar days. It was money that had been taken for weddings, and now after compounded interest, the amount owed totalled Rs 2000. My father and I were unwell and there was no one to give the creditor a reply, hence an ex parte decree was awarded. My father died of the shock.

I was already indisposed, and the shock of my father's demise increased my woes. We buried my father honourably, but now my life was in danger. By the time I recovered three months later, our house had been put up for auction. My houses, which were worth Rs 10,000, were sold for Rs 2000, which was given to our creditor. I didn't get a single paisa.

Now that I was healthy, I started worrying about ways of earning yet again. In those days, a new contract for tolls had come up in Delhi. I was employed here at a meagre salary.

In the same period, Hakim Ahsanullah Khan asked me to translate *Qissa Mumtaz* from Persian to Urdu at Rs 10 per section. When the toll contract ended a year later, it was handed over to another contractor who brought his own employees. I was once again unemployed.

For a few days, I earned money by writing. I was appointed the editor of a newspaper, *Jalwa-e-Tur*, which was published from Bulandshahr. I relocated to Bulandshahr. This newspaper made great progress.

The newspaper's circulation even extended to the state of Alwar, where it was read by the ruler, Maharaja Sheodan Singh. He asked, 'Who is the editor of this newspaper?'

A friend of mine, Mirza Ali Naqi sahib Tehsildar, happened to be present there. He told him my name and described my circumstances.

Maharaja Sahib Bahadur asked him to summon me to Alwar, where he would employ me. My friend asked me to leave my job in Bulandshahr and come to Alwar. He claimed that the Maharaja was a very generous patron. I made excuses for a while, but eventually circumstances forced me to go to Alwar.

My relatives, Mehdi Hussain sahib Majrooh and Mir Sarfaraz Hussain sahib, were already present when my brother Umrao and I reached Alwar. We presented ourselves before the Maharaja.

7

Employment in Alwar and a Description of the State

The Maharaja Sahib was an extremely refined and soft-spoken man with an excellent personality. During our conversation, he said, 'I am a noble of Mewat and you are a resident of Delhi. You are fond of pulao and *qaliya* (meat dishes), and in my state we eat *moth* and *bajra ki roti* (vegetarian dishes). If you accept this, then Bismillah! Please share it with us.'

I replied with folded hands, 'This bajra is better than pulao qaliya and equal to a thousand blessings. Even if I get only one meal a day, I will never let go of Huzoor's hem.'

The Maharaja said, 'If you are willing to take a job in the rural areas, then you can get a handsome salary. But you will be under the command of the rulers there, and if those officers complain, then I will have to take their side. If you want, you can serve directly under me. But you will get a lower salary.'

I replied, 'Huzoor, I consider being in your service a thousand times better than going to the rural areas.'

That very day, the Maharaja employed both me and my younger brother. Our names were written in the register. We were each given one priceless purebred horse from the stables. We began attending the Maharaja's darbar and lived a life of luxury, with not a care in the world.

Our days and nights passed in laughter, entertainment, playing ganjifa and chausar, watching dances, and going to fairs and *shikar*. Whenever the Maharaja went out, we accompanied him as his flunkies. About twenty to twenty-five young men of pleasing countenance and dress would be gathered around the Maharaja to keep him entertained and in a happy mood. The Maharaja was so fond of us that he would not part with us at any point during the day. He would give us the best of everything to wear and reward us generously at every function.

This was a unique, colourful assembly, which had to be seen to be believed. Maharaja Sheodan Singh Bahadur, the ruler of Alwar, had set up such a splendid assembly that even that of Abul Hasan Tana Shah (of Golkunda) would have paled in comparison.

The pomp and majesty of this small state had no peer in all of Hindustan—at least, none that I had seen or heard of.

The masters of every skill and accomplishment were gathered here. None of them had any equal in their art anywhere in Hindustan or abroad. The court had a calligrapher such as Agha Sahib (the disciple of the late Mir Panjakash, the most famous calligrapher of his time), who wrote the *Gulistan* at the cost of Rs 1 lakh.

Precious Objects

Ibrahim Shamsher Saaz's skilful hands had shaped a unique sword whose blade was encrusted with gems and pearls.

When one picked it up, all the pearls would gather at the hilt, and if one were to use the sword to strike, the pearls would run down the blade and start shining. I have seen that sword with my own eyes.

There were many other unique and beautiful swords shaped by Ibrahim Shamsher. They were kept in the armoury.

One carpenter had built a 5-yard-long and 1.5-yard-wide mechanical silver table. When one wound it up, a magical workshop would appear. On one side of the table he had built a baradari with a mountain behind it, a river flowing in front of it and gardens on either side. When it was wound up, clouds would appear on top of the baradari and mountain, accompanied by sounds of thunder and lightning. Water would even fall in the form of rain in the river and flow away with it. Small red and green fish could be seen in the water.

Dogs

The darogha of the sweepers in the hunting house had a talent for making street dogs fight against tigers, and training the dogs to win.

This happened many times. He would catch healthy pups as soon as they were born, and then he would fatten them up. The day the orders were given to make them fight against tigers, he would take four or five dogs and make them inhale snuff. They would go out of control as soon as they inhaled it and strain at their leashes, till they were released on the tiger. They would then leap and attack the tiger and tear it to pieces. A few dogs would die during the battle, but the darogha was not worried as they were street dogs and not expensive, pedigreed ones. There were always fifty to sixty dogs in the kennel at any point.

Horses

I have not seen a stable of the quality like that in Alwar anywhere else in any state.

There was a special stable with 400 highly pedigreed horses, which were trained and always ready for riding. These horses cost thousands of rupees, with the lowliest one fetching a price of Rs 500. The man in charge of the stables was a Khanzada[134] from a noble family.

I once heard the Maharaja tell a horse trader, 'If you bring me a pair of these horses, I will give you Rs 50,000.'

The stable boy and *Asp-e-Benazeer* were brothers from Kathiawar. The *Asp-e-Man Pyaara* and *Asp-e-Man Murad*[135] were also Khanzadas and half-brothers.

The horses were of different breeds and pedigrees. The horses used for drawing the carriages were also unique. There were Kathiawar and Marwari horses.

There were 1800 cavalrymen of the Khangi regiment who had state horses and beasts of burden. Behind the risala were two Kathiawar stallions; these were the horses who were used for breeding. The colts of these stallions were bred separately. The best ones would go to the special stable and the rest to the risala. From there, the better ones would go to the carriage division and the rest would be divided amongst the cavalrymen.

When the special horses came out for riding, it was a spectacular scene. The horses would be adorned with silver saddles studded with jewellery, silver decorative armour on the legs, bracelets with bells on the upper part of the legs, gold and silver ornaments around the neck, highly decorated martingales, and beautifully embroidered silver and gold covering for the saddles. Their handlers would lead them, prancing and dancing along. It seemed as if fairies from fairyland were dancing along the way.

Stables in the Hindustani states did not have such highly bred and pedigreed horses. Maybe the Sultan of Rum or the Badshah of Iran had such stables.

The daily procession of Sheodan Singh came out with such pomp and show every day that it could put every other noble procession to shame.

A little before dusk, all the courtiers would change their clothes, and wear beautiful, light-coloured turbans on their heads. A tray containing the finest itr would be presented before them, and they would pick up one bottle and dab it on their hands, one by one. When this was done, the courtiers would rub the fragrance on their dresses. A Banarsi dupatta would be tied around their waists, and putting their swords in the sword belt, they would come out of the palace. They would mount the special horses and go and join the Maharaja's procession, taking a place according to their station.

The procession would move slowly to the Moti Doongri,[136] and when it returned in the evening, it would be accompanied by servants bearing lighted candles and lamps on bamboo sticks. The Maharaja's horse would be in the middle, a band of friends riding behind him.

It looked exactly like a wedding procession and Sheodan Singh really looked every inch a bridegroom!

I have not seen such a procession being held by any other nobleman.

The entertainers included all the chosen singers, dancers and instrumentalists such as the sitar player, flautist, rabaab player, sarod player, singers and the *kalawant*.[137]

Amrit Sen and Lal Sen, who were famous sitar players, Ghulam Naqi, the famous flautist, and Gokiya Punjaban, a unique singer, were all present in Alwar. There were also beautiful courtesans from all over the world there.

The Maharaja would sit on his throne, his courtiers sitting on both sides. The entertainers would be in front of him, with about twenty-five to thirty beautiful, professional dancers and singers. They were fairy-like houris, shining stars of the firmament, who had angelic voices. They were elegant from top to toe, and it seemed as though a veritable garden of beauty and grace were flourishing there. It was more a theatre than a soiree.

There would be a 2–2.5-yards-wide, 1-foot-high platform made of rose petals in front of the throne. Around 20–25 ser of *mukaish* would be mixed with the rose petals. A mechanical silver device was kept in front of the throne. The Maharaja would turn it towards a person and press the button, and a fine spray of saffron or red would bespangle the person's white dress and throw handfuls of rose petals and mukaish on the courtiers. Whichever fortunate courtier was thus honoured, he would get up and present his salaam to the Maharaja. From head to toe, everyone would shine, their beards, turbans, dresses and faces luminous with the silver. As a result, the rose petals and mukaish would be used up in playing Holi and encrusted thus on the courtiers' dresses.

I don't think even Tana Shah would have seen such an assembly in his dreams.

The birthday, Dussehra and Teej assemblies were even more splendid. The Muslims would be treated to unique dishes, spread out in front of each person over a yard, and served in priceless porcelain dishes. They would also be presented with dresses and rewards.

I have never seen such a generous and benevolent man anywhere in the world.

Appreciation and Elevation of Poets

Maharaja Sahib Bahadur was extremely fond of poetry. He himself was an intelligent person with a high degree of understanding. His appreciation for poetry was such that he would become restless and immediately try to learn it when he heard it.

He never heard a qasida without giving a reward to the reciter. If anyone wrote a qasida for him, he would reward him suitably. I once read out a qasida on his birthday. When I went to pay nazr, he caught both my hands and asked, 'What do you want?'

I replied, 'Huzoor, you have caught both my hands. There is nothing left for me to ask. If someone catches one hand, then he patronizes him for life. Huzoor has caught both my hands! What more can I ask for?'

Maharaja Sahib Bahadur said, 'These are words of happiness. Please explain.'

I replied, 'You heard my qasida. How did you find it?'

He said, 'It is very well written.'

With great sincerity and humility, I replied, 'This qasida was not written by me. It was written by someone else.'

He said, 'He writes very well.'

I replied, 'Despite this, he is living a hand-to-mouth existence. In return for this qasida, would it be possible for him to make a living?'

'Who is this person?' he asked.

I replied, 'He is a sepoy in Daulah Khan Pathan's platoon.'

'Call him here,' he ordered.

The sepoy was called and given a fixed salary of Rs 20 per month. He was posted in the library.

Maharaja Sahib would also hold mushairas. The court poets were Mir Mehdi Hussain Majrooh, Mirza Qurban Beg Salik, Umrao Mirza Anwar, Miyan Ghulam Ahmed Tasweer, Miyan Khuda Baksh Tanveer and this lowly person, Zahir.

He respected poets very much, and he greatly appreciated their verses.

Quitting the Employment in Alwar

I spent three or four years in Alwar in ease and luxury, but fate couldn't countenance this happiness and my life was destabilized once again.

The Rajputs have always held a grudge against the Muslims and hostility and prejudice towards us is concealed in their disposition. They were envious and jealous and felt that the Muslims had become too close to the Maharaja, taking up all his time, and that the Maharaja Sahib had stopped paying attention to them. So they decided to find some way to turn the tables and began to conspire amongst themselves.

Lakhbir Singh Thakur was prepped for rebellion.[138] Sukhdev Singh Ra'ai gathered a group of 5000–6000 malevolent soldiers and attacked the state of Alwar. He began looting and plundering the Naraianpur Tehsil and Pargana Banwar and Lal Gaddi, and burnt the stables.

When news of this reached Alwar, Maharaja Sahib sent Captain Daulah Khan along with a platoon and Nawab Kamdar Khan with a risala of cavalry to stop the rebels. These brave men immediately brought the scoundrels under control. Dead bodies were strewn for many miles. Many of the leaders were beheaded and their heads sent to the Maharaja. Kundheer Singh baghi fled to Pratapgarh, Rajgarh after this defeat.

The brave soldiers followed him there and didn't let him settle down. Eventually, he was warned that if he ever set foot in the state of Alwar again, drastic steps would be taken against him by the state.

Embarrassed and despondent, he took refuge in the state of Jaipur, and from there the Rajputs sent petitions (to the British) stating that the Muslims were misleading the Maharaja of Alwar and had converted him to Islam. They begged that the Muslims be sent away from Alwar as there was strife in the state because of them. The Maharaja received an order from the British sarkar to send the Muslims away. He ignored the first order. The second order met the same fate. On receipt of the third order, we said in one voice, 'Why are you destroying your state because of us? Please give us permission to leave. We are attached to your feet and will return in a few years.'

With great difficulty, we managed to make the Maharaja agree to let us go. We came back to Delhi.

For a year, our salaries came to our houses. After a year, I asked Nawab Mustafa Khan sahib Shefta if he could help me get employment in the state of Jaipur. I would be forever grateful to him, I said. After all, who would keep sending a salary without getting any work in return?

Nawab Sahib was a very generous man. I had spent some time with him earlier, and he looked upon me kindly. He immediately sent a letter of recommendation to Nawab Faiz Ali Khan sahib Bahadur, *Madar-ul-Maham* (prime minister). His son, Nawab Mohammad Ali Khan, sent a letter to Bakshi Imdad Ali Khan sahib, the younger brother of the Nawab Sahib. On the fifth day after sending the letter, I was called by Nawab Mustafa Khan sahib Bahadur. He gave me the letter that had come from Nawab Faiz Ali Khan, summoning me. He said, 'Say Bismillah and leave for Jaipur. You will receive employment as soon as you reach.'

I left Delhi. When I reached Jaipur, I went to the house of my brother, Syed Ahmed Mirza Khan sahib. I met Bakshi Imdad Ali Khan sahib first, and then through his kind services, I met Nawab Faiz Ali Khan sahib Bahadur. Nawab Faiz Ali Khan put me on the waiting list, and after two months, appointed me thanedar of Khandar.

Employment in the Riyasat of Jaipur

Khandar is a pargana of Jaipur, and lies in the south-east. The Chambal River is at a distance of 3 kos from Khandar. It is also the confluence of the Banas and Chambal rivers. Another river flows into the pargana from Gwalior. The Rameshwaram Temple is built at this spot. Below this temple is the meeting point of the three rivers. The Chambal is the boundary between Jaipur and Gwalior.

There is a very strong and lofty fort built on top of a hill in Khandar. The army lives inside the fort. The pargana Khandar falls in the administrative district of Sawai Madhopur.

I could write a book on my days as a thanedar there. In short, it was an extremely respectable job where I was highly regarded.

I had an area of 12 kos under my administration, with 125 villages under the thana. I governed this pargana for five or six months. I enjoyed it so much that I forgot all the luxuries of Alwar.

Six months later, I was transferred from Thana Amriya and I returned to Jaipur. My family was already staying there in the house of Syed Ahmed Mirza Khan sahib.

I rented a house in Jaipur and shifted my family there. I left for Amer myself. When I reached Amer, I found that it was a sadar thana and was equal to the kotwali of Jaipur in status. Amer was an ancient capital of Jaipur state. Here, a bolster and cushions were provided for the thanedar. I performed my duties here for six months. Now it was time for the Dusshera festival. From my subordinates, I learnt that we should make arrangements for the same.

Maharaja Sahib Bahadur would honour the area with his presence and stay there for a few days. The thanedar was supposed to make all arrangements and be positioned at the deorhi of the fort.

All arrangements were made and the days of Dusshera began. On the first day, the employees of the thana said that we should go to the top of the hill and perform the Dusshera rituals. I had no idea of the rituals but they assured me that they would guide me.

I wore my turban, tied my sword and sash and went along with them. When we reached the market, the halwai had finished cooking about a maund and a half of sweets. He joined us too. A little further down the road, the Hindu butcher, the one employed by the state, joined in with about thirty to forty goats. I had no idea what was happening.

When we reached the top of the hill, I saw the entrance to the palace. I went inside. On top of the hill, there was a huge ground with royal buildings on all four sides of it. There was a majestic temple there with many nobles standing near it. This was the Mata Mandir and the Khas Mahal Darwaza of the palace was situated at her feet.

The people of the area live in the middle of the high mountains. The western mountain is very high and the fort is on its top, with palaces alongside it. In the shade of these

mountains, there is a huge pond with concrete sides. There
is an orchard near the pond and around it is a red sandstone
enclosure. When the water overflows from the pond, small
boats ply, helping people cross the orchard. This orchard is
under the palaces and is very beautiful.

When I entered the temple, I saw all these beautiful
surroundings. Towards the south is a hallway with aisles and
next to it is the room which houses the idol of Shila Devi.[139]

The priests took the sweets and put them in front of the
Devi. The goats were herded inside the temple courtyard.
I stood against a column in the courtyard outside, and saw
that the priests had lit many ghee lamps in a tray. They were
moving it up and down in front of the idol, chanting the
whole time. I couldn't understand what they were chanting.
Soon, bells and drums were being beaten and the whole
temple was lit brightly and filled with the smell of incense.
This went on for some time. When the priests had finished,
they came and stood next to me. There were men holding
lighted torches in the courtyard. A man came up, wielding
a large knife. A rope was tied to the horns of one goat and
pulled, while another man pushed from behind. The man
wielding the knife made a powerful stroke and the goat's
head flew. All the goats were slaughtered in the same
manner. They call this *balidan*.

Once this was over, the priests distributed the sweets and
gave us leave to go. I now realized what my job entailed and
the customs the thanedar has to take part in. I would go to the
temple every evening and come back late at night, after the
balidan and sweet distribution was over.

One evening, as the sky was reddening, a young Rana,
slim and of average height, wearing a red turban and red
Banarsi sash on his waist, came riding from the palace door

on a bay horse. He stopped at the thana. Amir Khan, the musketeer, gestured to me with his eyes, and I ran outside and held the reins to help the Rana dismount. I took the horse, but before I could stable it, the servant came and took it away. I presented my salaam to the Rana and offered the nazr.

The Rana said, 'I will take the nazr a little later. Untie my sash first.'

I took out both the swords and then untied the sash. I had spread a handkerchief on the platform and placed everything on it. Under the Banarsi sash, there was another white sash, which I undid. Under this was a silken tassel with a bunch of keys hanging from it. Below it was a tassel with the scabbards made of broadcloth. There were scissors, knives, daggers, nail parer, thread and God knows what else.

Below this, there was a red purse weighing 3–4 ser. When I opened it, I found it was drenched in perspiration.

The Rana said, 'Keep these in your custody. When Kishan Lal comes, tell him to store them properly.'

Saying this, he went inside the thana. The servants took the saddlecloth off the horse and put it under him. I kept standing there, guarding the things he had left. After a while, the army came and the entire courtyard filled with people. Then Kishan Lal Chela came on his horse and dismounted near me.

I said, 'Kishan Lal ji, please take care of these things.' I handed them to him. There were all kinds of useless things, including an English pen stand, pencil and paper inside the scabbard.

Inside the purse, there was an assortment of some Rs 200, more than 100 coins and a separate bundle of notes wrapped in a waxed paper which I couldn't count.

After some time, the Rana went inside the temple and a balidan was performed. When he came out of the temple, he was drenched in perspiration. He sat on the steps. I put down a handkerchief for him to sit on. Kishan Lal came and stood behind him, but the Rana ordered him to sit as well.

He then asked me, 'How many days have you been in this thana?'

I replied, 'Huzoor, it's been five months since I was transferred here.'

He asked, 'Which thana were you posted in earlier?'

'At the Thana Khandar.'

'Had Nawab Sahib recommended you from Shimla? I was the one who signed your orders,' he said.

'Yes, those orders were given for me.'

I was in the Maharaja's (for that is who the young Rana was) service for the five days he stayed here. Whenever he came, I would be in attendance to him. We would talk of everything under the sun. We would even play ganjifa and chausar. On his asking, I told him about myself, my ancestors and our services in the Mughal court, and he very graciously told me to consider this state to be the same as that I had left behind. He said that this service was the same as the one I had held under the Mughals and said, 'Once someone comes to this house, they don't leave it.'

The Maharaja was very pleased with a couple of services that I was able to render and hence gave me much respect. I was always called to do important tasks outside of the military service. In fact, one day there was an urgent problem and they were discussing who the best person would be to solve it. The Maharaja immediately said that I should be given the task as I would do it very ably.

I was on my way to Delhi on some work when this transpired. I had already gone some distance. A cavalryman of the royal regiment set out to look for me at night. As it was the Maharaja's order, the rider reached me at midnight at Acharwal and read out the task stating that I must set off for Jaipur immediately and reach that very night.

I wrote a letter to the thanedar, Chandwaji, stating that I had been given orders to go to Jaipur so I could not fulfil the task I had been given originally. I requested him to come and take it from me so that I could proceed to Jaipur. He could send the package I was carrying to Delhi and get the receipt. I asked the rider to rest for a bit, and left immediately with a servant for Amer. I reached by 4 a.m. After freshening up, I mounted another horse, which had been kept ready for me, and left in a rush from the valley gate, reaching Zoravar Singh's gate. I proceeded towards the deorhi and sent word to the Maharaja that I had arrived. Everyone was waiting for me, and hence I was immediately called inside.

When I went in, Huzoor was brushing his teeth with a *meswak* (tooth-cleaning twig). I presented my salutations.

He responded, 'You have come! You took a long time.'

I replied, 'I have come from a distance of 13 kos.'

He praised me, '*Shabaash!* [Well done!] Now you will be sent to solve a difficult problem. Resolve it in the same way that your ancestors resolved issues for the Mughal emperor. Go. I give you into the custody of God. Nawab Sahib will tell you what you have to do.'

Nawab Faiz Ali Khan sahib and Munshi Ramji Das caught my hands and took me inside Chandar Mahal. Here, they told me of the secret mission. This was not a usual time for the chief minister and other important ministers to be present in court, and I realized that they had stayed up with the Maharaja, waiting for me.

Nawab Sahib said, 'We will give you as much money as you think necessary to take with you. Also take as many men as you deem essential.'

'Neither men nor money are needed,' I said.

Nawab Sahib was shocked to hear this and asked, 'How will you do the work?'

'I don't want to spend a penny on the work, and neither do I want to take anyone with me. I want to complete my task without any of this, and if God wills, I will complete it to the best of my ability,' I said.

Nawab Sahib said, 'Two men will accompany you and one of them is from the agent of Jaipur. You can't accomplish your task without their help.'

'If I complete my task with their help, then what is my efficiency? If God wills, I will complete my work without any of them being the wiser.'

The Nawab Sahib said that I would at least need money for my living expenses and I should take it from the treasury. I said that they should deposit Rs 500 with the officer who could give it to these people when they needed it. But yes, I did need a letter from the council, telling the jagirdars and those subordinate to them and the superintendent that they should render me whatever assistance I might need. No one could ignore this. I was given the letter to carry along with me.

That place was a little distant from Jaipur. I left with my companions, and before reaching the scene of the incident, I did my job. When we reached the site, the two men with me found no trace of the incident they had gone to investigate.

They came back and reported that the suspicions had been unfounded and they found no trace to substantiate it.

When I came back and presented my salutations to the Maharaja, he said, 'If any chief of state had gone, he would have spent at least Rs 2–3 lakh.'

I performed many such tasks for the Maharaja. That is why he was very fond of me and gave me respect and extended his patronage to me.

He then said, 'You must get yourself transferred to Sanganer Thana, as I go there very often.'

I replied, 'Huzoor, that is your privilege.'

So the council was asked to issue an order stating that Zahiruddin Hussain Officer was transferred to Sanganer. Further, he couldn't be transferred, suspended or removed without direct orders from the Maharaja himself.

Many of the Maharaja's other courtiers became very jealous of our closeness. When he went out for a ride, I was often the sole person accompanying him. Everyone else, including Kishan Lal Chela, could only watch us go.

The Maharaja had some secrets that only God and I were privy to. However, I am a very unfortunate man. Had the Maharaja lived for a few more years, I don't know what kind of rank I might have achieved. When I was promoted to the post of deputy superintendent, he told me, 'I have not made you a deputy. I have made you a general superintendent. I will send you to Sirsa to collect the taxes. After six months, you will become the general superintendent.'

He died within three months of saying this.

8

Description of the Maharaja of Jaipur

Shri Sawai Maharaja Ram Singh sahib Bahadur was an extremely intelligent, broad-minded, visionary, honourable, far-sighted man, caring of his subjects, generous with his praise. He had no prejudice, he was clement and affable, rational, good-natured and a constant man. He had a pleasing countenance, was very good-natured and a wonderful amalgamation of all the best qualities and virtues that could be found in a man.

There is no other nobleman with this kind of temperament in all of India. The only man who came somewhat close to him was perhaps Nawab Yusuf Ali Khan sahib of Rampur.

The foundation of Maharaja Sahib's kingdom was his far-sightedness. He employed hundreds of informants to write a daily diary/journal, and he knew exactly what was happening at all times in every Indian state. He had informants in every state, including Hyderabad, Udaipur and the governor's office. His informants accompanied the Governor Bahadur everywhere and relayed every bit of information to the Maharaja, no matter how small.

Thousands were spent on this intelligence department and all informants were given the appropriate salary. There was not a single factory, department, administrative division or district in his own state which didn't have an informer. The *Darogha-e-Khabar* had instructions stating that if there was an important piece of news and the Maharaja was in the *zenana mahal* (the ladies' quarters of the palace), he should be woken up and given the information.

The Maharaja sent a daily telegram to Queen Victoria in London, inquiring after her welfare. No British agent or Resident could go against his will. He left no stone unturned in looking after and rewarding the British agents and Resident.

One of his most noble attributes was that all his life, he never uttered an uncultured word of abuse or criticism against anyone. He never addressed anyone with '*tu*',[140] and even the lowliest person was addressed with civility. If he ever got angry with someone, the most he would say was '*Tu jaa, bewaqoof*!' (Go away, foolish man!) Despite this mildness, his awe and majesty was such that everyone held him in great esteem and no one would step out of line.

Whenever the Maharaja fell silent, it was as though all hell had broken loose. People would understand that he was angry and every noble would tremble with fear.

When the Maharaja ascended the throne as a minor, Rawal ji Sahib (Rawal Bairi Sal) was the regent, and Jaipur was a desolate state. Its revenue was only Rs 24 lakh, and there was no department or administrative machinery in place. Everything was done verbally and the kingdom was in a bad way.

Whatever progress Jaipur made, its beautiful culture—all this was achieved during the reign of this Maharaja. When the Maharaja became an adult and Panditji the premier, then fifty-two departments, courts, administrative units, districts, tehsils and thanas were opened. Rules were framed for the administration of the state, collection of revenue, and regulations for civil and criminal courts, and officers posted to ensure they were complied with.

Crores of rupees were spent on building dams, tanks, and making arrangements for irrigation. Roads were built, sanitation was looked after, hospitals and schools were set up throughout the state.

Jaipur was lit up by gaslights and water was provided to the citizens via taps. Thieves, dacoits, thugs and highwaymen were brought under control by strict measures, and peace prevailed. Travelling out of Jaipur, which had been very dangerous, became safe, as all famous highwaymen and thugs were caught and hanged. The rebels were warned.

Maharaja Sahib was very caring of his subjects, and his instructions were, 'Give as good as you get and even more. I will take care of you.' Jaipur became so safe that one could walk about freely with as much gold and silver as one wished, and no one would touch it. Lambs and lions drank water at the same bank.

The quality of justice and equity was superior. There is a famous incident: A few butchers of the state of Tonk were taking cattle that they had bought in Jaipur back to Tonk. On the way, they rested at a spot, and after buying some grass, they fed the cattle. A bull from the local village came and started eating the grass and pushed away the cattle. When the butchers saw this, they hit the bull with a stick and drove him away. After a while, the bull returned and had to be driven away again. When this had happened a couple of times, one of the butchers got angry, and drawing his sword, hit the bull on his leg. The bull's leg was cut and flew away.

This resulted in a furore, as the Hindus were in control in the area. There was a minor riot and the butchers were caught and put in jail.

The thanedar prepared a charge sheet and sent it to the criminal court. As it was a religious matter, the court advised serious punishment for the butchers. This was sent to the court of appeals, which gave another verdict. Eventually, the case went up all the way to the council.

The council members said that it was indeed a religious matter, and religious texts should be consulted and punishment given accordingly. The religious scholars were called and they pronounced that the first level of punishment was a death sentence, the second level was dismemberment and the third imprisonment for life.

The final decision was left to the Maharaja, and the case was presented before him. He listened to everyone's comments and gave orders to summon the *shastri ji*, or priest. When the shastri ji came, the Maharaja said to him, 'Have you given this punishment according to Hindu law or Muslim Sharia?'

The shastri ji replied, 'I have given it as per the *Dharam Shastra*s [Hindu religious texts]. I have nothing to do with Sharia.'

The Maharaja replied, 'The criminal is not a Hindu and the condition of justice is that punishment should be given according to one's religion. This case should be decided on the basis of a fatwa by an Islamic judge, otherwise it is illegal. In their religion, it is permissible to eat beef. In my eyes, it is punishment enough that this case has dragged on for one-and-a-half years. The prisoner should be freed.'

The man was freed at once.

No other Hindu king could have given such a just judgement!

There were many such judgements given by the Maharaja. He was the Nosherwan-e-Adil[141] of his times.

Once, a poor traveller was desirous of presenting his petition to the Maharaja. He was unable to get an opportunity. One day, he was standing on the deorhi of the palace when the guard moved a little away. He seized the opportunity and entered the deorhi. He climbed the stairs and reached the special room where the Maharaja used to sit. It happened to be a time when ladies were present, so the area was cordoned off. The Chief Queen[142] was present there. The visitor immediately put a hand over his eyes and began to retrace his steps. The Maharaja saw him and came to ask him what he wanted. The traveller presented his salutations, but the Maharaja caught both his hands and asked, 'Who are you?'

The traveller said, 'I am a servant of Allah.'

The Maharaja said, 'Everyone is a servant of Allah, but who are you?'

He replied, 'I am a traveller and a maulvi.'

'Why have you come to this place?'

'I am a family man and am unemployed. I have come in hope of employment.'

'Didn't the guard stop you?' the Maharaja asked.

'It's not the fault of the guard,' the maulvi replied. 'I slipped in when he had gone to the other side. I am at fault, not him. I am the criminal. You can give me whatever punishment you deem fit. I am ashamed to have come at such a time. But Huzoor, the *Badshah-e-waqt*[143] and the Maharani are the parents of their subjects, and subjects have the same position as their children. And mothers don't need to observe purdah in front of their children.'

'You are a maulvi,' the Maharaja said. 'Where did you study?'

'In Lucknow.'

'Do you have proof?'

'Please test my knowledge,' the maulvi offered.

'Had you not been a maulvi, God knows what punishment might have befallen you. I consider the scholars of all religions to be my *peshwa*s.[144] Anyway, this was not a deliberate act, and I forgive you.'

He called out to his servants. When one came, he ordered him, 'Take Maulvi Sahib to Maulvi Rashidudin Sahib and tell him that I have sent him so that Maulvi Sahib's knowledge and capabilities might be tested. Please inform me of the result at once. If he passes the test, appoint him as a teacher in a madrassa and inform me.'

Maulvi Rashidudin examined the new entrant, praised his knowledge and appointed him as a teacher at a salary of Rs 30 per month.

Could any other ruler show such forbearance and generosity? This was only the generosity and magnanimity of the Maharaja.

Habits of the Maharaja of Jaipur

The Maharaja was of a Sufi bent of mind. There was always a variety of people in his service. They included a couple of dervishes, Egyptians, Muslims, some Hindu faqirs, *bairagi*s[145] and monotheists. His temperament was spiritual and he would spend a great deal of time discussing mysticism. He was free of the ego of the rich and powerful men, and though he wore clothes befitting his royal status, he shunned its other trappings. He would often sleep on his horse's saddle without worrying about bedsteads and canopies. He did not stand on ceremony himself and preferred those who were informal. He was an extremely humble person with no hauteur or airs and graces which could be considered a natural outcome of his royal position.

He would keep himself surrounded by a few faqirs, physicians, British men, courtesans, dancers and musicians, kite fliers and experts in different arts. This group would always accompany him, along with a few Rajput chiefs.

He was very fond of Muslims and his constant companion was an old blind faqir named Baju Miyan. It was Baju Miyan who served the Maharaja when he retired to his bedchamber. The Maharaja would wake up every morning only after looking at his face. Baju Miyan would get up for the dawn prayers, and after completing these and sundry other rituals, he would go up to the Maharaja and remove the sheet from his face. He would call out, 'Maharaja! It's morning. Wake up and take the name of Khuda and Rasool.'

The Maharaja would then open his eyes and look at the faqir's face. Only after that would he greet everyone else.

He would give lakhs of rupees to charity. Poor and indigent travellers in inns would be generously endowed. Hundreds of boxes, each containing 1 ser of grain, 250 gm dal, 1 chattank oil, 250 gm sugar and 2 paisa cash would be distributed every day. Apart from this, Jaipur's charity and charitable institutions were famous.

Moharrum

The Maharaja had twelve platoons of the army whose job was also to do *azadari*[146] during Moharrum. They were paid Rs 250 each. Money was spent separately on the Maharaja's personal azadari. These fifty men would be excused from service during Moharrum so that they could do the azadari.

Help for Those Going on Haj

Every year, Rs 20,000–25,000 were given to pilgrims undertaking haj. They would also be given leave of absence for six months.

As a result of all this charity, the state expenditure exceeded Rs 1 crore.

Death

When Maharaja Ram Singh left this world, his subjects were heartbroken. His affairs were well settled, the treasury was overflowing and the employees were prosperous. The city observed a three-day mourning period.

The city of Jaipur had no Indian peer in its prosperity, the grandeur of its monuments and the elegance of its people.

> If Paradise resides on the Earth
> It is here, it is here, it is here

May God keep this city safe. It is a protector of the poor.

After Maharaja Ram Singh's death there was a great revolution, and Maharaja Madho Singh Bahadur[147] ascended the throne.

During his rule, a stormy wind blew away the fine culture established by Maharaja Ram Singh. Everyone was ready to devour each other!

When Thakur Fateh Singh ji Naila became the diwan and Sales Sahib (1876–1883),[148] the British agent was looking after the administration of Jaipur and the state was plunged into indescribable darkness. There were thousands fighting for posts in Jaipur and they were even being advertised in newspapers. A job in Jaipur became a basket of oranges, and anyone who could pay the price could have one.

This tumult led to all the old employees of the Maharaja being replaced by the new ones who had bought these posts.

A Thakur chief became the general superintendent and he terminated the employment of the old guard. He took on new employees. There were four deputy superintendents, and all four of us were terminated in one go.

I mourned this termination for a year and a half.

Eventually, the agent was terminated along with Thakur Fateh Singh, and even the general superintendent was imprisoned. However, there was no relief for the complainants, and no one was re-employed. I had to leave after fourteen years in the service of Maharaja Ram Singh and three years in the service of Maharaja Madho Singh Bahadur. I was rewarded for my services by being terminated for no fault of my own, and thus became unemployed. The only consideration I received for my loyalty was that my son Sajjad Mirza was made a thanedar.

It was to be a new pasture and new hay for me once again.

Revenue of the Kingdom

It's been forty years since I went to Jaipur. I have seen every part of it. The kingdom's length stretched for 300 miles from the north to the south, and 150 miles from the east to the west.

The revenue of this state was approximately Rs 1 crore. It was divided in three parts of Rs 33 lakh, each for:

1. The expenses of the state
2. The salaries and expenses of the employees and the princes of the royal blood

3. The upkeep of the Brahmins and their expenses, worship of cows, maintenance of temples, and so on. This department also dealt with charity and giving rewards.

All the increase in land revenue under Maharaja Ram Singh was due to the charity that he carried out.

Nawab Ahmed Ali Khan Raunaq

I spent nineteen to twenty years in service to the state. In these years, I got very little time to write poetry. I could write barely forty to fifty ghazals and a few qasidas, and that too at the insistence of friends. I would write only when my friends and acquaintances pressed me to participate in some mushaira.

Hakim Mohammad Salim Khan sahib would often request me to write a ghazal. Though I was not inclined to write poetry, I was compelled to do so, because of my friends. One day, by a beautiful coincidence, I was in my thana at Sanganer and Maharaja Sahib was present in the fort. I was discharging my duty at the deorhi.

While I was smoking my huqqa at the entrance to the garden where the Maharaja Sahib was resting, I saw an impressive-looking gentleman of sixty to sixty-five years of age, in a cream angarkha, pyjama and turban, wearing the trappings of a hunter. He had arrived from Jesar. Getting off his tonga, he came towards me. I greeted him respectfully. He sat down next to me and said, 'I want to smoke a huqqa.'

I presented the nozzle to him and he started drawing from it. After a while, he asked me, 'What is your name?'

'Your humble servant is called Zahiruddin,' I replied.

On hearing this, he became attentive and asked, 'Why are you here?'

'I am a thanedar and am here in discharge of my duties.'

'Are you Zahir Dehlvi by any chance?'

Replying in the affirmative I said, 'Though I am definitely a Dehlvi, maybe you are looking for some other Zahir.'

He started laughing and recited:

The friend is in the house and we search the whole world,
The water is in the pot and we roam with parched lips[149]

Embracing me, he exclaimed, 'My elder brother, Nawab Abdul Karim Khan sahib, and I have been looking for you for ages. He passed away without having his wish fulfilled, but praise be to Allah that my wish has been granted and I have met you.'

I asked, 'Sir, how do you know of me?'

He replied, 'My brother and I heard one of your ghazals being recited by a Mughal in an assembly. From that day on, that poem mesmerized us and we wanted to become the disciple of the writer. I still remember a few verses of the ghazal:

However much you may avoid idolatry, trouble has a way
of finding you
These beauties will be your undoing; they have a way of
bewitching you'

He went on to say that he was so fond of Urdu poetry that it was an addiction. 'I went to Lucknow, and among the famous poets I met Sheikh Imambaksh Nasikh and Khwaja Haider Ali Atish. I have also written three diwans. Miyan Khuda Baksh Tanveer came to Tonk and worked for me for some time. I have been looking for you. Please accept me as your student and guide me.'

I replied respectfully, 'Sir, you are as old as my father. I am thirty-four to thirty-five years old and you must be over sixty years of age.'

'What do you recommend, then? Age and wisdom don't always go together,' he said.

The Maharaja saw us talking and called out, 'Miyan, why don't you come here? Come and partake of some paan with me.'

Nawab Sahib replied, 'I will present myself in a moment. I am smoking a huqqa with my ustad.'

Maharaja Sahib said, 'Why, Miyan? Is it forbidden to smoke huqqa near me?'

Nawab Sahib immediately exclaimed, '*Nahin* [No] Huzoor! I was just talking to him. I will come at once.'

The Nawab Sahib went up to the Maharaja. The Maharaja asked curiously, 'How is he your ustad?'

'You know that I am addicted to poetry,' Nawab Sahib explained.

Maharaja Sahib exclaimed in surprise, 'Aha! Is he also a poet? He has never told me that he writes verse. Nor has he ever recited anything for me. Call him here.'

Nawab Sahib called out to me.

When I went near, the Maharaja Sahib said, 'Thanedar ji, you have never even once mentioned that you are a poet.'

I replied respectfully, 'Such an opportunity has never arisen. It is not my habit to talk of myself or praise myself.'

When Maharaja Sahib ordered me to recite something, I requested permission to go up to the gate to bring some of my poems. When he gave permission, I came up to the thana and searched my bag. I found an incomplete qasida. I somehow completed it in two hours and took it to him.

When I recited it, both the Maharaja and the Nawab Sahib were very happy and praised me highly.

Nawab Ahmed Ali Khan said, 'Huzoor, he has written this extempore.' Maharaja was very surprised and said, 'I am also fond of poetry. Keep reciting to me. I have learned of your talents today, and I will now hold a mushaira. You must write for that.'

'As you wish, sir.'

Later, the Nawab Sahib said that he was staying in the nearby garden, and asked for leave to say his prayers. Both of us came out and went to the other garden. Nawab Sahib bought sweets worth Rs 5 from the nearby market and asked me to give *niaz* (consecrate in the name of the Prophet). After I gave the niaz, it was distributed to those around us.

Nawab Sahib now asked me to correct his ghazal.

I said, 'Nawab Sahib, you have seen with your own eyes that I am busy all day and no longer have time to write poetry. Now my younger brother, Umrao Mirza Anwar, has become a much better poet than me. You should let him guide you. He is coming to Jaipur and will undertake the task whole-heartedly. I will bring my brother to your house once the Maharaja Sahib leaves this area.'

After a few days, when the Maharaja had left for Jaipur, I accompanied him and sent for Umrao Mirza. I took him to Nawab Sahib's house, and he showed him his ghazal. Umrao Mirza made the appropriate corrections and suggestions and this impressed the Nawab Sahib greatly. He was a mature and worldly man and eager to learn.

When I met him a month later, he said, 'Ustad, your brother has lifted the veil from my eyes. I realize now that I was totally ignorant and so were the people around me. I have put away my old diwans and started writing anew. I write two ghazals every day, and they are immediately corrected and improved. I have fixed a time for writing poetry. I lie down in my bed at 10 p.m. and start composing a ghazal. A writer sits next to my bed and keeps writing as I speak the words out loud. I have one more diwan ready.'

I would often keep him company and listen to his verse. I had been so busy with my work that I was not able to write much myself. Now that I was free from my job, I started writing again.

Meanwhile, my brother had found employment in Delhi and I started attending mushairas in Bhopal, held under the aegis of Nawab Shah Jahan Begum, the ruler. Nawab Siddiq Hasan Khan[150] appreciated my ghazals and I stayed in Bhopal for four months. I had to return to Jaipur when I got news of my brother's demise.[151]

Nawab Sahib offered condolences on Umrao Mirza's death and said, 'Please stay with me now and don't leave me. I will look after you in the same way that I looked after your brother.'

I started living with him and advising him on his verse. He had already published one diwan with my brother's help. It was known as *Diwan-e-Raunaq*. He was preparing to publish another when he passed away.

Both his diwans are excellent, as my brother and I put in our best efforts to improve his work. We made it better than our own verses. One wants to work hard for such an appreciative and generous student. The late Nawab Ahmed Ali Khan gave me much more appreciation and respect than any other student has given to his teacher. There was nothing that he didn't share with me. In fact, when he took his medicine he would make me have them too! He used to get Rs 7 worth of Unani tonics for strength and general health every month, and out of that, he would give a portion to me.

His appreciation for me was such that if any unique and tasty dish was put before him, he would offer it to me first. When I demurred he would say, 'You taste it first so that some of the sweetness of your tongue rubs off on mine!'

I was sitting with him on his bed when he passed away. My hand was tightly clasped in his on his chest when he breathed his last. His eldest son was watching us.

Nawab Ibrahim Ali Khan had once asked Nawab Ahmed Ali Khan to let me go with him, but the latter had refused, saying that he could not bear to part with me. He had added that, 'Today you want to take him with you, but if you are not able to give him as much love and respect as I do, I will be anguished and there will be a problem in our relationship. You can call him after my death.'

This is what happened. When Nawab Ibrahim came to know of Nawab Ahmed Ali Khan's death, he sent a message to the latter's son, calling me. I went to Tonk in deference to his wishes.

Nawab Ahmed Ali Khan was extremely fond of attending mushairas. While I was with him, Nawab Sahib would ask me to write for them and I wrote around 200 ghazals at his request. My first diwan, *Gulistan-e-Sukhan*, was almost completed in his lifetime.

In the Maharaja's Service

When I was the thanedar and enjoying Maharaja Sahib's generous patronage, he would often give me important responsibilities to fulfil. He would send me on secret and important tasks. He knew that I would not be coerced or influenced by anyone.

There was an ancient tradition in the state of Jaipur that if any criminal went and took shelter in the village of one of the rural chiefs, they considered it against their ethos to have him arrested. This was considered indicative of their valour—that such and such house was a safe haven and no criminal could be arrested if he were sheltering there. This was especially true for those jagirdars who were considered members of the state.

Rawal ji Sahib and his brother Thakur ji, whose family had held the premiership of Jaipur since old times, would send me to capture these rebels and criminals.

By chance, I once came to know that three criminals were sheltering in the birthplace of Thakur Rawal ji, qasba Samode.[152] They had come there right after committing a crime. I went there and arrested them. Rawal ji was very surprised as no thanedar before me had been able to arrest any criminal in that place. He told me, 'Set them free. If the state wants them, they should send a summons for them, and then I will ensure that they are sent there.'

I replied, 'If I do that, then what of the law and order of the state? I will not free them on any condition. I will take them like this in handcuffs and shackles.'

As they saw that I was not going to be coerced, they offered me a bribe of Rs 3000 to set the criminals free. They were fearful of the dent in their reputation if it were known that criminals who had sheltered in their village had been caught.

I was affronted by the offer of the bribe and retorted, 'I would have handed them over to you earlier, but now that you have tried to bribe me I will never set them free. I have arrested and handcuffed and shackled them today, but tomorrow I may be the one in handcuffs and shackles.'

The argument grew heated. Rawal ji Sahib confronted me and said, 'Let's see how you take these three away. Scores of thanedars have come and we have dispatched them summarily.'

I retorted, 'I am sure no thanedar ever came here. They must be all disreputable, ungrateful wretches. I will take them, and take them in full view of all.'

There was a safe house in a temple's premises. I took control of it and locked the criminals in the room there. I put up a guard outside. I sent messages and intimated the thanedars of nearby areas. I also sent a missive with a rider to the general superintendent, asking for help. By afternoon, two neighbouring thanedars had come to my aid.

Now I had fifty horsemen and around 1000–1500 men. The employees of Rawal ji got the entrance to the city locked up and set a guard of 300–400 men at each entrance so that we could not take the criminals out of the city.

The grocery shops in Samode were instructed not to sell anything to the government employees. Now the horses and men were hungry. We were all worried, until we saw that there was a small grass manger in front of the temple. It belonged to a bania. It was the same bania who owned the village grocery store. We went and forcibly brought the bania to the temple. He was spread-eagled and a heavy stone put on his back. We threatened him, 'Hey you, we will die of hunger, but we will kill you first. We are the employees of the state and have come here in pursuit of our duties. No one can harm us. Either you give us provisions or we will plunder your shop and house.'

He started pleading and shouting, but Rawal ji's men didn't have the gumption to come and save the bania. They had only been indulging in false bravado.

When the bania saw that no one was going to come to his aid, he was reduced to pleading with us and asking for forgiveness, 'Please leave me; I will give you provisions.'

I replied, 'We can't leave you like this. You must get all the provisions right now.'

He called out to his brothers to come and take him out of this plight.

His brother and son came running and he told them to bring over all the provisions we needed. They quickly brought all the sacks of grain and other things, and set up shop in the temple itself.

I had the stone removed from his back and told the bania to provide us food for eight days. I told my cavalrymen, 'Bring as many haystacks as you need for your horses and pay him for it. If you don't have the money now, then register your name, your village's name and the name of your jagirdar in his accounts book.'

Once we had got all we needed, we released the bania. We were now sending a letter to the central superintendent, asking for help. As the gates were locked, we decided to send it with foot runners via the wicket gates.

This situation continued for seven days, and we received no reply or help from the central department.

Eventually, since we had no other choice, I sent one missive to Hakim Mohammad Salim Khan, Darogha-e-Khabar. I described our situation from start to finish and asked him to send the information to the Maharaja and let me know his orders straightaway.

My messenger reached Jaipur at three in the morning. The place we were in was 12–13 kos away from Jaipur. The Darogha-e-Khabar read it and immediately took it to the Maharaja. He sent a message to the Maharaja, saying that he had urgent news which he had to relay to him verbally.

The Hakim Sahib was immediately called into his presence. He read my message to the Maharaja verbatim.

The Maharaja summoned Shafi Miyan, the general superintendent, and sent a message to the bakshikhana saying that both the bakshis should prepare their cavalry and bring them to the palace.

As soon as the Maharaja gave the orders, the messengers started running about and preparations began. Meanwhile, the superintendent came and was taken to task by the Maharaja. 'My officers and men have been imprisoned for eight days and you have taken no action. Is this why we appointed the superintendent, so that my officers and men could languish like this without any help?'

The superintendent admitted, 'Huzoor, it was a matter of your courtiers. That is why I delayed.'

The Maharaja retorted, 'My courtiers are not more important than me. One soldier is equal to a courtier. These people had gone to fulfil their duties as per my orders. Go and have them released. And listen carefully: God save you if even one of my men is harmed. I order you to flatten Samode if you have to. There should be no signs of habitation left after you finish.'

The superintendent gave his acquiescence. 'It will be as you desire. Your servant is leaving to fulfil your wish.'

The Maharaja stopped him, saying, 'You are an old man; it will be too tiring for you. Send your son instead.'

His son, Ahmed Miyan, was also present and came forward. After presenting his salutations, he left. By midnight, he was on his way from the Chandpol Gate with his cavalry. By this time, the artillery had also received orders to get ready and leave.

Rawal ji Sahib was present in his Chini ka Burj in Jaipur. As soon as he heard of the force that had been dispatched, he came and fell at the Maharaja's feet. 'Huzoor, why have you troubled the army? I will present the criminals and employees who have disobeyed Your Majesty by afternoon.'

'There is no need for all that. The thanedar who has arrested them will bring them to me,' said the Maharaja. 'I will not break my thanedar's heart. He has done me such a great service. You go and wait in your house. By tomorrow, everything will be known.'

On the eighth day, I was sitting on the temple platform with five cavalrymen, smoking my huqqa after my morning ablutions. I was wondering what the day would bring, what the answer would be to my message, when I saw two men coming towards me from the wicket gate. They wished us and said they were travellers like us. They were craving a drag of the huqqa. I invited them to smoke with me. As they sat down next to us, one of them said he wanted to talk to me in private. Thinking him to be a traveller, I took him aside and asked him to state his intent. He told me quietly, 'Help has come for you but the gate to the city is closed. How can they come inside?'

Thinking that there would be around 50–100 cavalrymen, I inquired, 'How many men are with you?'

He replied, 'There are 5000 cavalrymen at the gate and infantry and artillery forces are on their way.'

I was stunned into silence, finding this unbelievable. Once I regained my senses, I asked, 'Is this true? Or are you joking?'

'You can see them with your own eyes, but you must first tell us how to enter,' he replied.

I advised them to bypass the gate and go towards the north gate, which was open. 'Come galloping in together in such unison that they are unable to close the door. I will be there myself. Take the Almighty's name and come in.'

I called my troops and told them to be ready for action, but to prepare themselves in such a way that no one would be alerted. I instructed them not to gird their horses as that would give the game away; they just had to be ready themselves.

Taking my sword in one hand and the huqqa in the other, I walked casually towards the gate. My servant was walking behind me with his gun on his shoulder. When we reached the gate, the 150–200 strong troops guarding it stood at attendance and saluted me and inquired, 'Thanedar ji, to what do we owe the pleasure of your company?'

'We are your prisoners and can't go out of the city. We are just whiling away time by wandering about,' I said.

The sentry at the gate said, 'Thanedar ji, who can imprison you? After all, you are a state employee. All this will die out in a few days.'

We were talking when I saw a deputy risaldar galloping towards the gate, followed by a regiment of cavalry who drew their swords as they came closer. The leader gave the war cry and the local soldiers could only watch in stupefaction.

'Don't you dare move, or you will be quartered by our swords,' the naib said. 'Just stay in your positions.'

No one dared to protest as the naib called on his troops to enter. A sea of cavalrymen entered Samode, the war drums being beaten by the *naqqarchi*. Each of the eight regiments had their own *naqqara* and naqqarchi beating the drums as they stormed in.

Ahmed Miyan came and greeted me.

3000 troops belonging to the jagirdars also came galloping in. Samode was now teeming with cavalry. Ahmed Miyan asked me to bring the criminals I had imprisoned. When I told him they were locked up in the temple, he requisitioned a cart and loaded the prisoners on it. He asked me to leave with him.

I asked him to wait for five minutes so that I could go and meet Rawal ji, the jagirdar of the area. When Ahmed Miyan agreed to wait, I requested him to send the naqqarchis with me.

I went up to Diya Bhai's house (the man in charge in Samode) with the naqqarchis and some horsemen. I found the doors locked. I called out to them to come and talk to me, but received absolutely no response. When there was complete silence, I shouted, 'Bhai ji, you had challenged me stating that no thanedar has been able to take criminals from your estate. I said I would do it in style as no loyal thanedar had come here yet. Here I am! I am taking these criminals away in pursuance of my word. Men of integrity always fulfil their promises. If you have the courage, come and take them from me.'

I ordered the naqqarchis to beat the drums to announce my victory. The city and mountains resounded with the beats as we set out from Samode with the criminals.

We set up camp in Rawal ji's bagh, which was at a distance of 1 kos from the city. Ahmed Miyan sent a message to Diya Bhai to ensure provisions were available for the troops—this was the condition if he wanted to stay safe. He added, 'In consideration of Rawal ji, I have brought my troops outside Samode, or they would have plundered it to the ground.'

A little while after I sent this message, provisions were rushed to the bagh. We stayed there at night and set off at dawn. By 11 a.m., we had reached Harmara (in Kishangarh tehsil, Ajmer district), where my thana was situated. The troops rested with their horses in the shade of the trees, and we partook of refreshments prepared by my men. We left from there at 2 p.m.

When we reached Amani Shah, we found a multitude of people, as though at a fair. Spectators had gathered from Amani Chowk all the way to Habib Chowk, and it was difficult for the troops to move their horses. Somehow, we managed to reach Habib Chowk and found that our Maharaja, along with Maharaja Jaswant Singh of Jodhpur, was waiting for us in the burj near the palace steps.

Ahmed Miyan, the officers and I went up to the burj and presented our salutations.

'What did you get yourself into?' asked the Maharaja Sahib.

'Huzoor, things like this can happen in your service,' I replied.

Prompt came his response, 'Shabaash! This is how loyal officers should be. Hand over the prisoners and go and rest; you have discharged your duty.'

The officer gave me a receipt for the criminals and I left for my home. When I reached, I found everyone praying for my safety. They were very happy to see me and started giving away *sadqa* (propitiatory offering) in my name.

A similar episode took place in Thakur Govind Singh's village. I could fill a register with it. I will attempt to describe it in brief.

There was a bairagi swami whom the entire populace had great faith in. Even the Maharaja had great faith in him.

Swami ji's buffalo was stolen and he took his complaint to the Maharaja saying, 'What kind of state is this? You haven't been able to protect a single buffalo.'

Maharaja ordered the superintendent to pay him Rs 10 worth of compensation, along with one rupee a day till the buffalo was found.

I asked the Swami ji why he had complained to the Maharaja instead of telling me of his problem. Swami ji replied, 'Baba, this is beyond you. I know where it has gone. My buffalo has been taken to a big man's estate. You can't bring it back.'

I asked him for some signs of the place so that I could recover his buffalo. Swami ji asked me to pardon a criminal who had an award on his head, and said that this man could take me to the right place.

I took the case to the council and asked them to pardon one criminal so that I could recover the buffalo. The pardon was given on the condition that the criminal would help me recover the stolen buffalo. I took the order to the swami ji, who called the wanted criminal, Baijnath, and presented him before me. He was not a criminal from my area. I took ten men from the special cavalry unit and left with Baijnath.

Baijnath took me to a village in the jagir of Thakur Govind Singh. This village was 14 kos from Jaipur. When we reached it that evening, I sent a message to the local taluqdar saying that we had come on official work and he should send word to his principal and come himself to help us complete it.

The taluqdar replied saying that he was busy and wouldn't be able to come till morning. In addition, he had no orders from his master to cooperate with us.

I sent another rider, asking him to come, but he sent the same reply. I asked my spy to point out the buffalo to

the police and get the animal under their control. My spy
said that the buffalo was no longer in the house where he
had seen it last. He continued, 'I had specifically told the
taluqdar that the buffalo should not leave this place. I had
also made this clear to the peasants and criminals who had
stolen it. They seem to have sent the buffalo away when they
heard of our arrival. That's why the taluqdar hasn't come
either.'

We camped there that evening. Though we could make
arrangements to feed the horses, the men went hungry.

When the taluqdar came in the morning, I saw that he
was a huge, well-built man. As he wished me and sat down,
I told him, 'Taluqdar Sahib, I have come to carry out specific
orders from the Maharaja Sahib, but you are delaying me.
First, give me reason for this delay. Only then will I talk to
you further.'

The taluqdar said that he didn't know I had come on
orders from the Maharaja. I asked him to hand over the stolen
buffalo and Kalinath Sarik.

'What buffalo? Who is Kalinath?' asked the taluqdar.

I retorted angrily, 'The buffalo belongs to the swami of
Sidhse, and Kalinath is the thief you have given refuge in your
village. You make him commit thefts and robberies and grow
fat on the proceeds.'

The taluqdar said, 'No Kaliya or buffalo has come to our
village.'

On hearing this, I asked my spy to reply to him.

Baijnath replied, 'Taluqdar ji, I saw the buffalo in this
village with my own eyes. I even asked you to ensure that it
didn't leave from here as it had been stolen. Kaliya was also
present at the time. I had specifically warned you not to let
either of them leave.'

'He is a liar. He is making false accusations,' said the taluqdar.

I said politely, 'Taluqdar Sahib, I request you as a friend to hand the buffalo over to me, otherwise even the Thakur Sahib will get into trouble. This is the Maharaja's order.'

'Aji Hazrat, I have seen scores of officers. None have had the guts to get the Thakur Sahib into trouble,' said the taluqdar.

'You have never seen an honest officer, or you would have been in prison by now,' I retorted angrily.

'Handcuff me,' challenged the taluqdar.

'Insha'Allah, if I am an officer worth my salt, by tomorrow that piece of jewellery will be adorning your wrists.' Having said this, I left.

I entered Jaipur at four in the evening and went straight to the council, along with the spy and two cavalrymen.

As soon as he saw me, Nawab Faiz Ali Khan asked, 'Have you recovered the buffalo?'

I described the state of affairs. The cavalrymen corroborated my account. It was then the turn of Baijnath to be questioned: 'Did you see the buffalo with your own eyes?'

Baijnath replied, 'Not only did I see it, I ran my hand over the buffalo and told the taluqdar and peasants to look after it.'

His statement was taken down.

The Nawab Sahib left the council and went to the Maharaja. On his return, he gave the order stating that we were to go and surround the Thakur Sahib's village on all four sides. We would tell them that the siege would continue till the buffalo and Kalinath were brought to Jaipur.

As soon as these orders reached the Thakur Sahib, he sent horsemen and camel riders to bring the buffalo, thief, taluqdar, peasants and the village accountant to him before dawn.

After receiving these orders, I came home and went to sleep. The next day, I slept in, as I was very tired. I was still sleeping when the superintendent's messenger came to call me.

I got ready, tied my turban, picked up my sword and went to attend to the superintendent's summons. Mir Ahmed Ali Khan, the superintendent, was already holding court when I reached, and the taluqdar, village headman and village accountant were all present.

I presented my salutations to the superintendent. The latter asked me, 'What conversation did you have with the taluqdar?'

I described the discussion.

The superintendent asked, 'What did you say?'

'I said that if I am a loyal officer, then I will have you wearing the jewellery tomorrow.'

'All the jewellery is here,' the superintendent said. 'You can present to him whatever you believe fit for the taluqdar. You may fulfil your promise.'

I picked up a heavy leg shackle and took it up to the taluqdar. An orderly immediately put it on his legs and sealed it. The peasants were also put in shackles. The courthouse was filled with such demonstrations.

Eventually, the taluqdar owned up. 'We left the buffalo in the village of Thakur Ranjit Singh. It is still there.'

As soon as I heard this, I went to the council and told them everything, including that the buffalo was still in the village of Thakur Ranjit Singh ji. Thakur Ranjit Singh was the leader of the council and present when I made this statement.

Nawab Faiz Ali Khan Bahadur questioned the Thakur Sahib. 'Waah waah, Thakur ji! You shelter thieves, despite being the head of the council?'

Thakur Ranjit Singh told me, 'Bhaiya, if the buffalo is in my village, it will reach your house tomorrow. Set your mind at ease.'

I saluted the officers and went home. I was summoned to the office of the courthouse again the next day. When I reached it, the superintendent greeted me with the words, 'Come and take custody of this buffalo and give a written receipt of it to Thakur Ranjit Singh's men.'

I gave the receipt and went to the council, where I told the Nawab Sahib that I had got the buffalo back by the majesty of the Maharaja. It was up to the council to mete out punishment.

Nawab Sahib caught my hand and took me to the Maharaja. As soon as I presented my salutations, he asked me with a smile, 'Have you brought the buffalo?'

With folded hands, I replied, 'By Huzoor's majesty, it is here.'

Maharaja Sahib began laughing. 'Nawab Sahib! I had told you he would bring it back, even if he had to produce a new one!'

I was ordered to hand the buffalo over to the swami and take a *razinama*.

Swami ji was called and told to take the buffalo and give a razinama in favour of Thakur Govind Singh ji. However, the swami refused to give a razinama. The thakur's lawyers and men began pleading with the swami ji, offering money, but he refused to take back the buffalo or give the acknowledgement of its return.

I asked the swami ji why he wasn't giving the razinama now that his buffalo was back. The swami ji said, 'They have cut off the horns and tail of my buffalo and killed its calf.'

I offered to get him a compensation of Rs 80.

However, the swami ji said, 'I have my reasons for not giving the razinama. I don't care about this one buffalo. If ten of my buffaloes were stolen, I wouldn't have complained. I receive daily complaints from local peasants whose cattle, camels and grain are stolen. That is why I have raised my voice. Until these robberies stop, I will never agree to give a razinama. This same Kaliya who stole my buffalo commits crimes everywhere and terrorizes the villagers of the Kahwar qasba. He is in cahoots with the guards of that qasba. His brothers and relatives have disowned and disinherited him and thrown him off his property. His inheritance and fixed income have been taken over by others and now he loots it with the help of the guards and sentries posted there. He has important supporters in the villages. He steals from the Alwar area too.

'The government should either arrest him or give him back his share so that he ceases his looting and plundering and the villagers can rest in peace.'

After I heard this, I relayed it to the rulers. I was ordered by the council to go and investigate the matter and restore Kalinath's hereditary lands to him. We were to rehabilitate him so that he could give up his erring and mischievous ways and bring succour to the villagers.

I went back to the same area and put up posters in the village, informing Kaliya that he should come within eight days and reclaim his hereditary lands. If he did this, all his crimes would be forgiven. If he didn't, his lands would be confiscated and given over to others appointed for the purpose and his excuses wouldn't be accepted.

Three days after the poster was put up, Kaliya came to my thana and fell at my feet. I reassured him and told him to stay in my thana while I went to his area and arranged for his lands to be returned to him.

I went to the Qasba Bijnor and called all the village elders. I ensured that Kaliya got back his share of the property and was rehabilitated. The rulers were very happy with my actions.

There was misadministration in the Qasba Navali in the administrative area of Balipura, as the sub-revenue collector's tyranny had removed all the guards. The subjects of the area were greatly oppressed.

The landed gentry of Navali asked the council to transfer me to their area.

I was very harassed and over-worked there. I would be touring the area the whole night with fifty men, and was still unable to catch any thief. They would run away to another area as soon as I reached.

Eventually, I asked the council to reinstate the guards. I put up posters advertising the position, and by evening, there was a group of twenty to forty young and old women and men who had come to plead for their reinstatement. I had them reinstated.

From that day on, law and order was restored in the qasba and no more robberies took place. Some of the villages in the district were rebellious, but I soon brought them back to order.

The law and order situation of the areas I was posted in was always very good, and there were very few incidents of crime. If the law was broken, I would not let up on the guards until the real criminals were caught.

When I became the deputy superintendent of Samadri (in district Barmer), a man came to me with a problem from the council. His problem was that there was a dispute between the two *thakurani*s of a jagirdar. The army was on the side of one thakurani while the *kaamdaar* were on the side of the other. There were 7000–8000 men involved in this conflict

222 Dastan-e-Ghadar

and I was asked to resolve it before bloodshed took place and the peace of the place was ruined forever.

My orders were to prevent any rioting or fighting. The same orders were sent to Mir Ahmed Ali sahib.

We took a force of 400 cavalry and infantry and left for the place. There, we found that forces from both sides were entrenched. There were 6000–7000 men facing each other, their artillery in place for an attack. Only one light was needed to set off the cannons! The entire city was in a state of panic and people were fleeing to Bikaner with their families and possessions. Even the merchants, traders and shopkeepers were transporting their merchandise away from the city. The residents were running away to other villages.

I was once again reminded of the ghadar.

I spurred my horse into action and went and stood between the two opposing forces. I called out in a loud voice. 'We have come to settle affairs. Now whosoever steps out of line or makes the first move to attack will be an offender of the Raj. We will ensure suitable steps are taken and you will be facing the might of the Raj. Please come and state your problems to us, and we will resolve them. Please remove the men from these battle positions.'

I was able to move the forces some distance. In the evening, all the army officers and a lawyer of the *Badi Thakurani* (elder wife) came to me with her *odhni* and her message. Thakurani Sahiba sent her greetings and said, 'Deputy ji, you are my brother in religion. I am a widow. I have called you my brother and now you have to protect me and honour this odhni. Now, either you or Khuda will protect me.

'Thakur Sahib died two years ago and he left behind a five-year-old son, born from the Chhoti Thakurani (younger wife). As soon as this boy was born, Thakur Sahib put the baby in my lap as mine. Now these kaamdaar have got together with the Chhoti Thakurani and are harassing the army and the people.

'It's been ten months and the army has not been paid. The kaamdaar have confiscated all lands given by the Thakur. They are plundering the jagir and enjoying the spoils. Eventually, the army had no choice but to face them militarily. The kaamdaar too have gathered a force and are ready to kill or die.

'Now it is up to you to settle the affairs once and for all. I have sent Rs 300 for your meal, and promise to bear the entire expense of your sojourn here.'

After listening, I replied, 'Please convey my salaam to the Thakurani Sahiba. She has called me her brother and it is our custom that money belonging to a sister, daughter or niece is haram for us. Please return the money to her. If God wills, this place will not suffer or be harmed in any way. The enemy will be routed and your writ will prevail. But you will have to comply with my words.'

While this conversation was taking place, the kaamdaar went to Nazim Sahib and asked him to arrest the army officers and take them to Jhanjha. 'The road will be clear for us, as the soldiers can do nothing alone. We can then control this area and administer it as per our wish without any impediment.

'The Thakurani is a purdahnasheen lady and cannot interfere or control us. She will just languish in house arrest.'

I received news of this plan at midnight. A risaldar of the army came and told me that the kaamdaar intended to arrest the officers but they would not find it so easy. 'After all, we are soldiers and ready to kill and be killed. If Nazim Sahib decides to arrest us, we will not have any consideration for the government and will not leave Nazim Sahib, who has joined hands with the kaamdaar. Everyone is equal for us at the moment. If the Jaipur state army comes up against us, then we are warning you that we will attack, no matter whether it's the Nazim Sahib or you.'

I reassured him that such a situation would never come to pass and told him that he should set his mind at ease. I would ensure that things were sorted out much before that. He went away on hearing this.

When I was enjoying my huqqa in the morning, a man came running to me with a message from Nazim Sahib, asking me to come quickly with my forces as fighting had broken out. I quickly called out to my force to be ready and armed.

I left with my force and found that though Nazim Sahib was also loading his weapon, he was trembling with fear.

As soon as he saw me he cried out, 'Weapons have been fired and there has been bloodshed! Let's go quickly.'

I requested him to stay where he was and let me go with my men. 'It's better that you don't come. Your presence might inflame the already excited men. I will go with my men. If I get caught in the fighting, you can come to my aid.'

When I reached the scene of the action, I found that fighting was about to start. The two groups were standing facing each other. They were 100 steps away from each other. All this was happening in the middle of the bazaar.

The army had brought the artillery with them and the cannons were loaded and ready. The army was standing behind them.

The forces of the kaamdaar were standing with their weapons on either side of the shops in the bazaar.

I took a stand between the two groups. A man from the army called out, 'Deputy ji, careful! Don't come closer, or we will light the cannons.'

I replied, 'All right! I will leave my men behind and come alone. I want to talk to you.'

My men were not willing to let me go alone. 'The state will never let us live. We will be accused of murdering our deputy,' they said.

I pacified them and managed to make them let me go. I then called out to both the groups and said, 'My force is standing between the two of you. Whoever starts the fighting will in effect be fighting with me.'

I made my force stand in the middle and went up to the army officers.

'Look here,' I said. 'You are soldiers, and normally soldiers are not very well educated. Don't take a step which will result in death with corpses lying all around for vultures and dogs to eat. Your families will be destroyed and your women's honour violated. Do something that will help you achieve your objective without loss of face. I think that you should go to Jaipur and present your petition to the army headquarters there.'

The officers said, 'We are ready for this if the kaamdaar agree. In fact, they want to arrest us.'

I agreed to stand guarantee that this would not come to pass; I would send them off to Jaipur first. The army men were ready to go if the kaamdaar went too.

I went towards the kaamdaar and threatened them with dire consequences if they didn't leave for Jaipur at once. 'Why are you bent on destroying your own land? Send off these rioters who are ready to fight.'

I ordered my men to get the rebels out of the shops. I took the two warring parties to Nazim Sahib and said, 'It's to everyone's advantage that the kaamdaar be sent with your horsemen to Jaipur. I will send the army officers with my men. The fight will end. I will get both sides to disarm and disband.'

Nazim Sahib agreed to my proposal and asked the kaamdaar to settle their fight in Jaipur and make ready to leave.

I got the cannons removed and placed in the topkhana while my men dispersed the rioters. I relayed a message to both thakuranis to send their legal representatives to Jaipur.

That very day, the two warring factions, along with their representatives, were sent off to Jaipur.

I often settled such affairs during my employment in the state.

Once, during my thanedari in Sanganer, the general superintendent Shafi Miyan dismissed me from my post and appointed one of his relatives instead.

I was not worried, as I knew it wouldn't be easy to dismiss me from my post without the Maharaja's permission. I sat at home for two months. Finally, I wrote about my dismissal in a qasida and took it to the Maharaja.

The Maharaja was in the hunting lodge of Khatipura District at the time. Nawab Ahmed Ali Khan and his nephew Naib Obaidullah Khan were present in Jaipur then. They also came to the hunting lodge. In the evening, I presented myself to the Maharaja. When I had completed my salutation he asked, 'Thanedar ji, how are you here today?'

I replied, 'Huzoor, I have not been able to present my salaam to you for many days. I have also written something in your honour.'

'Very well. Let the lamps be lit. I will sit down and listen.'

In the evening, Huzoor sat down with Nawab Ahmed Ali Khan in the Khanapur bungalow. I sat down on one side of the lamp that was kept in front of them, and Nawab Obaidullah sat on the other. Babu Rao Kanti Chandra

Bahadur was also sitting near them. Munshi Nawal Kishore, the owner and publisher of *Awadh Akhbar* was sitting next to me. Maharaja Pratap Singh of Jodhpur was sitting near the Maharaja, talking to Thakur Fateh Singh, when the Maharaja called out to me to start.

I read out my qasida and everyone praised it. Munshi Nawal Kishore exclaimed, 'Waah! What a qasida. It seems to be in the same style as that of Firdausi. It is the Maharaja Sahib's good fortune that men of talent gather around him.'

The Maharaja was delighted to hear these words. However, when the lines about my dismissal came, he turned towards Nawab Ahmed Ali Khan in surprise and asked, 'What is he saying?'

Nawab Ahmed Ali Khan replied, 'He was dismissed from service two months ago and has been sitting at home.'

'Who dared to dismiss him without my permission?' Saying this, he turned towards Babu Kanti Chandra and said, 'I had given instructions that no one is to be appointed or dismissed without my permission.'

Babu Sahib responded that he had already got this order written by the council.

Maharaja Sahib said, 'Shafi Miyan is a very imprudent man. Make arrangements to give him the two months' worth of salary from Shafi Miyan's, so that it may be a lesson to him to not do such a thing in future. Fix a stipend of Rs 20 per month for him [Zahir Dehlvi], which will be separate from the salary he gets for serving the state, if he continues to work.'

I got up and presented my salaam to him. Then, taking his leave, I went home.

Shafi Miyan came to Nawab Ahmed Ali Khan's house and summoned me to go back to the thana and resume my duties.

I replied, 'Please excuse me. Maharaja Sahib has fixed a stipend for me and now I don't need to work. I will not go back to the thana.'

Shafi Miyan was not willing to accept my refusal and requested Nawab Sahib to send me to Sanganer. 'Let him come to Sanganer. Then even if he gives his resignation, I will be acquitted of this task.'

Nawab Sahib somehow coaxed me to return to my thana.

A year later, Huzoor promoted me to post of deputy superintendent and sent me to Torawai. He also sent a message, 'I am keeping tabs on your service, and Insha'Allah, you will rise to a very high post.'

However, it was my misfortune that he passed away within six months of this and I got stuck in this mess. I worked for one year in Torawai, and then for three years as a deputy in Sheikhawani.[153]

Maharaja Madhav Rao Singh, his successor, was a minor, and there was a state of chaos in Jaipur. All of the employees appointed by Maharaja Ram Singh had been terminated. A new superintendent was appointed, who terminated my services along with those of the other three deputies and old thanedars. He appointed new men to these posts.

There were many complaints and petitions against this, but to no avail. He appointed his brother in my place even as the complaints continued. After two years, I gave up and went home. The only concession that the state made was to appoint my son as thanedar.

During this period, when my services had been terminated, I decided to travel to Bhopal. I stopped in Jaora on the way. I met Nawab Ismail Khan Bahadur, the ruler of Jaora. I wrote and presented a qasida in his praise. He was very pleased, and

I remained his guest for eight days. He also gave me Rs 50 as a reward when I left.

I stayed with a friend in Bhopal, and here I met Nawab Siddiq Hasan Khan sahib. There was a mushaira held under the aegis of Huzoor Nawab Shah Jahan Begum[154] every Friday. Only five or seven people would attend it. Nawab Sahib asked me to attend it.

I had written a qasida on the occasion of Eid Qurban and read it in the darbar of Nawab Shah Jahan Begum. She rewarded me with Rs 200 in appreciation.

After three months, I left for my house (in Jaipur) with this money.

I wrote a qasida on the occasion of Nawab Ahmed Ali Khan's eldest son's wedding. Nawab Sahib rewarded me with Rs 50 and told me to stay in his state and stop my wanderings. As a result, he did not let me leave him as long as he lived. I lived comfortably in Jaipur.

May God bless Jaipur! It is a unique city. It has no equivalent. It's a peaceful city with every conceivable luxury needed for a good life. The weather is also very pleasant.

The most unique aspect of Jaipur is that there are people here of every religion, community and section of society and they all live in perfect harmony. I have never seen any bigotry or communal tension in the city. Hindu, Muslim, Shia, Sunni and the British all get along with each other and are happy. There has never even been a discussion on communal tensions.

There have been riots and fights in the states under the British during Holi, Dussehra, Moharrum and Ram Lila. People are killed in these riots. Yet, there was never even a simple quarrel in Jaipur. This was because of the Maharaja's strong sense of justice, administration, statesmanship and love for all his subjects, irrespective of religion. It is because of this strong foundation that Jaipur is still such a wonderfully run state.

Maharaja Madho Singh is slightly prejudiced against the followers of Islam, but he has not let it reflect in matters of state. No difference is made when dealing with Hindus or Muslims.

When a famine struck Jaipur, people of every religion were given the same help; everyone was given Rs 2 from the state for three years.

In fact, during the famine, Maharaja Madho Singh's nurturing of subjects was unparalleled. No ruler has looked after his people so well. He spent crores of rupees on the welfare of his subjects. He filled the markets with grain at very low rates and even gave some away for free.

Veiled women would go and work under the cover of the night and return before morning with their wages. There was a general order that anyone could cut trees from the forest and sell them and live off the proceeds. Apart from this, there was an ongoing langar of free food. There were free shelters put up everywhere and thousands of blankets were distributed to the poor.

Maharaja Sahib was a very generous man and could not bear to see anyone in distress. He never uttered a word of censure or abuse. He never got angry at his employees and was very appreciative of their efforts. Everyone got their due from him.

The Fort of Ranthambhor

This Qila is considered one of the best forts. If an enemy wants to attack it, he will find it impregnable on all sides. If the defenders of the Qila have sufficient ammunition and provisions, they can defend it forever.

This Qila is built over an area of 7 kos, and is surrounded by steep and high mountains. Since these mountains are fertile, with streams and waterfalls, they are dotted with villages.

There is only one approach to it, which is through the main darwaza of the Qila. It is so high that it is beyond the reach of cannon fire. There is a minar in the middle and it seems as if these sharply steep mountains that surround and protect the Qila on all four sides also rise up like the minar. The only slope is the one which leads to the entrance.

To the south of the Qila, in its front, there is a huge ground with a grand and majestic pond. There are many mango trees on the sides of the pond. This place is so beautiful and verdant that even Kashmir cannot compare to it. A multitude of keora and ketaki trees spread a beautiful fragrance over the mountains. The land is verdant with flowers of every colour, as though it were painted by an artist. It is difficult to find such an attractive and soothing place anywhere else.

There is space and provision for a huge army to camp inside. There are two deep buildings named Jawahar Bawahar, which can accommodate thousands of maunds of grain, ammunition and crores of gold coins.

On the top of the Qila, there are two shrines to the revered saints with whose help the Qila was conquered. One is Syed Sadruddin sahib.

Adjoining the Qila is the Ran Mountain. There is a distance of 200 yards between the two. It's a strange experience to climb the two. If one climbs the Qila, the Ran Mountain seems low, but when you climb the Ran Mountain the Qila seems to be in a hollow.

Sultan Alauddin had conquered the Qila, wresting it from Raja Hamir. The valley is filled with the graves of the martyred soldiers. It was conquered after the death of lakhs

of people, due to the blessings of the two Saiyyed saints. The
Sultan's forces reached the Ran Mountain and fired their
cannons from there. The Rajputs found it difficult to defend
it from that position.

The mountains are full of natural vegetation, streams and
waterfalls that have resulted in a multitude of animals and
birds, especially the animals hunted in shikar.

This Qila is 40 kos from Jaipur and lies towards the south-
east. All the British officers who come to Jaipur make it a
point to visit it and stay on for eight to ten days for the shikar
of tiger, bear, deer, antelope, cheetah and black bull that are
found here in large numbers.

The Mountains of Babaraiya

There is a pargana named Babaraiya[155] in Jaipur, 24 kos from
the city. There are ancient ruins and remnants there, which
are 5000 years old. The Pandavas, who are mentioned in
history, once lived here. The battle between the Kauravas and
Pandavas took place in this district. The houses of Bhima and
Arjun are still present here. There is a small hill which has a
large cell carved into its side. They say that this cell comprised
Bhima's living quarters.

There is a spring on this mountain, which is 10–12 yards
long and 1.5–2 yards wide. It is extremely deep. There is a
lot of exaggeration about its depth and it is said that even
if you tie a stone to the rope of seven charpoys and throw it
down, it wouldn't touch the bottom. No one has been able to
fathom its depth so far. Legend has it that Bhima kicked the
mountain in anger and the bottom of the earth cracked and
this spring came forth from it.

There's no doubt that the spring flows all year round and people use its water and take it away too. In spite of this, the water never diminishes.

There are huge, rounded, 5-yard boulders on this hill. According to legend, the Pandava brothers played with these stones.

There is another hillock around 50x50 yards in size. At the top of this round circle, there are four burjis, one at each corner. The uniqueness of this place is that it seems as though it is floating in the air and there is nothing between it and the earth, except for that one point which rests on the hill. To me, it seems as if a *khasdaan*[156] has been kept upside down on the mountain.

A little ahead, on another mountain, one can see stone drums, and a life-size stone elephant. There is a 6-yard stone obelisk on the hill above it. When investigations were made, it was discovered to be the ladle with which dal is pureed, and the drums were of pure iron. The elephant was the one used by the Pandavas. Later on, they all turned to stone.

Sheikhawani

This large district lies to the north of Jaipur. Its western border adjoins Jodhpur and Bikaner and its northern border lies along Hansi, Hissar and pargana Loharu. This is a desert area, covered with sand dunes. When a strong wind blows, the sand of one dune blows on to another. A man sleeping in the sand can be buried, and no one would be the wiser.

Here, water is as scarce as it was in Karbala. Wells are very far apart and water is found at great depth, and that too does not always happen. There are huge leather drums kept at the sides of the well and whenever water is spotted, the drum is beaten and people gather to fill water.

Every village has one well with a platform with four minars around its rim. The water is pulled out and filled in tanks. The place has been built in such a way that there are concrete water canals on the four sides of the tank, and water overflows into them.

The Thakurs, Brahmins, *baqqal*s (grain merchants), *sahukar*s, Muslims, Sheikhs, Saiyyeds, Mughals and Pathans all come and fill water from these tanks. There is no discrimination between Hindus and Muslims here.

In some places, there may be a drought as the water there is not potable and is as salty as seawater, very bitter and unhealthy. Anyone drinking it falls sick with diarrhoea. In these places, large, sloping concrete tanks have been built in the open ground. Next to them are very deep wells. The walls and the bottom of the well have been made of concrete.

During the monsoons, these tanks fill up with rainwater, and there are channels covered with mesh which run to the well. Water is strained through the mesh and falls into and fills the well. At the mouth of the well is a window that is always locked. The villagers open it in the morning and distribute water. One pot of water is given to each family and they have to make sure the needs of their entire household are met by it.

If there is no rain and the wells run dry, the villagers leave their homes and journey to other places where water is available.

In this state, camels and not oxen are used for agriculture. In some places, the fields are not ploughed, and people just plant seeds with their hands in the sand piles.

By the grace of God, bajra and *moth* is grown here. After a small shower of rain, the bajra seeds are sown. The bajra plant can grow taller than a man on a horse. The bajra is so sweet that it tastes better than wheat or rice. This is the staple diet of the people. Over here, bajra roti and moong dal taste so delicious that pulao and biryani pale in comparison. They say that if one eats too much wheat and rice here, they fall sick.

The herdsmen keep cows and buffaloes, and tasty, creamy milk can be found in plenitude here. A lot of ghee is produced.

The sheep here are the most beautiful I have seen anywhere. They are pure white in colour and have very fine coats. Their meat, as well as that of the goats, is very tasty and better than that of fish and chicken. It is very easy to digest. Such tasty mutton is not found anywhere else in India.

A kind of watermelon called *metra* is grown in the desert. SubhanAllah! It's extremely sweet and cooling. Its sherbet is also delicious. It grows in the sand piles and can be found hidden inside them. Those who know about them can find them. When water is unavailable for huge distances during travel, this fruit can quench thirst. Its juice is also given to the horses. I have often done this during my own travels.

The men of this country are very hard-working, determined, courageous and productive, particularly the community of sahukars. That is why they are very prosperous.

The people of Sheikhawani are spread all over the world, except in the eastern countries. They work in these countries and bring back their earnings to their land, where they build magnificent houses and mansions.

I lived in this area for three years as the officer-in-charge.

9

Employment in the State of Tonk

The talk of the town is that the wounded Zahir
Shall recite the tale of his broken heart

After the death of Maharaja Ram Singh ji, I stayed in the employment of Jaipur. For two and a half years after that, I stayed at home in Jaipur, looking for work.

I spent six years under the patronage of Nawab Ahmed Ali Khan. During this period, I was prolific in my writing and my collection of poems was impressive.

After the demise of Nawab Ahmed Ali Khan sahib Bahadur, Nawab Mustatab Nawab Hafiz Mohammad Ibrahim Ali Khan Amin-ud-Daulah Saulat Jung, ruler of Tonk, may God preserve his rule, summoned me.

A message was sent to the eldest son of the late Nawab Ahmed Ali Khan to send Ustad Zahir to Tonk.

I had often visited Tonk and met the Nawab Sahib. Most of his sons were my *shagird*. I had visited Tonk when Nawab Obaidullah Khan Wazir Jung invited me to his son's wedding. He had looked after me with a great deal of respect. I had written a *qasida tahniyat* for the wedding and he had given me Rs 50 and a shawl as a reward.

When I reached Tonk this time, I went to the house of one of my shagird and met Naib Sahib[157] afterwards. Naib Sahib greeted me with warmth and said, 'You have made us wait for a long time. Huzoor Purnoor has been expecting you.'

I met Munshi Mohammad Yusuf sahib, the mir munshi, and Captain Syed Moinuddin sahib Fasih-ul-Mulk, one of the Nawab Sahib's courtiers. They heard my verses. They were very well versed in poetry and even wrote themselves. They were very impressed by my work. They said that they found me better than my fame promised, and that the next day, they would take me into the presence of the Nawab Sahib. I was to read something for him.

The next day, I was fortunate enough to enter the presence of the Nawab Sahib. Huzoor was very happy and read out his own verses to me, which I praised.

'If you have liked it, then it must undoubtedly be special,' he said to me.

The next day, there was a mushaira in the house of Sahibzada Ishaq Khan, the Nawab Sahib's brother. I was ordered by Nawab Sahib to read my verse there.

There was a huge crowd at the mushaira. Many members of Nawab Sahib's family, as well as those from other noble houses, were present. Nawab Sahib himself was there as well.

There were curtains over the entrances to the tent when the poets started reciting their ghazals. The first ghazal to be read to great acclaim was the Nawab Sahib Bahadur's. After that, Sulaiman Khan sahib Asad, the shagird of the late Munshi Muzaffar Ali sahib Asir, read out the ghazal of his shagird, the Naib Sahib, and then his own. I praised them both and was asked to recite my ghazal.

As soon as I read the matla of my ghazal, there was a tumult of praise. Nawab Sahib made me repeat it numerous times. My next verse elicited the same response. The third verse received even more praise.

A Sahibzada, who has since died and whose name I don't remember, stood up and said, 'Sulaiman Khan Sahib says that the real praise of a poet is when the walls start echoing with commendations and swaying in appreciation.'

The whole ghazal was received with such generous praise and appreciation.

After that, others read their ghazals and the mushaira was concluded.

Nawab Sahib Bahadur called me inside the royal tent and showered me with much appreciation.

Then began the celebration of Nawab Sahib's birthday. I was a part of this too. As was customary, a nazr was made, and on the third day, a mushaira was held in the house of Sahibzada Ahmed Yaar Khan.

I had written a special qasida for the occasion. As soon as I read it out, there was a clamour of acclaim with shouts of appreciation and applause. I was sitting next to the curtain and reciting the qasida while Huzoor praised it from within the tent. The public echoed him from outside. When it was done, the Nawab Sahib asked the attendees who were inside the tent with him what reward he should give me for this qasida. He claimed that my work was on the same level as that of the ustad poets. Mirza Mohammad Ali Khan sahib and Nawab Najaf Khan sahib, members of the council, said, 'Huzoor, this qasida has been written by Zauq. Why are you rewarding him?'

SubhanAllah! Nawab Sahib's generosity was such that he said, 'It could be written by anyone, but it was read here in my praise, so I have to reward him. Give him Rs 250.'

This order was noted.

Mirza Mohammad Ali Khan sahib came out and described to me what had taken place within.

Three months later, I received the money. However, though I had been attending the darbar and reciting my verses in every poetic gathering, I had still not received a salary or letter of appointment. Eventually, I asked the Naib Sahib how long I would have to wait. After all, I was a traveller. He said, 'I will make arrangements for your departure.'

I repeated this discussion to Munshi Mohammad Yusuf, who told me strictly, 'Don't take this step. You have come here because the Nawab Sahib called you, so you will get paid as an employee. Naib Sahib doesn't want you to stay here. He is Sulaiman Sahib's shagird.'

Consequently, Nawab Sahib summoned both Sulaiman Sahib and me after four months and gave us salaries for two months each. He said we would get paid in the same manner after every four months.

This is the same year and date when Dagh Sahib attained success in Hyderabad. I received a letter from him while I was in Tonk, telling me of his employment in Hyderabad. I replied in the same vein, stating that I had found employment in Tonk.

In this period, Nawab Khatoon Zamani Begum Sahiba, sister of the late Nawab Kalb Ali Khan Mahal Khaas of Huzoor Nawab Sahib, became my shagird. I started getting a salary from this appointment too. I began correcting her masnavi.[158]

I was happy and content here and was living a good life. My son was also earning well as a thanedar in Jaipur. His services were terminated later, but since I was earning, it didn't matter. My second daughter was married and she went off to Delhi with her husband.

I decided to travel for pleasure. I took a three-month leave of absence and went to Bombay via Baroda and then on to Hyderabad.[159] I met many noblemen there. Maharana Bhagwan Sahai Bahadur and a few other men became my shagird.

I met Khan-samaan Mohammad Ibrahim Khan sahib. He met me very affably and asked me to wait, telling me that he would mention my name to Huzoor and try to get some employment for me here. He asked me to write a few poems and ghazals for Huzoor, which he would then take to him. Five months passed while I waited, and I started getting messages from Tonk, asking me to return. A telegram came, along with a letter from my son. In it, he informed me that he didn't need my earnings, and that I should return.

I left Hyderabad after receiving these letters. When I reached Tonk, salaries were being distributed after six months, but I didn't get mine. I only got it in the next half-yearly distribution. I suffered financially and was now facing a debt of Rs 900.

The wheel of cruel fate now dealt me such a blow that I was devastated. I received a letter informing me that my second daughter had fallen sick. She had come to Jaipur for treatment, and passed away there. As soon as I got this letter, I felt as if the life had left my body and I had no wish to live. I wept and mourned but there was nothing I could do. When I went to Jaipur, I saw my wife was crazed with grief. I somehow managed to console her and contain my sorrow. We had had eleven children, of whom only four had survived—the eldest son and three daughters. The youngest daughter hadn't been married yet. A beautiful baby girl survived my second daughter. I gave strict instructions to my wife and daughter to look after this child and consider her in place of her mother. I employed a wet nurse for her and left to go back to my job.

A year later, this baby also died and our wounds bled again. We could do nothing except bear this loss with equanimity. My wife finally joined me in Tonk.

Sahibzada Ahsanullah Khan, the nephew and son-in-law of Nawab Sahib Bahadur, was my shagird. My wife stayed with his mother. Begum Sahiba was very generous and hospitable towards her. However, she asked me to send her home after a month in Tonk. I booked a seat in a coach, and after tying purdah around it, I seated my wife inside, along with a Mughal lady who was to keep her company. I joined three other men sitting outside the coach. I had a good sword at my side.

When we crossed the river and got back on the coach, it was dusk. We travelled 3 kos more, and at 10 p.m., we heard loud sounds and calls of 'Kill them!' Highwaymen surrounded us and started beating us with their sticks. The coachman and sentry both fell down under this rain of blows. The highwaymen started hitting at the roof of the coach. A man and woman sitting at the back of the coach fell down. The travellers in the coach were all falling on top of each other under this rain of blows. I was pressed down by three men. The men who had been sitting on the outside of the coach were all slaughtered.

There was one young British soldier, on a mission to recruit sepoys, travelling in the coach. He had a stick in his hand, and using this, he hit out at the bandits and managed to kill one of them. But what could he do alone? They were forty men and they overpowered him. The British soldier fainted from the blows.

I somehow managed to writhe out from under the men but I couldn't find my sword. I came outside the coach on to the plank and was struck by a blow on my shoulder. A second blow struck my head and blood started pouring out of the wound. I was alert when the third blow came so I managed to avert it. It struck the chain of the coach instead, and I caught on tightly. Now I was holding on to one side of the stick, and the other was in the bandit's hand. Two or three of the others came and surrounded me and managed to get me off the coach. They wanted to hit me, when my wife came and fell over me. One of the bandits said, 'She's an old lady; she will die if you hit her.'

I was pulled upright and searched for money. I told them I had nothing with me and they dragged me ten steps away and threw me on the stones. Two men with sticks came and stood on my head and threatened to kill me if I moved. My wife came crying and said, 'These bandits are killing and looting everyone while we are sitting and watching.'

One of the men found my sword and was waving it around, threatening to behead everyone. All the passengers had been pulled from within the coach and thoroughly looted. No one had anything left. The Mughal lady had had Rs 500–600 worth of goods with her, and all of it was taken. A Brahmin lady was stripped of the jewellery she had been wearing. The robbers had had to leave her anklets, as they couldn't pull them off.

When the man waved my own sword at me, my wife started crying and pleading with me. 'May God help you to escape. At least your life will be spared.'

'Where can I run?' I asked her. 'He will follow me with his sword and kill me.'

In this time, one more traveller came up to me. The bandits guarding me ran towards him and hit him on his back and snatched his sword. They took Rs 5 from his pocket.

We heard people running towards the bandits and they finally ran away. The villagers had come to our aid. However, they refused to continue chasing them, saying, 'We won't go after them unless the police is with us.'

They had looted all our clothes and jewellery. My wife was left with an old burqa that she had made for travel. We stayed there that night, and in the morning, we tried to find clues to where the thieves might have gone.

I saw my broken and looted boxes lying some 200 steps away from where we had been attacked. The bandits had even looted the *paandan*! There was no trace of the clothes, jewellery or money.

However, they had done me a huge favour. They had left behind my most precious possessions—my ghazals, qasidas and other writings. They took the cloth they were kept in but left all the papers under a stone. When I saw my life's work, I heaved a sigh of relief. I picked up all the papers and left the looted box to rot.

I came back and told the other travellers, 'Bhai, I have recovered my wealth.' When they asked me what it was, I showed them my papers and asked them to look for their things. But they had nothing of value left.

When Sahibzada Abdur Rahim Khan sahib, the faujdar of the state, came to the scene of the crime, he had all the materials and dregs picked up. We went back to Tonk and registered our complaints in the criminal court.

Eight days later, I sent my family off to Jaipur.

A year later, I took my horse to sell it at the Jaipur fair. She was tied there and I left the servants to rub her down with the other horses. I was making tea for myself on the common fire when the flames leapt up and my kurta caught fire. I tried to put it out, but was unsuccessful. By the time help came I was badly burnt and had fainted from the pain. My son-in-law, Jeevan Ali, was with me. He rushed to the dispensary and brought back some ointment and medicine. He applied the ointment and gave me the medicine to drink. It brought temporary relief. He took me home in a carriage.

There was a tumult of crying at home when they saw my condition. It took three months for me to recover from my burns. In the meantime, news had spread of my death. It even reached Tonk.

When I went back to Tonk, everyone, including the ruler, was very happy to see me.

Mir Jeevan looked after me very well during my sickness. I could not even lift myself after my burn injuries. Alas! I couldn't look after him. When I went back to Tonk, he fell ill and passed away in fifteen days. There was to be no end to my sufferings and anguish. He left four young children behind. I had no life left in me.

'O Lord of the Worlds! I am old, ready to die, and my young daughter is widowed. Who will look after these children?'

The Death of Sajjad Mirza

I was still struggling with this grief when the cruel fate decided to give me another blow from which it was difficult to recover.

A year after Jeevan Ali's death, I had arranged the marriage of my youngest daughter. Sajjad Mirza was in service at that time. He wrote to me when I was in Tonk, saying that he would make arrangements for some jewellery for the wedding, and that I would have to manage the rest. He decided to take leave and come home to Tonk for the wedding. I made arrangements for money, silver jewellery, some silk clothes and gold–silver lace for their decoration. I was waiting for a loan before I left for Jaipur. The dastardly sahukar, however, kept postponing its grant. In this time, my son reached Jaipur.

The general superintendent transferred Sajjad Mirza to Borwane,[160] refusing to listen to his protests that his sister was getting married and that he had to be present in Jaipur. The superintendent requested him to go for a month, after which he would be transferred back to Jaipur.

Death was on his head, and Sajjad Mirza didn't even wait for my letter. Despite his mother protesting that he wait for me to reach, and for the wedding to be performed, he left. He kept saying that there was time for his father to come, and that he would return by then.

He departed for Borwane and reached Khandela.[161] I sent the things I had bought to Jaipur with Abdul Qadir Khan sahib, the risaldar's brother. I also passed along a message, saying that I would be there in a week. When Sajjad Mirza reached Khandela, he got the news that Deputy Sahib had died. He was astonished since Deputy Sahib had just transferred him and summoned him to Borwane. He reached the place in two days. On the third day, Sajjad Mirza and Singh, the officer in whose place he had been transferred, and the Deputy's brother all came back to Khandela and stayed the night at Deputy Sahib's house. The next day, Deputy Sahib's brother took his ashes to the River Ganga and told Sajjad Mirza that he would return and take his brother's effects from him.

Sajjad Mirza asked Singh to hand over charge of the area. Singh asked him to wait for a few days. Sajjad Mirza wanted to know the reason behind the delay as he had already been transferred.

This led to a heated argument. People there had warned Sajjad Mirza that Singh had poisoned the Deputy.

The unfortunate Sajjad Mirza retorted, 'Hand over the charge without posing any problems, or I will handcuff you and send you to Jaipur.'

Singh understood that he had learned of his dastardly act. He terminated Sajjad Mirza's assistant on a small pretext.

Sajjad had only brought along his two young nephews, Basharat Hasan and Ishtiaq Hussain. One day, when Sajjad Mirza had gone to meet the deputy superintendent of another region and Basharat Hussain was cooking meat, Singh came to the house. He asked him to put water in the vessel since the meat was burning. When Basharat got up to bring water, Singh put in a pinch of poison in the pot and stirred it. When Basharat returned, Singh left.

When Sajjad Mirza came back in the evening, he asked if the boys had cooked the food. The boys replied in the affirmative and they all sat down and ate dinner. The food had just gone down their throats when they started vomiting. At midnight, when they were a little better, Singh came to inquire how they were. Sajjad Mirza replied that he was suffering from heartburn. Singh advised them to drink lime juice. He added some more poison to the beverage before giving it to him to drink.

This second poisoning was fatal and Sajjad Mirza died in extreme pain. He was all alone, without a friend. There was no one to take care of him and his nephews. Misery was their only companion. The children were very sick but they survived the initial poisoning, since they hadn't drunk the juice.

The thanedar came and made arrangements for Sajjad Mirza's burial and took the two children to the thana. The next day, the Munshi in the thana hired a camel and an escort and sent the boys off to Jaipur. They reached the next day. When the children reached the mohalla, my wife's brother, Ahmed Mirza Khan, was sitting outside with some friends. He asked the children, 'Where is your mamu?' The nephews replied, 'He has died.' Ahmed Mirza Khan fainted from the shock and a clamour of crying erupted all around.

By the time the children reached the house, there was a crowd of local men and women gathered there. Everyone kept asking the children to describe the events. They were frightened and unwell themselves and could only give the bare details.

Ahmed Mirza Khan sent a letter to me to come post-haste. In it, he stated that Sajjad Mirza was very ill. I was in a state of shock when I saw it and immediately took leave from Tonk. I left for Jaipur in the evening. I was going by camel cart, which was painfully slow. The cart driver decided to change camels, but as it was late the villagers asked us to stop over for fear of highwaymen.

We left in the morning and changed camels on the way. Though the other passengers were eating breakfast, I could not swallow even a single morsel.

A wedding party from my mohalla was passing, making its way from Jaipur to Tonk. I saw them and inquired about my son. They didn't tell me of Sajjad Mirza's death exactly, but their words were such that I was in absolute distress over his fate.

I reached Jaipur the next day and went straight home. My wife had forbidden anyone to tell me of Sajjad's death. Hence, I was met by silence. I sent for Ahmed Mirza Khan and Ahmed Sultan. Again, in spite of my repeated questions, no one was willing to tell me the truth. Everyone said that Sajjad was in Khandela. When all the men had gathered, I entreated them to tell me the truth for God's sake. I had a premonition, a hint from their stony silence, that Sajjad Mirza was no more.

I couldn't bear it any longer and hit my head on the floor. My head started bleeding and I said, 'If you do not tell me the truth, I will kill myself right here.'

My relatives caught my hands and said, 'Bear it with fortitude. We will tell you.'

When Ahmed Mirza Khan told me the events as described by the children, I started weeping and wailing.

My niece brought Sajjad Mirza's young children before me. His youngest son was a year and a few months old. I had not seen my grandson before this, but blood is thicker than water. He crawled up to me and climbed on to my lap. I embraced him and his four-year-old brother. I felt some respite from the grief raging in my heart.

Ahmed Sultan asked me to look for Sajjad Mirza in these children and to expend my energies in bringing them up. He said that if I killed myself in grief, these boys would have no one to look after them.

A few days later, when I had come to my senses and contained my grief, I decided to complain about the events to the ruler. My wife asked me to desist from it and just bear the grief patiently. She said, 'They will exhume the body to check for poison and disturb my son's journey to the afterworld. My heart is against this. Don't go and complain. Just let things be as they are.'

No one let me go to the court to lodge a complaint.

Days after my arrival in Jaipur, I wanted to make arrangements for functions to pray for the departed one's soul, but was told that it had already been done before my arrival. Now people came to offer their condolences to me.

The next day, a messenger came from the superintendent, calling the nephews. I took both boys to the court. The superintendent already knew of the events in Khandela, and had taken prior permission from the Maharaja to exhume the body and conduct a post-mortem. The children were questioned gently and the report was filed. The investigations began.

The post-mortem report gave proof of the poisoning and of a murder. I went to the council and lodged the report of my son's murder. I asked for justice as well as some compensation for looking after the young widow and orphans. Orders were given stating that after investigations were completed, my complaint should be followed up and justice given to me. The case was filed in the criminal court and the children and I were summoned for questioning.

I took my grandchildren to the residence of Babu Rao Kanti Chandra Bahadur and asked him who would look after them and their mother. I was old and feeble. Babu Sahib asked two members of the council, who were sitting with him, about my appeal. They confirmed the events and said that I was in the right.

Babu Sahib said, 'Zahiruddin, don't cry. The state of Jaipur is not unjust. We will look after these children and their mother. The murderer will be punished in a fitting manner. He wasn't just your son. I will give witness too.'

He ordered a member of the council to check all the papers. 'Once Maharaja Ram Singh had given orders that Zahiruddin was to be given Rs 20 per month for life. Get those papers out and resume that stipend.'

I said that I didn't want any blood money for my innocent son's death. If the state was in accordance with it, they should just give a regular amount to my daughter-in-law and grandchildren for their expenses. Babu Sahib agreed to my request.

They searched for the stipend papers for four months in the council office, but they could not be found. Babu Sahib said he could do nothing, as I was not willing to accept blood money. Eventually, half of Sajjad Mirza's salary as a thanedar, which was Rs 12 and 2 annas, was fixed as a stipend for his sons. They would receive it till they reached the age of eighteen years. I received this order. I still have it. It said that I would be given the amount for Sajjad Mirza's family, and after my demise, it would go directly to them.

Singh was charged with Sajjad Mirza's murder and sentenced to life imprisonment.

This tragedy destroyed my life. I had no further desire to live. From this day on, I lost my senses and my eyesight, and my hearing almost failed. I am now skin and bones, but I am still condemned to live.

Can anyone imagine someone writing poetry in such a state?

Poetry in Tonk

I wrote a lot of poetry in Tonk and recited it in the mushairas held under the Nawab Sahib's patronage. Due to Allah's grace, my ghazal was never overshadowed by anyone else's.

The poets of Tonk would put in great effort to write their poems, and bring them to the mushaira. But when I read my ghazal at the end, all their efforts would pale into insignificance.

In many mushairas, poets would bring their own supporters to praise their ghazals. These men would be given strict instructions not to praise mine. But when I recited them, the unconnected people standing at the back would praise the verses so loudly that it would make them all envious.

A mushaira was once held in the presence of Nawab Sahib. The participating poets read good ghazals. My shagirds had also written good verses. When Iftikhar Hussain Khan Muztar read out his ghazal, it was unique. His supporters raised slogans of 'SubhanAllah!' and '*Kya kehna!*' at every verse. No poet could compete with this. There was so much praise all around. My shagird Ahmed Saeeh Khan Aashiq's ghazal was no less than Muztar's; in fact, it was better phrased.

When my turn came, I said, 'O all those assembled here. You are young and enthusiastic. I am old and feeble, made senile from the sorrows that have struck me. What verse can I recite? Please excuse me from reading here.'

Nawab Sahib sent orders from inside his tent. 'You will have to recite your ghazal. Recite whatever you have written. I organize these mushairas only to hear your ghazals.'

I had no choice but to recite my ghazal and read out the matla. As soon as I read it, there was a clamour of praise and Mirza Mohammad Ali Khan sahib, a council member, called out, 'An ustad's matla is equal to another person's complete diwan. Those who were screaming praise for the previous poets, tell me, how good is this matla? *Sau sunaar ki ek lohaar ki.*' (100 blows of the goldsmith are comparable to one blow of the blacksmith.)

The matla was:

> That love is false in which one laments
> That fire is half-lit which emits smoke

Iftikhar Husain Khan sahib exclaimed that this is why we were acclaimed as ustads! It is such verses that are the pride of shayri. This happened to me on many occasions in Tonk.

Except for Nawab Sulaiman sahib Asad, Bismil Sahib[162] and Muztar Sahib,[163] all of these poets were my friends. There was never any tension or conflict between us, but there was a lot of envy on the part of people who, though they never visited Lucknow, felt that they owed allegiance to these poets from Lucknow.

My shagird Sahibzada Ahmed Saeed Khan procured a Diwan-e-Zauq so that he could compare the qasida for which I had received a lot of praise, since I had been accused of plagiarism from Zauq's qasida. There was a world of difference between the two. Ustad Zauq had written a qasida of recovery from illness, and mine was on the Nawab Sahib's birthday.

Ahmed Saeed Khan asked me to accompany him to the house of the person who had accused me. I replied, 'Miyan, let it be. The envious behave like this.'

He refused to listen to me, and finally, I had to go with him. He told the people standing outside the house, 'Here you are, Hazra. Here are the qasidas and the person you accused of theft. What is the name of the person who accused him?'

One man came forward and said, 'I made the accusation.'

Ahmed Saeed asked him, 'On what basis did you say that this qasida was written by Ustad Zauq?'

He replied, 'The language, subject and style of the ustad themselves provide testimony. None of the contemporary poets could write such a verse.'

Both qasidas were read out and this person had to agree that I had not copied from Ustad Zauq.

Nawab Ibrahim Ali Khalil

May the Almighty keep Nawab Ibrahim Ali Khan Bahadur, ruler of Tonk, safe and sound, and may his state prosper.

Nawab Sahib is an amalgamation of all commendable qualities found in a man. He should be included in the category of angels. I have not seen a ruler who was not only spiritual, pious, devout, devoted to Islam and the Prophet (peace be upon him), but extremely honourable, just in all his dealings, merciful and generous. He is very courteous in his dealings with all and steadfast in his relations with his friends.

My pen does not have the capacity to write all his praiseworthy qualities. First, the glory and majesty of his state is unparalleled on this earth, yet his humility is an example to all. He is creation incarnate.

He never misses a single namaz and reads the morning prayers on time. He spends his time in remembrance of God. He must rest for only four hours at night. He is awake by four in the morning. His attendants have strict instructions to wake him up at that time so that he can say his morning prayers. There is a masjid in the garden where he reads his namaz five times a day, along with a congregation. I have seen him weeping in the masjid at odd hours, completely immersed in worship.

His mercy is such that if he ever gets angry (which is rare) and hits an attendant over some mistake, he asks him for forgiveness later. 'Miyan, forgive me for the sake of Allah,' he says.

He gets a fixed amount of Rs 5000 every month for his personal expenditure and uses this on his family, as well as to give presents and rewards to his courtiers. He doesn't take money from the state for any of this. He is extremely generous and gives away a lot in charity. He has never been heard to say anything discourteous or hurt anyone with his words.

It is said in Tonk that if anyone commits a crime, he will receive complete justice. Inebriation and intoxication are punished. If someone skips fasts or saying his prayers (without a valid reason) during Ramzan, he is arrested and taken to the kotwali. He is kept under arrest and made to fast in the kotwali. He is released once the Eid moon has been sighted. Women engaged in prostitution are arrested and married off.

Nawab Sahib is very fond of *milad* and a gathering is held once a year. Delicious food is served and sweets are distributed. For the first twelve days of Rabi-ul-Awwal,[164] milads are held and grand preparations made for the same.

There is an arrangement for elaborate illuminations in the Nazeer Bagh, which is open to everyone. 1 ser of sweets is given to all those who attend. For seven days, there is a mehfil for men. The next five days are for the women. The women are able to move around freely and need not be in purdah at this gathering. The men are given strict instructions not to venture into the designated area.

Verses in praise of the Prophet (peace be upon him), known as *Hamd* and *Naat*, are read out at this gathering. The Nawab Sahib is not only fond of poetry, but writes quite well himself.

Alas! The state has suffered losses and its revenue has come down. It once had revenue of Rs 22 lakh, but it is only worth Rs 10 lakh now. The first reason for this is the terrain of Tonk. It's not a compact state. The boundaries of its parganas are not adjacent to one another and other states come within their borders. The people living in these areas leave Tonk in times of need and go to the other states. They have no loyalty to Tonk. Nearby areas such as Bhopal have benefited from this.

Secondly, the Nawab Sahib's family has increased, and hence, so has the expenditure. The Nawab Sahib could not give an allowance to each prince, and they had to live on their mother's money.

The first ruler, Nawab Mohammad Amir Khan, had twelve sons and many daughters. Each of them got an allowance, which continued down the generations. Now there is no money left in the treasury. It is just a state in name, and has no money.

All that was left has been destroyed by the rail tracks, which have been built in the state.

Still, no change has made itself felt in the present Nawab's generosity or charity. Any traveller who visits him leaves with something or the other. Even an ordinary poet can get the Nawab Sahib's attention, and even if he doesn't get employment, he is given some money for his expenses. Nawab Sahib is extremely fond of poetry and thinks it is haram to listen to a qasida and not give a reward in return. Unlike the nobles of Hyderabad, Nawab Sahib knows the value of poets.

I was living very happily in the state of Tonk and received a salary of Rs 30 from Nawab Sahib and Rs 10 from Begum Sahiba. My servants were paid by Sahibzada Ahsanullah Khan sahib, and I stayed in the latter's house. I didn't have to pay rent and I used the conveyance of Ahsanullah Khan to go wherever I wished. I had one tonga that had been given to me by the state as well. Khwaja Abur Rahim Khan sahib sent me Rs 15 every month from Dhaka. My family was in Jaipur and I could visit whenever I wanted.

Nawab Sahib Bahadur accorded me great respect. It often happened that if I were sitting at a distance and Nawab Sahib saw me, he would summon me close to him. Even if I gave excuses, he would smilingly say, 'Come closer to me. You are now deaf and won't be able to understand my verses.'

My life was very comfortable, but misfortune made me shift to Hyderabad.

Many of my friends wrote to me, telling me about the generosity and patronage of the nobles of Hyderabad. Poetry was cherished there and many assemblies were held. My friends said that the nobles were eager to hear my verses and they were very appreciative. Finally, I decided to leave for Hyderabad.

I was worried about my family as I had reached an advanced age and wanted to make arrangements for them. If nothing else, at least they could get some employment in Hyderabad. I took on a debt and made travel arrangements for them as well.

It took me four months to leave Tonk. I came to Jaipur to meet my family. In Jaipur, I found that my wife was unwell. She died within eight days of my reaching. My house was now desolate. I spent all the money I had taken as a loan for my travel on her burial and other funeral arrangements.

I now lost all appetite for travel. I sent a letter to Hyderabad, informing my friends about the tragedy. In return, I got a reply which said that whatever fate had ordained had happened, and I shouldn't change my programme.

10

Arrival in Hyderabad, Deccan

Since I had no option, I left for Hyderabad.[165] On the way, I made a stopover at Baroda, where Raja Bhagwan Sahai Bahadur arranged for me and my attendants to stay in the Bagh.

Initially, my monthly expense was Rs 80–90, but I later sent off one of the men. Raja Bhagwan Sahai Bahadur gave him money for his travel expenses. He was my sponsor for a whole year and took care of all my expenditures.

Maharaja Kishan Pershad and *Aala Hazrat* (Nizam) had to go to Delhi, so I decided to leave as well.

The people who had invited me here remonstrated with me, telling me that it was unwise to have left for such a reason. They said that I should wait for the Maharaja to return.

I stayed behind. The Maharaja Sahib Bahadur returned after three months. Meanwhile, Maulvi Bartar sahib returned to his native land. He had told me that he would make arrangements for me. He had asked Raja Murli Manohar sahib to extend his patronage to me. He said that other nobles would also extend their patronage to me. The Maharaja Sahib would take care of the rest and I would be able to live comfortably. However, all of these were empty promises, and no one besides Raja Bhagwan Sahai even inquired after my welfare. I was told that it would be difficult for me to find employment, but I would be sent off with adequate compensation.

Eight months passed in hope, but all the promises turned out to be empty ones. I also received notice from Tonk, informing me that my name had been struck off the register and there was no point in my returning.

I was faced with disappointment on every side. The people who had called me to Hyderabad also started avoiding me and refused to meet me. Eventually, I wrote a petition to the government, laying out my problems as well as describing my termination from Tonk. The government considered me destitute and fixed a small allowance for me. I was able to live my life. All my friends had deserted me by now.

I somehow managed to keep body and soul together, and for this, I give thanks to my benefactor, the government.

All the hopes I had from the people of Hyderabad turned out to be false. Whatever little appreciation I got was from Yamin-us-Sultanate, Madar-ul-Maham Maharaja Kishan Pershad Shaad. The latter appreciated the art of poetry and employed many poets in his court. He himself writes fine poetry too. He is very well-versed in poetry and prose and Persian and Arabic. He is a very accomplished man of excellent character and bearing. His courtesy, generosity and charity are legendary. He donates generously to Sufi shrines and towards the urs held there. Thousands are fed during the urs and gifts are given to the visitors.

Urs Maula Ali

When Maharaja Kishan Pershad Shaad went up the mountain to the shrine of Maula Ali, he spent a number of months there. He was accompanied by the entire paraphernalia of the government and officials. Everyone was well looked after and fed by the state.

The urs of Hazrat Ali Murtaza Sher-e-Khuda Salatullah Alaihi was celebrated with great ceremony. The place was beautifully decorated. Thousands of people came to pay their respects and were looked after by the state. Dancers and singers and courtesans also came. Tents were set up for all these people to stay in.

Huge amounts of food were cooked for both meals and distributed to the pilgrims. This went on for many days. After the urs was over, Maharaja Sahib gave gold coins to his courtiers.

Today, no noble can afford to spend so lavishly, even though some may have more money than the Maharaja. He was called *Hatim-e-Waqt*.[166]

I had had huge expectations of Hyderabad when I left for the state. I knew that if I could get the patronage of even one or two nobles, I could live comfortably.

There is no state as prosperous and grand as that of Hyderabad. It is considered to be on the same level as Iran. Many rich and important nobles live there. It is not difficult for anyone to get a job with a salary of Rs 400–500 per month.

In Hyderabad, there were jagirs worth Rs 25 lakh. The rest of Hindustan has jagirs of Rs 4–5 lakh and must maintain their status and responsibilities within that amount. However, when I reached the state I found that it was all empty show.

Not only did I not receive any patronage, but I reached the stage of having to starve. I was asked who had told me of such green pastures that they induced me to leave my comfortable home to come and starve here!

Mir Mahboob Ali Khan

He was an extremely intelligent and visionary man. He was a patron of the arts, extremely just and very pleasant. He was merciful and concerned about his subjects.

He was known for his lavish lifestyle and was fond of dance and music assemblies. He kept the city well-lit and decorated. He was extremely loyal to the emperor. The people of Hyderabad were very happy and affluent and they did not face shortages of any kind.

The City's Population

The city is another world altogether. There are bazaars and residences for miles all around it.

It wouldn't be unsuitable to say that there is a jungle of men here. Thousands of horse carriages and sedans run from evening to midnight. The pedestrians find it difficult to walk because there are so many carriages doing the rounds.

There are people going somewhere or the other day and night. The number of employees is much higher here than anywhere else in Hindustan.

The wealthy are divided into three categories:

Tabqa-e-Aala – These are the nobles and jagirdars who are related to the royal family, such as Nawab Shamsul Umara's family. He is the jagirdar of fifty-two villages, and the biggest one. He is the son of the Aala Hazrat Qadr-e-Qudrat's (the Nizam's) sister.

This category includes hereditary jagirdars such as Maharaja Shiv Ram Bahadur Dayanatwant Asif Jahi, Rao Laxman Rao Bahadur Dayanatwant Asif Jahi, Maharaja Chandu Lal Bahadur's family and the family of Salar Jung.

Tabqa-e-Do'am – This category includes jagirdars and mansabdars who earn between Rs 3 lakh and Rs 50,000. Members of the government and employees earning Rs 5000–Rs 200 are also included in this category.

Tabqa So'em – Employees, soldiers, government officials earning a salary of Rs 200–Rs 5 come in this category.

In Hyderabad, an employee who gets a salary of Rs 100 is equivalent to someone getting a salary of Rs 30 elsewhere in Hindustan. The reason for this is that Hyderabad is much more expensive than other cities.

Economic Conditions

Now let us take a look at the prices of commodities here in Hyderabad. Meat, which used to sell at the rate of 8 ser for Re 1 in the rest of Hindustan, was sold at 4 ser for Re 1 here. However, prices have gone up now, and it costs 8 annas per ser everywhere.[167] It is possible that the prices in Hyderabad are double this.

The other grains, which sold at the rate of 17–18 ser for Re 1, were 10 ser for Re 1 in Hyderabad.

A small comparison can be made. Washermen take 4 annas per month to wash an ordinary man's clothes. In Hyderabad, however, the washermen ask for Re 1 per month.

On top of that, they wash the clothes only twice a month and only after much persuasion.

A barber takes 1 anna to trim a beard and moustache. That's the rate in Delhi too. A poor man gives 1 paisa for a haircut in Hindustan, while the better off give 2 paise.

In Hyderabad, most people are comparatively more affluent than the rest of Hindustan. The people of the *Tabqa So'em* are much better off than their counterparts across the country. People with strained resources can't hope to live comfortably in this state. That is why travellers and those who come in search of employment face a tough time trying to make ends meet. No one is willing to come to their houses to serve them.

The Grandeur of the Nobles

The nobles of the *Tabqa Awwal* and *Tabqa Do'em* are very fond of pleasure, hard to please and enamoured of grandeur and luxuries. They rarely think of the plight of the poorer people. In fact, the poor have no hopes of even reaching the darbar to present their problems.

How would such nobles have time for refined activities such as poetic soirees?

> O unwise nightingale, hold your breath in your throat
> The fragile hearts of kings can't bear to hear your song

No one appreciated poetry or literary activities here. There were no patrons for the men of letters in this city, however accomplished they may have been. The only ones who received their due were *marsiya-khwaan*,[168] who were called upon to recite *marsiya*s during the ten days of Moharrum. There was a catch here too, as only those marsiya-khwaan were called whose ancestors were also famous in this genre. This happened even if the descendants were not very skilled. They were patronized and rewarded irrespective of whether or not they were talented. The nobles are only concerned with their own reputation and fame as there is a competition over who has called a more famous and expensive marsiya-khwaan! No one else stands a chance against them, no matter how talented.

Marsiya-khwaani is all that these nobles appreciate. They don't seem interested in other religious ceremonies during this month. In every other city, the rich and poor alike feed the poor and destitute during Moharrum and spend thousands of rupees in offerings and consecrations to the Prophet's family.

Unlike the nobles of Hyderabad, those of other places in Hindustan have various hobbies and pursuits and patronize accomplished people from every field of art and music. Some are fond of kite-flying, pigeon-flying and hunting. Some are fond of horse riding and buy expensive breeds from different countries and employ experienced people to look after them. If some noble is fond of bird shooting, he spends thousands of rupees in pursuit of his passion. In brief, the nobles indulge in various hobbies and passions and collect and patronize accomplished people in that field. They shower riches on them.

The Hyderabad noblemen have a European education and emulate the British in every respect. They guard their purse strings and don't spend a single paisa on unnecessary pursuits. It is impossible for a man, however accomplished he may be, to receive even a small reward from them by displaying his talent. Jugglers and performers have no hope of winning a single paisa by displaying their sleight of hand or tricks.

The nobles are very wise and have ensured that travellers and seekers don't come to their doorstep for help. The generosity and charity shown by other rulers is missing in Hyderabad.

An Explanation of My Writing Style

When I recall my life, I realize it can be divided into different phases. The first phase is my childhood and youth, which was spent in the lap of luxury, enjoying myself. The second phase was nomadic, when I was uprooted from my home and spent my time in errantry and the search for livelihood.

In the third phase, I benefited from my skill and passion for poetry. I spent these years writing, reciting my verse, honing my craft and was mostly in the company of poets and those who loved shayri.

I became interested in poetry at an early age and was a student of Sheikh Ibrahim Zauq Khaqaani-e-Hind. In those days, I was young and ignorant and had no knowledge of the drawbacks in my writing. Even though I was not able to learn much from my ustad, and my work was never really corrected, I gained a lot from observing and listening to great poets. After the demise of my ustad, I gained a lot from being in the company of poets.

When I returned to Delhi four or five years after the ghadar, I found that that there was a greater focus on poetry. I spent a lot of time in the company of Mufti Sadruddin Khan sahib Azurda, Nawab Mustafa Khan sahib Shefta and Hafiz Ghulam Rasool sahib Weeran. I also met Mirza Asadullah Khan sahib Ghalib on many occasions. Even though I did not ask anyone to revise or correct my verses, I learnt a lot by listening to the work of these great poets. I heard the verses of the three ustads of our times, Zauq, Momin and Ghalib, and developed a style of my own.

I adopted the language and metaphors used by Sheikh Ibrahim Zauq, the delicacy of thought, impassioned style and subjects of Momin Sahib, and copied Mirza Ghalib's composition and arrangement of verses.

Apart from this, I tried to write as well as I could within the rules, as per my limited understanding. I stringently rejected any verse which didn't sound good to the ear or wasn't well composed.

I do not claim to be the reviver or innovator of my era, nor do I ask that anyone copy my style. I have never used an inappropriate word in my verse, but others have the right to use such words or reject them. I spent twenty years in the service of Jaipur state. I had no time during this period and may have written just twenty to twenty-five ghazals and a couple of qasidas at the insistence of my friends. When I left this service and accepted the patronage of Nawab Ahmed Ali Khan sahib Raunaq, I set my focus on writing and my verses became famous. My fame spread and many poets became my students. My grasp of poetry increased day by day. My first diwan, *Gulistan-e-Sukhan*, was prepared when I was in service to the Nawab Sahib of Tonk. He gave me the necessary resources. It was published under the aegis of Raja Bhagwan Sahai Bahadur and Khwaja Abdur Rahim Khan sahib. It became popular all over Hindustan.

My second diwan was also made ready, but I could not get it published. By the grace of God, I have material for three diwans and enough *marsiya*, *salaam* and *rubayi*[169] to make up one book. If God Almighty makes some arrangements with His divine providence, then these will be published as well. I can see no other resource except divine help.

I spent my life in service to the Badshah, kings and important nobles. I have lived with respect and dignity all my life. Rich and important men appreciated my poetry and rewarded me. A noble once gave me Rs 1000 for a ghazal of nine verses. I have often been rewarded with gold coins for a new ghazal.

Nawab Ahmed Ali Khan sahib Raunaq had an income of Rs 3000 a month. Apart from my salary, he would give me

Rs 200 a month, or whenever any of my children got married. He would reward me separately for my qasidas.

Raja Bhagwan Sahai Bahadur sahib Garam and Khwaja Abdur Rahim Khan sahib Aseem[170] always patronized me. I lived my life with the help of these kind patrons.

Now, I have a few days more to live and my end is nigh.

I have had my share of fame and my students are present in every area, from Dera Ghazi Khan, Dhaka, Shimla and all the way to Madras. My students respect me and revere any corrections I make to their work. My verses have reached every corner of the country and people eagerly await my ghazals. Each line is appreciated. There is no poet who doesn't know of me.

What greater fame could I ask for?

By the grace of God, my students have reached such peaks of excellence that they have become ustads themselves. Each one has 100–200 students and they no longer need my guidance. It is their respect for me that leads them to send me their verses for correction. Their work is no less than any other poet. In fact, it is often superior. They are incomparable in the writing of qasidas.

Maulvi Nadir Ali Bartar, Najmuddin Ahmed Saqib Badayuni, Sahibzada Ahmed Saeed Khan Ashiq Tonki are all ranked in the first level of poets. On the second level are Munshi Ramzan Ali Khan, Akhtar Ajmeri, Munshi Ibrahim Dabeer Rodkoti, Nain Miyan Uns, Sukna Bada Awadh, Munshi Sultan Ahmed Nashaad Sukna Calcutta and Nawab Khwaja Abdur Rahim Khan sahib Aseem, the Nawab of Dhaka, and Hakim Asad Ali Khan Sahib Dehlavi Muztar, Syed Hasan, Syed Bhopali, Mahmood Khan Mahmood Hyderabadi. I can't enumerate the students in the third level, as they are innumerable.

I have passed seventy years of age and I have become physically and mentally very feeble. My memory is such that

I forget something as soon as I have uttered it. The grief of losing my children has broken my heart. Worry over my family has made me lose my senses.

I am ready to leave this world at any time now. I have lost my hearing and sight. Despite this, I drink tears of blood and have managed to write some verses. Yet, the response has only been envy and jealousy.

The world is extremely unappreciative and I have lost interest in writing poetry. I eventually gave up writing. I retired from active life and now no longer write poetry.

Poetry

When I arrived in Hyderabad, I became instantly famous and an army of people would come to meet me. From morning to eleven at night, there would be a crowd of people in my house. They would request me to recite my verses and I would comply.

During this period, my well-wisher, Nawab Abdullah Khan Zaigham, organized a mushaira and informed everyone of my attendance. A huge crowd gathered in this assembly, but I was delayed. The mushaira had started when I arrived, but everyone welcomed me respectfully.

I saw something very strange here. Before one ghazal could be completed, the next poet would come and pull the *shama-e-farozan*[171] towards himself and start reciting his work. Before he could finish, someone else would come and start his own ghazal. They kept reciting regardless of whether they were receiving any praise from the audience. Around 150–200 verses were recited in this fashion. The poets kept reciting and paid no attention to the lack of response. Their behaviour was totally against all norms of etiquette. They did not wait to be invited or give a gap between the ghazals. Another strange thing was that once they had finished reciting, they would leave for home instead of staying on to hear the rest.

La Haula Wala Quwwata Illa Billah! (There is no might and power but that of Allah!) What kind of uncouth and uncivilized people are these who don't know the etiquette of a mushaira?

I was very ashamed and embarrassed to have come to this mehfil. I somehow spent the evening there, but I was in agony. When my turn came, it was nearly dawn and there were hardly eight to ten people left. They had come simply to recite their own verses and had no interest in my work. However, I am grateful to God that my ghazal was greatly appreciated and even though there were very few people present, my verses became famous throughout Hyderabad.

My ghazal was never inferior to that of other great poets in Hyderabad. The fame of my qasidas spread all over the city, and there is no need for me to write about it.

Many of the poets gathered in Hyderabad are from Lucknow. Only Dagh Sahib and I represented Delhi.

Dagh Sahib[172] didn't attend mushairas; I was present at all of them. The result was that other poets stopped coming to mushairas.

The Maharaja held many assemblies, and I was successful there too, by the grace of God. Those who attended them know the reality of the praise I received there. Alas! I got no reward or compensation except jealousy and envy.

The late Dagh Sahib was also envied by most people and criticized by them. I am in the same boat. If they were envious or jealous of Dagh Sahib, it was understandable, as he was a man of means. But I was so unlucky that I could hardly feed myself. Their hostility towards me was totally unnecessary.

Hyderabad turned out to be an empty dream.

I now spend my time in prayer, waiting for my end.

Timeline of the Ghadar in Delhi

11 May 1857 – The soldiers arrive from Meerut early in the morning. The rebels kill Frazer, Capt. Douglas, Rev. Jennings and a few others in the quarters above Lahori Gate.

11 May – William Brendish and J.W. Pilkington, two assistants at the telegraph office near the magazine, manage to send a message to Ambala about the revolt in Delhi. This message is later sent to Shimla and results in a force being dispatched from Punjab to fight the rebels in Delhi.

12 May – A dusty, unused, silver throne lying forgotten in a corner of the Diwan-e-Khaas is brought out by the rebels and Bahadur Shah Zafar proclaimed Badshah-e-Hindustan.

16 May – The rebels slaughter forty-nine European men, women and children who had been confined in the Qila.

30 May – British troops arrive and meet the Indian rebels in Ghaziabad. This is what is referred to as the First Battle in the text.

8 June – By 2 a.m., the Indian soldiers begin firing at the British troops from their position in Badli ki Sarai. The Indians are routed by a bayonet charge by the Seventy-fifth Regiment of Foot, who capture the rebel battery that was raining fire on them. It is a decisive win for the British as they retake strategic position on the Ridge. This is referred to as the Second Battle in the text. There are continuous skirmishes after that for the next few days.

19 June – The Indian soldiers attack the British forces on the Ridge from three sides and come very close to winning when the British infantry and guns drive them back to the walled city.

23 June – Another major attack by the Indians from Sabzi Mandi. This is a fierce attack, as it was believed that on the centenary of the Battle of Plassey the Indians would gain freedom from the British.

2 July – Arrival of Bakht Khan with the Rohilla regiment of 15,000 soldiers from Bareilly. They cross the river with bands playing and colours flying.

14 August – The British troops are joined by the Punjab Moveable Column, numbering 4200 and consisting of British, Sikh and Punjabi units under General Nicholson.

25 August – Battle of Najafgarh. The forces of General Nicholson and General Bakht Khan face each other in this battle and the British forces under Nicholson inflict a heavy defeat on the Indian army. The Indian guns are captured and the Indian army suffers grave losses.

6 September – The British siege train, consisting of fifteen 24-pounder guns, twenty 18-pounder guns and twenty-five heavy mortars and howitzers, with almost 600 ammunition carts, arrives. Reid's Battery, established on the southern end of the Ridge over the next few days, demolishes the two Indian positions at Mori Bastion and engages the Kashmiri Bastion.

7 September – British forces occupy Ludlow Castle and Qudsia Bagh. They set up batteries there.

11 September – The Second Battery established outside Ludlow Castle opens fire against the Kashmiri Bastion and Water Bastion. The British begin an assault from a third and fourth battery against the Indian side which is by now running out of options. Assault continues for two days and nights at intervals of fifteen minutes each.

14 September – The final assault. Kashmiri Gate is breached.

17 September – The British enter Shahjahanabad and the emperor flees from the Qila and takes refuge in the house of Mirza Ilahi Bux in Hazrat Nizamuddin Basti.[173]

19 September – The emperor goes to Humayun's tomb.

20 September – Delhi falls into the hands of the British and the rebels are cleared out.

21 September – Major Hudson captures the emperor.

22 September – Hudson executes the Mughal princes.

Historical Notes on Some Key Figures

Zahir Dehlvi was twenty-two years old when the rebels came to Delhi. Based on this, his year of birth would be 1835. His full name was Syed Mohammad Zahiruddin Husain Rizvi and he was called Nawab Mirza. His takhallus was Zahir. He was awarded the title of Raqim-ud-Daula Syed Zahiruddin Hussain Khan Darogha-e-Qauzbegi, and he is often referred to as Zahiruddin Khan.

Zahir's family had been in service to the Mughals, holding high positions for several generations. His grandfather, Mir Imam Ali Shah, was one of the most famous calligraphers of his age, and Badshah Bahadur Shah Zafar was his student. Zahir's father, Syed Jalauddin Haider, was also a famous calligrapher, and after his father's death, he was given the position of ustad to the Badshah in calligraphy. Zahir himself was a student of the emperor in the art of calligraphy and was therefore a frequent visitor to the Qila-e-Moalla from the age of eight.

At the age of fourteen years, he became a student of Sheikh Ibrahim Zauq to learn the art of poetry. After Zauq's death, he went to Mirza Ghalib for correction of his verse.

Though he was a student of Zauq, he was influenced by the style of Momin Khan Momin.

He spent four years in the employment of Alwar state, around nineteen in Jaipur state and around fifteen or sixteen years in Tonk state. From Tonk, he went to Hyderabad in search of patronage and died there.

Though he doesn't mention his physical appearance, Mirza Farhatullah Beg describes him in *Delhi ki Akhri Shama* as being exceedingly handsome—tall, slim, broad-shouldered with a wheatish complexion, aquiline nose, very bright eyes and sporting a trimmed beard.

In August 1863, he was responsible, along with Anwar Dehlvi and Hafez Ghulam Rasool Veeran, for putting together *Nigaristan Sukhan*, which had portions of the diwans of Ghalib, Momin and Zauq. Since 1857 had resulted in great loss to poetry and literature with diwans and books being burnt, this was a very important contribution.

Zahir's poetic work was destroyed in 1857, but towards the end of his life he once again became prolific during his service to the ruler of Tonk. His first diwan, called *Gulistan-e-Sukhan*, was published while he was there. Later, two diwans were published in Karimi Press, Bombay. His fourth diwan was with his grandson Mir Ishtiaq Hussain Sahuq Dehlvi, which could not be published.

After a life which reads like a piece of fiction itself, with its considerable ups and downs, he breathed his last in March 1911.

Hakim Ahsanullah Khan learnt the art of *hikmat* or functions of a physician from his father. His reputation as a doctor was such that a person who could not get cured by any other doctor would come to him to find relief. The residents of Shahjahanabad would flock to him for treatment.

His reputation reached the ears of the Mughal emperor, Moin-ud-din Mohammad Akbar Shah, who appointed him as his personal doctor.

After his father's death, Bahadur Shah appointed him as his doctor as well. Ahsanullah Khan gained prominence and promotions, and the emperor gave him the titles of *Ehteram-ud-Daula Sabit Jung*. There came a point when the emperor would consult him on everything, whether it had to do with his health or the kingdom. When the prime minister, Mehboob Ali Khan, fell sick with dropsy, the emperor put Ahsanullah Khan in charge of all the affairs of the Qila and made him prime minister.

Hakim Ahsanullah Khan is a highly controversial figure and has been accused of having been in league with the British. He gave evidence against the emperor during his trial.

After the emperor was exiled to Rangoon, the venerable, thin and white-bearded hakim moved to Baroda. He died there and was buried in 1873 at the age of seventy-six.

Maharao Raja Sheodan Singh (1845–1874) succeeded as a minor in 1857 and reigned from 1863 until his death in October 1874. Maharao Raja Shri Sheodan Singh ji was learned in Persian and Hindi and had a special love for painting and music.

According to the *Imperial Gazetter of India*, under his father, Maharao Raja Viney Singh (1815–1857), 'The Government had previously been carried on without any system. But with the aid of certain Musalmans introduced from Delhi and appointed ministers in 1838, great changes were made. The land revenue began to be collected in cash instead of kind and civil and criminal courts were established.'[174]

Sheodan Singh was a boy of twelve when he became the Maharaja, and is perceived to have fallen under the influence of the Muslim diwans. There was an insurrection against him in 1858. This resulted in the expulsion of the Muslim officers and the formation of the Council of Regency by the British.

Maharao Raja Sheodan Singh assumed independent power on 14 September 1863, and the regency was abolished soon after. He recalled the Muslim diwans with whom he was still in contact and gave them high offices. This once again led to unrest among the Rajputs, and in 1866, Thakur Lakhbir Singh invaded Alwar. He was defeated, but in 1870, there was a general uprising of the Rajputs with the result that the British government had to interfere once again. Major Cadell was then appointed the political agent in 1867, and with the sanction of the government of India, a council of management was formed, with the political agent as president and the Maharaja having a seat on the board. Sheodan Singh resented this interference. He fell ill soon after and died in October 1874, at a comparatively young age.

Maharaja Sawai Ram Singh II of Jaipur (reigned 1835–1880) succeeded as Maharaja in 1835, though a council of regency controlled Jaipur until 1851. He was decreed a Knight Grand Commander of the Most Exalted Order of the Star of India in 1877. He was also dubbed a Counsellor of the Empress in 1877 and a Knight Grand Commander of India in 1880. He was the first to use the title of Maharaja of Jaipur.

Maharaja Ram Singh was responsible for turning Jaipur into a well-administered and prosperous state. His prime objective was the welfare of his people. He would look into the details of every department of the state and kept himself well informed on what was going on in the different sections of the administration. He would roam incognito on the streets to check on his officials and that kept them on their toes as well as ensured the wellbeing of his subjects.

He built the Jaipur water works (1875), gas works (1878), the Mayo Hospital, the Ramniwas gardens with the museum, the School of Arts, public library, Ramprakash Theatre, Maharaja's College (1844), Sanskrit School (1865), the Nobles' School (1862) and the Girls' School (1867). The public works department was established in 1860. Roads and highways between Jaipur, Ajmer and Agra were constructed during his reign. Besides this, dams for irrigation purposes, public buildings and offices were also built.

The Maharaja was an ardent devotee of Lord Shiva.

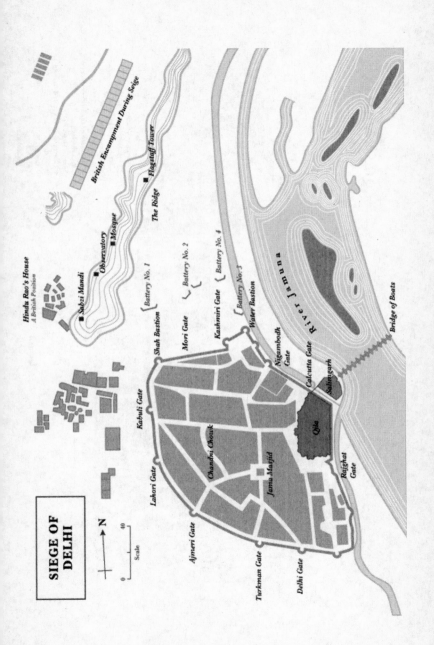

SIEGE OF
DELHI

N

Scale
0   40

Hindu Rao's House
A British Position

British Encampment During Siege

Sabzi Mandi

Observatory

Mosque

The Ridge

Flagstaff Tower

Kabuli Gate

Shah Bastion

Battery No. 1

Mori Gate

Battery No. 2

Kashmiri Gate

Battery No. 4

Lahori Gate

Battery No. 3

Water Bastion

Nigambodh Gate

Chandni Chouk

Calcutta Gate

Salimgarh

River Jamuna

Ajmeri Gate

Jama Masjid

Qila

Bridge of Boats

Turkman Gate

Rajghat Gate

Delhi Gate

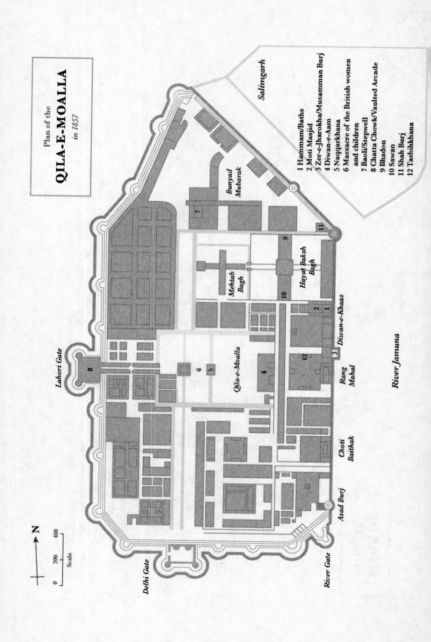

Plan of the
QILA-E-MOALLA
in 1857

1 Hammam/Baths
2 Moti Masjid
3 Zer-e-Jharokha/Musamman Burj
4 Diwan-e-Aam
5 Naqqarkhana
6 Massacre of the British women
  and children
7 Baoli/Stepwell
8 Chatta Chowk/Vaulted Arcade
9 Bhadon
10 Sawan
11 Shah Burj
12 Tashikhana

Salimgarh

Buryad
Mubarak

Mehtab
Bagh

Hayat
Baksh
Bagh

Qila-e-Moalla

Diwan-e-Khaas

Rang
Mahal

River Jamuna

Choti
Baithak

Asad Burj

Lahori Gate

Delhi Gate

River Gate

N

0   200   400
Scale

Plan of the Qila-e-Moalla and Shahjahanabad

Qila-e-Moalla

Lahori Gate – The main gate (so called because it faced the direction of Lahore, which was to the west of the Qila), is the gate from which the prime minister of India addresses the nation on 15 August. Outside it was a large open square where the nobles put up their tents when it was their weekly turn to mount guard.

Akbarabadi Darwaza (now called Dilli Darwaza) – The gate to the south of the Qila.

Apart from Lahori Darwaza and Akbarabadi Darwaza, the western half of the fort also housed the workshops designed to serve the royal manufacturers, the royal guard house, stables, a section of the emperor's army and the administrative offices.

Khizri Darwaza – The Qila gate that faced the east.

Salimgarh Darwaza – The Qila gate that faced north.

Chatta Chowk – A vaulted arcade, which was built as a shopping area for the royal ladies and princes. Curios and handicrafts are sold here today.

Naqqarkhana – This is the gate where drums were played. It was here that the visitors had to dismount and enter the Diwan-e-Aam/Diwan-e-Khaas on foot. Between it and the east end of the vaulted arcade (Chatta Chowk), there was a court, 200 feet in length and 140 feet in breadth. It was surrounded by arcaded apartments which served as quarters for the nobles on duty on the emperor's guard. It was broken by the British to accommodate the barracks. There used to be a tank, which was the scene of the massacre of the Europeans described in the book. The British filled it up.

   Much to the annoyance of the emperor and courtiers, the baghis would ride their horses all the way up to the Diwan-e-Aam and would not give consideration to the courtesies due the emperor.

Mehtab Bagh – On the left side of the naqqarkhana was the Mehtab Bagh, or Moonlit Garden. It was filled only with trees, shrubs and plants with white flowers. The *nahr-e-Bahist* or stream of paradise flowed through it. This stream interspersed with exquisite marble and silver fountains flew throughout the Qila complex. The British destroyed the Mehtab Bagh and built barracks in its place. It was here that the baghis came and camped at first, causing much distress to the Badshah by trampling over the flowers. Later, they moved to Salimgarh Fort.

Diwan-e-Aam – Once one entered the naqqarkhana, there was a waiting area in front of the Diwan-e-Aam. There was an enclosure with a marble railing around it, beautifully decorated with golden finial on its kiosks. The nobles, ministers and emissaries stood here in order, according to their official status. Nothing remains of this. A garden has been planted here. From here one went to the main Diwan-e-Aam where the throne was kept. There was a strict protocol for entering it and standing in position when the emperor was in court. Again, this was not observed by the baghis.

Gulal Bari – The Gulal Bari was an ante-court built outside the Diwan-e-Aam and reserved for minor officials. The general throng attending the darbar stood outside this last enclosure. It is no longer present.

Hammam – To the south of the Diwan-e-Khaas is the hammam, or baths. The emperor used it for private conferences as well as rest and solitude.

Hayat Baksh Bagh – This was a beautiful garden behind the hammam, and adjoined the Mehtab Bagh.

Lal Purdah – This was the entrance to the courtyard nearest the Diwan-e-Khaas. It was known as *jilaukhana* or abode of splendour, and was kept screened by a red curtain. This is the courtyard where nobles of the highest order waited on the emperor. No one could enter without being given permission or being announced. It plays an important role in the events after 11 May as the scene of many incidents, and was the cause of the emperor's displeasure as the sawars entered the Diwan-e-Khaas without observing protocol.

Diwan-e-Khaas – The heart of the Qila-e-Moalla was the Diwan-e-Khaas, a beautifully decorated marble edifice. It is here that the emperor granted special audience. It is also the place where the peacock throne was used on special occasions. On the eastern side, the building overhung the Jamuna. The doors on that side had finely carved marble screens with glass inlay work in their perforations.

Towards the west was a courtyard that was 70x60 yards, and around it were mansions and arcades of red sandstone. Towards the west was the entrance, which connected it to the Diwan-e-Aam by a passage.

Deorhi – To the south of the Diwan-e-Khaas was the passageway leading to the Royal Harem. In front of this entrance, towards the courtyard, was a marble enclosure called Chaukhundi Diwan-e-Khaas. All of these structures were removed or altered after 1857.

Tasbihkhana – This was on the same terrace as the Diwan-e-Khaas, and lay towards the south. It was the rear portion of the royal khwaabgah. In the middle of this hall there is an engraved weighing scale made of marble with *Mizaan-e-Adl* (Scales of Justice) written on it. It led into the royal apartments of the emperor and the harem.

Musamman Burj/Saman Burj – This burj, or pavilion, is to the east of the wall of the harem and is made of marble from top to bottom, and covered with beautiful decorations. As it was octagonal in shape, it was called musamman. Three sides of the tower are turned towards the harem, and five overhang the river. There are marble screens over the five sides and one of them houses a balcony that overlooks the river. It was to this balcony that the emperor came for jharokha darshan, and where he was sitting the morning of 11 May 1857 when the baghis came from Meerut.

Baithak – There is a set of three rooms behind the Musamman Burj, which includes the Khwaabgah or private apartments of the emperor, and a hall that is open on one side and is called the Badi Baithak.

Shahjahanabad

There was a broad road running from the Lahori Darwaza to Fatehpuri Masjid on an east–west axis. This divided the city into two halves. There was another road, which ran from the Lahori Darwaza to the Delhi Gate of the city on the north–south axis. Access to the city was through the two principal bazaars along the east–west, north–south axes.[175]

Urdu Bazaar – The first section of the bazaar between Lahori Darwaza of the Qila to Kotwali Chabutra was known as Urdu Bazaar or Camp Market.[176]

Kotwali – This was the old kotwali of Shahjahanabad. Its courtyard was the magistrate's office and platform. Cases were heard here and punishment meted out in public. In front of the kotwali was a wooden pole to which culprits were tied and flogged. It was near the present-day Gurudwara Sis Ganj.

Tripolia – This was a lofty building with three archways or gates, standing opposite the kotwali. It was probably demolished after 1857.

Khooni Darwaza – This Khooni Darwaza should not be confused with the one near Feroz Shah Kotla. This led to Dariba Kalan and was so called since there had been so much bloodshed near it during Nadir Shah's massacre of the inhabitants of Delhi. It would be near the Sunehri Masjid in Chandni Chowk today.

Dariba Kalan – This was one of the broad streets of Shahjahanabad and was accessed from the northern gate of Jama Masjid. A gateway in Dariba Kalan led to Dariba Khurd or Chota Dariba. Chota Dariba is today known as Kinari Bazaar. The opposite side led to Moti Bazaar and then on to Jauhri Bazaar. There was another market called Chota Dariba.

Kucha Chela'n – This was an area where the disciples of Emperor Shah Jahan had built their havelis. It is in present-day Chandni Mahal, in Chandni Chowk.

Maliwaara – This may originally have belonged to gardeners, but by the mid-eighteenth century, it was a locality with many mohallas which were inhabited by members of the Jain community.

Paiwala'n Bazaar – This was a bazaar near the northern gate of the Jama Masjid. The traditional goods sold here were bedsteads, wooden settees and bedposts or *pai*, which led to the name.

Khanum ka Bazaar – This was situated between Khas Bazaar and Urdu Bazaar and sold arms and weapons.

Khaas Bazaar – This was to the east of Jama Masjid.

Matia Mahal – This was a palace dating from pre-Shahjahanabad days. The name stuck and is still used to designate the area opposite the main gate of Jama Masjid.

Glossary

Angarkha	A male dress
Arz beg	Petition officer
Azadari	Observance of rituals connected with mourning in the month of Moharrum
Baal-e-huma	Fly swatters
Badshah	Emperor
Bagh	Orchard
Baghi sawar	Rebel cavalrymen
Baithak	Sitting room
Bakshi	Paymaster
Bakshikhana	Paymaster's office
Balidan	Sacrifice
Bania	Trader
Baraat	Procession
Baradari	A twelve-arch pavilion
Barfkhana	Ice factories
Baridar	Servant

Bazaar	Market
Begum	Queen
Bhang	A drink made from the leaves and buds of the female cannabis plant, very popular in India
Bismillah	The ceremony which marks the start of formal learning; also, an exclamation meaning 'In the name of Allah!'
Burj	Pavilion
Chabutra	Platform
Chatta	A covered lane or passage
Chillum	The part of the hookah which contains the tobacco and fire
Choubdar	Mace bearer
Chowk	Square
Darbar	Court
Dargah	Shrine of a saint
Dariba	Street
Darogha	Superintendent
Darogha-e-Khabar	Superintendent of Intelligence
Darogha-e-Mahi-Maratib	An official of the Order of the Fish, or the superintendent of the royal fish emblem

Darogha-e-Qauzbegi Peshgah	The head of the attendants who could reach the last station near the emperor, which an ordinary person in the court could not reach.
Darwaza	Monumental gate
Deorhi	Entrance, passageway to a specific place
Diwan	Collection of ghazals
Diwankhana	Salon
Farashkhana	The room where carpets are kept. Farashkhana is also the name of a locality in Shahjahanabad/Old Delhi so called because the carpet makers/sellers lived there.
Faujdar	Superintendent of the army
Fil–baan	Elephant keeper/mahout
Ghadar	Mutiny
Gora	A white person. Here, the term is taken broadly to refer to the Europeans in the East India Company army.
Hakim	Doctor
Halwai	Sweetmeat or snack vendor

Hammam	Bath
Haram	Forbidden
Hauz	Reservoir
Havaldar	Sergeant
Haveli	Mansion
Hawadar	Sedan chair
Howdah	A canopied seat
Huzoor	Royal presence
Huzoor purnoor	Illuminated royal presence
Jagir	Land grant for services rendered to the ruler, mostly military
Jagirdar	Owner of a jagir
Jamadar	Head of a unit
Jharna	Fountain
Jharokha	Balcony
Kaghazi	Paper merchants
Kaamdaar	Officials
Kachori	Stuffed savouries
Kalan	Big
Kalima	Creed recited by Muslims testifying to the oneness of God
Kampu	A body of infantry trained in the European fashion in service to the native princes
Khaas	Special

Khalifa	Successor (in the art of calligraphy)
Khan-samaani	Department of household expense
Khilat	Dress of honour bestowed by a superior
Khurd	Small
Khwaabgah	Royal harem, or private apartments
Khwaja-sara	Eunuchs employed in the court of the emperor
Kos	A measure of length equal to about 2.25 km
Kothi	House/cottage
Kotwal	Head of the kotwali/ chief police officer
Kotwali	The chief police station in town
Mahal	Palace
Mamu	Maternal uncle, or mother's brother
Marsiya	Elegy recited during Moharrum
Marsiyago/ marsiya-khwaan	Those who recite marsiya
Mehfil	Assembly
Mir munshi	Royal scribe/clerk
Mohalla	Locality
Moth	A kind of pulse

Mukaish	Thin metallic strips used for embroidery
Mukhtar	Agent
Munshi	Scribe
Mushaira	Poetic symposium
Nafiri-wala	Trumpeter
Naib	Deputy
Najib	Irregular soldiers/ volunteers
Naqqara	Drum
Naqqarchi	Drum players
Naqqarkhana	Drum house
Nazr	Tribute
Odhni	Shawl
Padri	Christian priest
Paan	Betel leaf
Panah	Shelter/refuge
Pankha	Fan
Pargana	District
Patri	A concrete strip running along the side of the Qila which marks the division of the Qila from the river.
Pul	Bridge
Purbia	As the rebel sepoys who mostly belonged to Awadh and Bihar regions were called

Purdah	Segregation
Puri	Puffed fried bread
Qalamdaan	Pen and ink stand
Qasba	Town
Qasida	Ode in praise of someone
Qila	Fort
Qiledar	Commandant of the palace guards
Raiyyat	Subjects
Razinama	A deed of acknowledgement of cause being settled by a plaintiff or prosecutor
Risala	Troops
Risaldar	Troop commander
Riyasat	Princely state; also refers to government.
Roza	Fast kept in the month of Ramzan
Rubayi	Quatrain
Sadar	Central
Sahib	A term of respect
Sahukar	Moneylender
Salaamgah	Different stations from where the nobles had to present their respects before going into the court

Sarai	Inn
Sarkar	Government
Ser	A measure of weight equivalent to 0.93 kg
Shagird	Student
Shahr Panah	City of refuge
Shastri	Hindu priest
Sher'r	Couplet
Shikar	Hunting
Subedar	A junior military officer in the British Indian army
SubhanAllah	Glory be to God
Sultanate	Kingdom
Taluqa	An estate
Taluqdar	Landlord of an estate
Tasbihkhana	Prayer house
Tehsil	An administrative division
Thakurani	Wife
Thana	Police station
Thanedar	The police officer in charge of the police station or thana
Topkhana	Artillery
Ustad	Teacher
Wali Ahad	Heir apparent
Zer-e-jharokha	Under the balcony

Poems and Verses in the Text[177]

The verses in this section are the transliterations of the verses used in the text. The verses quoted from the Quran are not included in this section. For instances where more than one verse appears on a page, the page numbers are followed by (a), (b), (c), as per their order of appearance.

p. x (a)
Sultanat-e-Shah-e-Alam
Az Dilli ta Palam

p. x (b)
Ya mujhe afsar-e-shahana banaya hota
Ya mera taj gadayana banaya hota

p. xx
Darog bar gardan-e-ravi

p. 3
Shanidah ke bood manind-e-deedah

p. 6 (a)

Hum se phiri chashm-e-yaar dekhiye kab tak rahe
Gardish-e-lail-o-nahar dekhiye kab tak rahe

p. 6 (b)

Sohbat-e-agyaar-o-yaar dekhiye kab tak rahe
Mujhse yeh daar-o-madaar dekhiye kab tak rahe
Ghair se dil tera yaar saaf hai aaina waar
Meri taraf se ghubaar dekhiye kab tak rahe

p. 7

Diwan-e-Zahir Faryaabi
Dar-e-Mecca beduzd gar yaabi

p. 8 (a)

Hawa-e-mausam baaraan se kuchh baeeid nahin
Bane jo khana gulshan nigarkhana-e-chiin
Naseem aaya Subhana Rabbi-al-Aala
Gulo'n ke kaan mein karti hain subah dum talqee'n

p. 8 (b)

Naseem mast nikalti hai josh-e-masti mein
Lapat lapat ke jawaana'n-e-bagh se har baar

p. 8 (c)

Saal mein ek mahina Ramzan ka thahra
Hukm karta hai pai saum Khuda-e-muta'al
Aur mujhe chaar mahine mutawatir guzare
Aakhiri maah Jamadi se laga ta Shawaal
Roze rakhwaaye mujhe chaar mahine paiham
Lekin aaya iftar ka ab tak na khyaal

p. 9 (a)
Khoon bahaaye aashiq nashaad kya
Dilbaro'n ki daad kya fariyaad kya

p. 9 (b)
Chaahat kya ajab maza hai jab ho'n woh bhi beqaraar
Dono'n taraf ho aag barabar lagi huyi

p. 17
Jahan khodo wahin buniyaad ke pathhar nikalte hain
Bahut maamura-e-hasti hai ujde ghar nikalte hain

p. 18
Ke ek shakhs hai baais soobe ka khawind
Rahi na iske tasarruf mein faujdari kuul

p. 24
Kahan woh Khusrau Aali Nazar Bahadur Shah?
Kahan woh sarwar Nekuser Bahadur Shah?
Kahan woh Badshah daadgar Bahadur Shah?
Kahan woh dawar-e-wala gauhar Bahadur Shah?
Kahan se baaghi be-deen aa gaye haaye haaye
Ke naam iska jahaan se mita gaye haaye haaye
Yeh kaisi aatish fitna laga gaye zaalim
Jahaan mein ek qayamat macha gaye zaalim
Garz ke naam khilafat utha gaye zaalim
Sabho'n ko mitne se pahle mita gaye zaalim
Kisi pe qahr Khuda ka na aafat aayi thi
Yeh khandaan-e-Taimur par qayamat aayi thi

p. 25
Meri aulad na-haq aarzu sultanat ki rakhti hai

Yeh karkhana aage ko chalne wala nahin hai
Mujhi par khatma hai
Az Taimur taa Zafar

p. 39
Shaan-e-qudrat dum ke dum mein kya se kya paida kare
Jo na ho wahem-o-gumaan mein barmala paida kare!

p. 47
Inqilaab-e-dahr ne dikhlaaye wo nai-rangiyaa'n
Jab zabaan par laaiye apna naya fasaana hai

p. 49
Na rakho aaj ki kal par, ke kal kisko khabar kya ho
Mareez-e-jaan ba-lab ko sabr-e-umeed sehar kya hai

p. 50 (a)
Chu subah az dum gurg barzad zabaan
Ba khaftan dar aamad sag was paasbaan
Kharus-e-ghanwadah far-o-kuft baal
Dahl-e-zan baz-o-bar tabira dawal

p. 50 (b)
Kya tan-e-nazuk hai jaan ko bhi hasad jis tan pe hai
Kya badan ka rang hai tah jiske pairahan mein hai

p. 51 (a)
Kya chahiye inhe sar-e-angusht barahna
Jis begaana ke khoon mein chaahe dubo liya
Yeh shahr woh hai ke guncha tha husn-waalo'n ka
Yeh shahr woh hai ke takhta tha nau-nihaalo'n ka

Yeh shahr woh hai ke majma tha mah-jamaalo'n ka
Yeh shahr woh hai ke marja tha zi-kamaalo'n ka
Yeh woh zameen hai, zameen jiski zar ugalti hai
Yeh khaak woh hai ke akseer haath milti hai

p. 51 (b)
Kuchh niraala hai jawaani ka banao
Shauqiya zevar hain iss sinn ke liye

p. 51 (c)
Fashr-o-panja marjaan zabir-e-mar vareed
Qamar za zeb shab ashkbar paida shud

p. 52
Subah huyi gajar baja murgh-e-seher ka gul huwa
Karne lage chaman chaman murgh-e-chaman navagiri
Masjid-o-khanqah se shor utha salat ka
Daer mein jaake barhaman karne lage 'Hari, Hari!'

p. 59
Ba-yak gardish-e-charkh-e-nilofari
Na nadir baja manad wa ne nadiri

p. 60
Tadbeer se taqdeer mitayi nahin jaati
Bigdi huyi qismat ki banayi nahin jaati

p. 71
Jahaan mein jitne thay ubaash rind na farjaam
Dagha-shiyaar, chughal-khor, badmaash tamaam
Huye shareek sipah-e-sharar wa bad-anjaam
Kiya tamaam sharifo'n ke naam ko badnaam

p. 88

Dil zamaana tha Dehli pe yeh tabaahi hai
Na samjhe dil mein Tilangani pur jafayi hai
Ke dil ko loot-te hain khana Khudai hai
Khuda ke ghar ko bigada sitam kuhayi hai
Nahin jahaan mein wallah is jafa ki panah
Jo intiqaam ho iska toh bas Khuda ki panah

p. 96

Sutun-e-Khan nisfat gira diye yaksar
Chiragh bazm-e-adalat mein bujha diye yaksar

p. 100

Hai dhawa che mana darad?

p. 104

Ze sam satunra'n dara'n pahan dasht
Zameen shash shudah-o-aasmaan gasht

p. 120

Bhang aise pijiye jaise Kunjpura ki keech
Ghar ke jaane'n mar gaye aur aap nashe ke beech

p. 129

Nikalna shahr se khilqat ka be sar-o-samaa'n
Woh jaana purdahnasheen ka be sar-e-uriyaa'n

p. 130

Na roz-e-hashr se kam thi azaab ki surat
Khuda dikhaye na iss inqilab ki surat

p. 133

Gulo'n se jismo'n pe ek murdari si chaayi thi

Woh mah se chehro'n pe goya chhoote havaai thi
Gazab woh purdahnasheeno'n ki be ravaayi thi
Garz ke aane se pehle qayamat aayi thi
Bayaan kijiye naseebo'n ki kya buraai ka
Woh dasht aur woh phirna barahna paai ka

p. 138
Nihaal-e-gulshan-e-Iqbal pamaal huye
Gul-e-riyaaz-e-khilafat lahu mein laal huye

p. 139
Kar gaya dadhi wala
Pakda gaya moocho'n wala

p. 142
Har ek shahr ka peer wa jawaan qatl huwa
Har ek qabeela wa har khaandaan qatl huwa
Hare ek ahl-e-zabaan khush-bayaan qatl huwa
Garz khulasa yeh hai ke ek jahaan qatl huwa

p. 143
Darog bar gardan-e-ravi

p. 147
Woh dhoop aur woh reg-e-tapaa'n, woh garam hawa
Woh fauj fauj har ek su se narga-e-aada

p. 150
Zamaana mard-e-masaaf ast-o-man ze saada-dili
Kanam ba joshan-e-tadbeer o ham dafa mazaar!
Ze manjaniiq-e-falaq sang-e-fitna mii baarad
Man ablahaana gurezam dar aabgeena hisaar

p. 155

Chu aajiz reha nandeh danam tera
Dareen aajizi chu'n na khwanam tera

p. 199

Gar firdaus bar ru-e-zameen ast
Hameen ast, hameen ast, hameen ast

p. 202 (a)

Yaar dar-e-khana wa maa gard-e-jahaan mi gardeem
Aab dar kuuza wa ma tishna lab mi gardeem

p. 202 (b)

Buto'n se bachke chalne par bhi aafat aa hi jaati hai
Yeh kaafir woh qayamat hain, tabiyat aa hi jaati hai

p. 236

Tonk mein dhoom hai kal se ke Zahir-e-khasta
Sarguzasht dil mahzun hain sunaane wale

p. 251

Woh jhoota ishq hai jisme fughaa'n ho
Woh kachhi aag hai jis mein dhuaa'n ho

p. 262

Ai andaleeb nadaa'n dam dar gulu faroband
Nazuk mizaj-e-shahaa'n taab-e-sukhan nadarad

Acknowledgements

A fascination with the character of Bahadur Shah Zafar, the last Mughal emperor of India, led me to this book. I am grateful to have been able to immerse myself in the Delhi of his times and thus get a glimpse into the syncretic culture I so zealously try to preserve.

This book wouldn't have been possible without the help of a lot of special people who encourage and motivate me to write.

I would like to thank Abdus Sattar sahib, an Old Delhi resident and collector of books. It was he who gave me a copy of the Urdu book published by Areeb Publishers, Delhi, and generously helped me with information on Shahjahanabad.

I wanted to read as many print copies of the *Dastan-e-Ghadar* as possible before translating it. Usman Rana from Pakistan responded to my request immediately and sent me a copy of *Dastan-e-Ghadar* published by Sang-e-Meel Publications, Lahore.

I am very grateful to Mohammad Shahid Saharsavi who helped me during the translation of this book.

My little Zunaira has grown up to be such a talented young lady and has made such spectacular maps to enhance my tale. All the best to you, Zunu!

Though he was studying for his exams, Syed Faizan was always available for me at the drop of a WhatsApp message, helping me not only with the translation of verses but also with deciphering complex words which I couldn't understand. I wish him all the best always. Thank you.

Prof. Shamsur Rahman Faruqi is undoubtedly an authority on all things to do with the Urdu language. His knowledge of terms, customs and historical references are unparalleled. I am blessed that I could go to him with my doubts and am deeply indebted to him for helping me out with the explanations of some terms and correcting a few errors that had crept in because of ambiguity in the text.

Manimugdha S. Sharma has always been my go-to man for any questions regarding military terms and events. There were many terms he helped me understand. Thank you, Mani.

I am extremely grateful to Prof. Ali Nadeem Rezavi, professor of medieval history at the Centre of Advanced Study, Department of History, Aligarh Muslim University, Aligarh, for always responding to each and query of mine and I always had plenty.

From being a stay-at-home wife and mom to a busy writer and explorer, my family has always supported my every endeavour and encouraged me.

When my children Baqar and Subuhi say that they are proud of me, I feel I have achieved every award that there is in this world. I am proud of you both!

My husband, Gazanfar, has always encouraged and supported me and given me space to grow. May we grow old together, InshaAllah.

My sisters, aunts, cousins, nieces and all the wonderful ladies of my family who share my happiness and inspire me—more power to us!

Kanishka Gupta and his faith in me kept me motivated to finish this translation. Did I tell you it makes me feel very grand to have a literary agent!

I owe a debt of gratitude to Achala Upendran.

I am really indebted to Mriga Maithel who has added immeasurably to the manuscript by making it crisper and raising pertinent queries, due to which I feel we now have a better text.

And last but not least: Thank you, Ambar Sahil Chatterjee, for all the help in presenting my work in the best possible light and for all your wonderful support. It's a dream to work with Penguin Random House, whose books have been such a huge part of my growing up. Thank you, Team Penguin.

Notes

1. Syed Khwaja Hasan Nizami, *Delhi ki Jan Kuni* (1922), transl. A. Sattar Kapadia, *The Agony of Delhi* (Delhi: Delhi Printing Press Works, 2003), available at: https://www.scribd.com/doc/44684266/Agony-of-Delhi-Khwaja-Hasan-Nizami. This book is a series written by the author on the events of the mutiny as told to him by eye witnesses and survivors.

2. *Qila-e-Mualla ki Jhalkiyan* by Arsh Taimuri, a direct descendant of Bahadur Shah Zafar, confirms that a treaty was signed between Lord Hardinge and Mirza Fath-ul-Mulk, heir apparent of Bahadur Shah Zafar, declaring that he and the rest of the Mughal family would vacate the Qila-e-Moalla after the death of Bahadur Shah Zafar and they would live in Mehrauli. This agreement is reproduced by Mirza Qumqaamuddin in his book *Khalf Shahzada Fath ul Mulk Bahadur*. He heard it from Mirza Khursheed Alam who had seen this agreement with his own eyes.

3. *Sarguzasht-e-Delhi: 1857 ke Andolan ki Kahani Jeevan Lal ki Zabani*, ed. and trans. Dr Darakhshan Tajwar (Rampur, UP: Rampur Raza Library Publications, 2005).

4. 'Peace be upon him.' This is used by Shias as a mark of respect with the names of the twelve Imams and some members of the Prophet's family.

5   *Hallaj-ud-Daula* means dispeller of difficulties of the state.

6   Zahir clubs together the names of the two books mentioned above.

7   Shah Naseer (1756–1838) was a prominent poet of his age. He was Mughal Emperor Shah Alam's court poet. He was also a very revered Sufi. His students include Momin Khan Momin and Sheikh Ibrahim Zauq.

8   Matla is the opening verse of a ghazal and is the only couplet in a ghazal, which has a qaafiya—the word that establishes its rhyme pattern. The last verse of the ghazal is called a maqta and it contains the takhallus or pen name of the poet. Nowadays, the tradition of using a pen name is disappearing from ghazals.

9   Zahir-al-Din Abu-al-Fazl Tahir *ibn* Mohammad was a famous twelfth-century Persian poet, renowned for his qasidas in praise of the Seljuq Emirs. Zauq likens Zahir Dehlvi to him in high praise.

10 These are names of months as per the Islamic calendar. The last month of Jamadi refers to *Jamadi-ul-Aakhir*. Its preceding month is called *Jamadi-ul-Awwal*.

11 Mirza Zainul Abidin Khan Arif was the nephew of Ghalib's wife and adopted by Ghalib as their son. He was also Ghalib's student in *shayri*. He passed away in his prime and this was one of the biggest sorrows of Ghalib's life.

12 Shujauddin, urf Umrao Mirza, was the writer's younger brother and a student of Ustad Zauq and, for some time later, Mirza Ghalib.

13 Jharokha darshan (the practice of meeting the subjects face to face) was an old practice of Indian rulers adopted by the Mughals. Akbar was the first to appear in a balcony and listen to the petitions of the citizens. This was continued by his successors. The forts in Lahore and Agra had balconies for this purpose. The one in Agra is also called Musamman Burj. In the Red Fort, a covered balcony overlooking the river

Jamuna was added in 1808–09 by Akbar II in the Musamman Burj and the practice of jharokha darshan here was called *Zer-e-jharokha* or 'under the balcony'. Jahangir had a bell hung with ropes in Agra Fort, which the supplicants could ring.

14 Ganjifa is a pack of cards with eight suits, and chausar is a game played with sixteen pieces, three dice, and a 'board' in the shape of a cross.

15 *Shab-e-Baraat*, or the night of celebration, is a full moon day in the Islamic month of Shabaan when, it is said, the fortunes of men and women are decided and sins forgiven. The Shia Muslims celebrate it as the birthday of the twelfth Imam. It is considered a blessed night and is supposed to be spent in devotion.

16 Qila-e-Moalla was a term for the entire fort complex. The residential areas inside that were called *mahal*, or palace. The mahals in which the ladies resided, or seraglio, were out of bounds for males except the emperor and those boys who had not attained puberty. Zahir would have gone to the area such as tasbihkhana and deorhi where special male visitors were allowed to visit the emperor and where the begums would not be present.

17 *Sanchak* and *mehndi* are pre-wedding ceremonies accompanying Muslim weddings, and are still followed today. *Chauthi* takes place after the wedding when the bride goes back to her home for the first time.

18 His father seems to have remarried and his second wife is referred to as mother by Zahir henceforth.

19 Term used for sister-in-law. Many trusted servants would address the ladies of the house with terms used by the family.

20 These lines warn the people to take heed from the lessons of the past and the punishment of the tribes of Banu-al-Nadir.

21 During the trial of Bahadur Shah Zafar, C.B. Saunders, the commissioner of Delhi, gives the emperor's income as Rs 1 lakh per month in pension from the British and Rs 1.5 lakh

per annum from the Crown lands near Delhi; rent, etc. were separate.

22 The original peacock throne, called *Takht-e-Murassa* (jewelled throne), had been taken as part of plunder in 1739 by King Nadir Shah. The one described here is a copy based on the original and was used by the later Mughals.

23 This was an area of the Diwan-e-Khaas where visitors waited to meet the Emperor. A red cloth curtain was used as a screen, which led to its name.

24 The royal fly swatter was made of yak's tail, though called *baal-e-huma*, an allusion to the mythical phoenix or *huma*. It was also called *morchal*.

25 It is not mentioned whether it is Diwan-e-Aam or Diwan-e-Khaas, but in all probability it was the Diwan-e-Aam.

26 Sehra is a genre of Urdu poetry recited in praise of the bridegroom for a happy wedded life. The same word is used for a veil of flowers tied on the forehead of the bride and bridegroom. Tahniyat is congratulatory verse.

27 The writer calls the court *kaiwan*, which means the planet Saturn (which is said to be in the seventh sphere or heaven); hence, the seventh heaven.

28 The Badshah or emperor is addressed by various terms of respect such as Hazrat, Huzoor, Huzoor Purnoor, etc., throughout the text. This was a common practice in writings of those days when writing informally.

29 Sir Thomas Theophilus Metcalfe was the Resident of Delhi from 1835 to 1853.

30 Khaqaani was a celebrated twelfth-century Persian poet.

31 Fath-ul-Mulk was made heir apparent after the death of Mirza Mohammad Bakht, the emperor's eldest son and first heir apparent.

32 *Ali mad ki kasrat* was an exercise in which one stands absolutely erect and tilts the head in such a way that the body forms the word Ali.

33 The tasbihkhana or prayer house consists of three rooms facing the Diwan-e-Khaas; the row of three rooms behind the former are known as the *khwaabgah* (private apartments) and the adjoining hall, half the width of the khwaabgah is known as baithak or *tosha khana* (garment hall). The exquisite marble screen separating the tasbihkhana from the courtyard outside has the *Mizaan-e-Adl* or Scale of Justice carved on it, and the emperors would sit here and dispense justice.

34 This is a mythical belief and has no truth.

35 Though the term *mast* is used for a rogue elephant, I doubt that Maula Baksh was a rogue. It is probably used in the sense of carefree and playful.

36 The elephants were trained to pay respect to the emperor with their trunk, which resembled a salaam.

37 C.B. Saunders, commissioner and agent of Delhi.

38 Again called *kaiwan*.

39 The Ottoman emperors took the name Qaiser-e-Rum or Caesar of the Byzantine Empire.

40 This Khooni Darwaza was at the entrance to Dariba Kalan, near the Sunehri Masjid. It was so called because there was bloodshed here during Nadir Shah's sack of Delhi.

41 The Prophet's birthday.

42 A death anniversary of a Sufi saint is celebrated as a grand occasion as the soul is now headed for a union with the beloved (God). Urs has been derived from the Arabic word for a wedding.

43 After the death of Qutbuddin Aibak, the mosque and Qutb Minar were completed by his successor, Iltutmish.

44 The writer is confused between Qutbuddin Aibak and Alauddin Khilji. The latter had grand plans for expansion of the mosque, which were left incomplete on his death.

45 Though Zahir says that the script is Sanskrit, it is written in Brahmi script.

46 Refers to the story of Raja Dasrath and Rani Kaikeyi where she vowed that if Rama were not sent into exile, she would stay in the Kop Bhawan and never tie her hair.

47 The Jharna was so named as there was a waterfall with the excess water from the Hauz-e-Shamsi falling here. Beautiful pavilions had been made here. There is no longer a waterfall, but it is still known locally by that name. The Auliya Masjid is still a functioning mosque. Both these places are near the Shamsi Talab in Mehrauli.

48 Kabuli Darwaza is now famous as Khooni Darwaza near Feroz Shah Kotla; the famous Dariba market is a thriving bazaar in Chandni Chowk; Kucha Bulaqi Begum and Khanum ka Bazaar are still surviving as localities in Old Delhi. Only the haveli of Khan Dauran Khan has ceased to exist.

49 This is a prayer: '*Allahummah fazna min kulli bala ad duniya.*'

50 Jeth is the third month in the Hindu calendar and coincides with May and June in the Gregorian calendar.

51 He was the chief of the palanquin bearers.

52 His Majesty the son of God and representative (on earth).

53 Area between the *khwaabgah* and Diwan-e-Khaas.

54 The bridge of boats or pontoon bridge was built by Jahangir to facilitate access to Salimgarh from the Yamuna bank. It was renovated by Shahjahan when he built the Red Fort.

55 Captain Douglas, commandant of the palace guards, referred to as the qiledar.

56 There are various terms used for the rebels—*sawar, baghi sawar, sawaaran-e-fauj baghiya, fauj-e-baghiya*. The sawars were mostly cavalrymen. But baghi or fauj-e-baghiya include the other soldiers too.

57 Shadow of God (on earth) and protector of his subjects.

58 Prior to 1857, the East India Company had divided their territories in India into three administrative divisions: Bombay, Madras and Bengal presidencies. Each had its own army. The soldiers involved in the ghadar were mainly from

the Bengal army. Unlike its name, the army hardly had any ethnic Bengali soldiers. The majority of the soldiers were recruited from the upper-caste Hindus (Brahmins, Rajputs and Bhumihars) and Muslims from the regions of Bihar and what is now East UP. Many were from Nawab Wajid Ali Shah's army, which had been disbanded after the annexation of Awadh. That is why they were referred to as Purbias. The soldiers of the Third Bengal Light Cavalry posted in Meerut were the ones who rebelled against their British officers and came to Delhi.

Manimugdha S. Sharma has kindly broken it down into percentages for me to clear misconceptions on the composition of the sepoys who took part in the uprising. He explains:

The Bengal Army was the largest of the Presidency armies, even larger than the combined strength of the Bombay and Madras armies.

The Bengal Army comprised several arms, such as Bengal Foot Artillery, Bengal Horse Artillery, Bengal Native Infantry, Bengal European Infantry, Bengal Light Cavalry (Native), Bengal European Cavalry, Bengal Irregular Infantry, Bengal Irregular Cavalry, etc. Apart from these, there were two other arms that functioned as part of the Bengal Army but swore allegiance to the Crown. These were regular British Army units both infantry (regiments of foot) and cavalry (Dragoons and Hussars). These were the King's troops.

Of the seventy-four native infantry regiments, only twelve continued to exist after 1857; the rest of them either mutinied, or were disarmed or disbanded to prevent insurrection. The native infantry regiments had 75 per cent Hindus, with 60 per cent of them coming from the upper castes (Rajputs, Brahmins and Bhumihars).

> There were ten regiments of regular native cavalry and Muslims comprised three fourths of the troop strength. They were primarily Hindustani Muslims (the name given to North Indian Muslims), Ranghars and Kaimkhanis from Delhi and its surrounding areas.

59 Under the Doctrine of Lapse, adopted children were not considered legal heirs and many women and their adopted children lost their inheritance after the husband's death. However, these women were wives of erstwhile rulers, many of whom joined in the War of Independence. Here the reference may be to the employees and serving women of the dispossessed women.

60 The first British Resident was David Ochterlony (1803–1806) and at the time mentioned here, the Resident was Simon Fraser (November 1853–May 1857).

61 Captain Douglas, commandant of the palace guards.

62 A term of endearment used for European children, it was also paternalistic in nature, used here in all probability to calm down the rebels.

63 The rebel cavalrymen, hereafter referred to as baghi sawar or simply sawar or baghi.

64 All the Darwazas or gateways in the Qila, walls of the city or street entrances had a small wicket gate set in it for easy entry as the Darwazas themselves may or may not be kept open all the time for security purposes.

65 Apart from Fraser and Douglas, the sawar also killed Reverend Jennings, his daughter Annie Jennings and her friend Miss Clifford.

66 Short form of salam aleikum.

67 I have been unable to find a reference to any Barburton or Warburton but a George Wagentrieber is mentioned in William Dalrymple's book, *The Last Mughal* (New Delhi: Penguin Books, 2006): 'George Wagentrieber helped fan

such flames from his new *Delhi Gazette Extra* printing press in Lahore: "Our army is exasperated almost to madness by what they have seen of the brutality of the insurgents," he expostulated in one editorial.' So, perhaps, the reference is to him.

68   Probably the Chatta Chowk.

69   Nainsook was a soft, fine, lightweight form of plain weave cotton which was very popular in those days. The word nainsook is first documented in 1790, and derives from the Hindi and Urdu 'nainsukh', which literally means 'eye's delight.'

70   The citizens of Shahjahanabad called the rebels purbia, as most sepoys had come from Uttar Pradesh or Bihar. The Indian sepoys in the British army in 1857 were also called Telingani as the earliest recruitment by the British had been done from Telingana for the Carnatic Wars. It basically meant outsiders. I have used the term purbia as written by Zahir Dehlvi.

71   Koriya Pul is a bridge near Kashmiri Gate.

72   Zahir uses the word *mem*, which was a term used for married European women.

73   In all probability, the word Miss refers to a European or Anglo-Indian girl.

74   This Khooni Darwaza, no longer extant, was in Chandni Chowk near the Sunehri Masjid, so called because of the bloodshed that happened near it during Nadir Shah's massacre of Delhi.

75   Mr Beresford was the manager of the Delhi bank. He was killed along with his wife and children. The other officers present were killed too.

76   George Willoughby and nine other officers of the British Ordinance Corps defended the magazine from 10 a.m. till the afternoon. At 3.30 p.m., when they realized that it was

in danger of falling into the hands of the Indian soldiers, they blew it up, killing many rioters and onlookers, and badly damaging nearby buildings. Surprisingly, six of these British officers managed to escape. One was killed on his way to Meerut. The survivors were awarded the Victoria Cross.

77 'There is no God but Allah, and Mohammad is his prophet.' The *shahada/kalima* or creed recited by Muslims testifying to the oneness of God.

78 According to Prof. Shamsur Rahman Faruqi whom I asked for help, this was the distortion of the Sappers and Miners, a British division, whose soldiers joined the rebels.

79 A non-Muslim subject of a state governed according to the sharia who is granted the freedom to worship and is entitled to the protection of life and property by the state, although constrained to pay a special tax and not granted the full legal status accorded to Muslim subjects. See: http://www. thefreedictionary.com/Zimmi

80 Direct descendants of the Prophet (peace be upon him).

81 The European men, women and children had been kept captive in the kitchen, a spacious building near Mehtab Bagh.

82 The murder of these prisoners was the gravest charge against Bahadur Shah Zafar in the trial conducted against him by the British after they gained control of Shahjahanabad. It was as if Zahir had foreseen a turning point in the fortunes of the Badshah.

83 This was the battle of Hindon on 31 May.

84 This was the Battle of Alipur.

85 This story is corroborated by Mainodin Hassan Khan in *Two Native Narratives of the Mutiny in Delhi* by Charles Theophilus Metcalfe (Westminster: Archibald Constable and Co., 1898). Khan names him as Ahmed Khan, a risaldar in the Fourth Cavalry.

86 A three-arched doorway built by Nazir Mahaldar Khan. It is now on the Delhi–Karnal road.

87 The word Siyah Burj is not mentioned in any text or map that I have read, but in the vicinity of Kabuli Darwaza, there was a Shah Burj (not to be confused with the one in the Red Fort). It is marked on a map giving positions of both armies in the siege of Delhi. It is possible that it got blackened with smoke and fire and so renamed Siyah or black.

88 Mirar is located in the region of Uttar Pradesh. Uttar Pradesh's capital, Lucknow, is approximately 230 km away from Mirar (as the crow flies). The distance from Mirar to New Delhi is approximately 631 km (as the crow flies).

89 Zahir is very vague on dates and locations. It is impossible to pinpoint exact dates or locations, but from Jeewan Lal's diary in *Two Native Narratives of the Mutiny in Delhi*, we get detailed accounts. There was a fierce day-long engagement with the British on 28 June near Qudsia Bagh and on 30 June near Suneri Mundai.

90 Bakht Khan was a subedar in the British army and had forty years of experience in the Bengal horse artillery and had served with distinction in the battle of Jalalabad in the First Afghan War. He replaced Mirza Mughal as the commander-in-chief of the rebel forces.

91 A very sparse, ascetic dwelling place of faqirs.

92 Mirza Fakhru was the heir apparent.

93 After the Battle of Karbala in AD 680, the Prophet's grandson Hussain was martyred along with the male members of his family. His sister, wives, daughters and other women of the family, along with his ailing son, were taken prisoners by Yezid, the ruler of Damascus. They were made to walk unveiled from Iraq to Damascus and suffer various indignities like common prisoners.

94 This is an oft-quoted remark, but the speaker was never identified. Zahir identifies him as Bakht Khan. However, Prof. Irfan Habib (of the Centre of Advanced Study, Department of History, Aligarh Muslim University, Aligarh) says that Bakht Khan who was a much decorated officer in the British army was a very sophisticated man, who spoke many languages including English and as such could not be the uncouth purbia described here. He had reached the rank of Subedar Major, which was the highest position an Indian could reach in the British army at that time. He was made the commander-in-chief of the Indian forces by Bahadur Shah Zafar and given the title of *Sahib-i-Alam Bahadur* (Lord Governor General). Zahir must have been confused as much time had elapsed between the actual events and his writing them down.

95 At various times during this period, the emperor wanted to retire to Zafar Mahal in Mehrauli or even to proceed to Mecca for pilgrimage, but was always persuaded to stay on.

96 The famous battle of Najafgarh.

97 It's a tributary of the Yamuna and is rain-fed.

98 A report in *History of the Siege in Delhi* says that Hakim Ahsanullah Khan had visited the place just shortly before it was blown up and so the needle of suspicion fell on him. But the diary of Jivan Lal does not corroborate that.

99 Munshi Jeewan Lal writes in his diary that the emperor hid Hakim Ahsanullah Khan behind the throne. The sepoys surrounded the palace, and after hours of resisting their demand, he gave up Hakim Ahsanullah Khan on the condition that they spare his life. That night, the emperor called his son to protect his life. 'There was panic in the city, every shop was closed. The Mohammadens passed every hour in fear, and fully expected that the soldiers would kill the King and massacre the citizens.' (Charles Theophilus Metcalfe, *Two Native Narratives of the Mutiny in Delhi*).

100 Zahir is vague about location and dates but Jeewan Lal mentions briefly a night attack by the British on the Kishanganj Battery on 28 August. He also mentions that the sepoy force was put under arms in expectation of an assault from the English (Metcalfe, *Two Native Narratives of the Mutiny in Delhi*).

101 This is a term for Mazhabi Sikhs who were basically non-Jat Sikhs taken into the army by the British.

102 The name of the Darwaza is not mentioned.

103 This was built in the reign of Jahangir as an inn by Farid Khan and later repaired and used as a jailhouse by the British. It lay outside the walls of Shahjahanabad. It no longer exists.

104 Stage of Sufism where you become oblivious to the world.

105 Connaught Place is located in what was Jaisinghpura, the estate of Sawai Raja Jai Singh of Jaipur.

106 Every other account mentions Major Hudson as the officer who captured the emperor and killed the Mughal princes. Here, Zahir is probably confused as C.B. Saunders was the commissioner and agent of Delhi that time.

107 He was the mir munshi of the governor general. As per the books on 1857 by Khwaja Hasan Nizami, Maulvi Rajab Ali and Mirza Ilahi Bux were British spies. They had accompanied Major Hudson to Humayun's tomb. They had been told by the British that they would be rewarded if they prevented the emperor from escaping with Bakht Khan and so did their best to persuade him to surrender to the British.

108 General Bakht Khan, the commander of the Indian forces in Delhi, had exhorted the emperor to come away with them before he left the Qila. He had said,

> Although the British have taken the City, militarily it is not a big blow to the Rebel Army as the whole of Hindustan is up in arms against the British and everyone is looking up to you for guidance. Travel with me to the mountains from where the fight

can be continued in such a way that the British would not be able to break through.

The emperor was inspired by the speech and asked Bakht Khan to meet him in Humayun's tomb the next day. The tomb, at the time, was located on the outskirts of the city.

As soon as Bakht Khan was sent off by Bahadur Shah Zafar, it was all over for him.

Mirza Ilahi Bux and Munshi Rajab Ali, spies for the British, overheard the exchange and carried the news to their masters, promising to persuade Bahadur Shah to stay in Delhi.

Mirza Ilahi Bux was the emperor's father-in-law and was furious with him for the preferential treatment given by the emperor to Zeenat Mahal, the youngest wife, and her son. Ilahi Bux's grandson and the emperor's heir apparent had been poisoned to death a year before, in which Zeenat Mahal was suspected.

The emperor trusted the two when they implored him to stay in Delhi, despite warnings from his khwaja-saras. While Major Hudson waited at the western gate, these two entered the tomb and convinced the emperor with their oratory that the best course for him lay in going back to the Qila with Hudson and not forward with Bakht Khan.

See: Nizami, *Agony of Delhi*, p. 19.

109   Major Hudson is credited with this act in all other sources that I have read.

110   Shah-e-Mardan is the present-day Jor Bagh. The area was called Aliganj and had an enclosing wall. Najaf Khan's mausoleum used to be within it. The walls are no longer

standing and Najaf Khan's mausoleum now falls in Lodhi
estate.

111 There was excessive looting after the fall of Delhi for
four days by individual soldiers and officers. Later on,
'prize agents' stepped in. Their job was to collect all the
loot, auction it, and distribute the proceeds among the
victorious soldiers in proportion to their rank.

112 'He was famous for his calligraphy, so much so that his
works were sold by being weighed against Gold or Silver.
He would write a single word and give it to a beggar who
could then use it as cash.' (Nizami, *Agony of Delhi*, p. 31).

113 Munshi Zakaullah has written:

> The main cause of the crisis was that Nawab
> Shamsher Jang Khan's son and Hakim Fateh Allah
> Khan had injured a British soldier who had tried
> to enter the female area of their house with evil
> intentions. When the Commanding Officer heard
> this, he ordered that all the men from this area
> should be either killed or captured.
>
> This order was carried out in a brutal way. The
> soldiers either,[*sic*] entered the houses and murdered
> the men on the spot or they captured them and
> took them in front of their Commanding Officer.
> He ordered that these men should all be taken to
> the banks of the river and shot dead. This was done
> straight away.
>
> These people were tied with ropes and made
> to stand in a line on the banks of the river. Then
> the British opened fire and killed them all with the
> exception of two who were not hit by the bullets.
> When the soldiers left, they got up and ran away.
> These two were Mirza Mustafa Beg and the other
> was Maulana Shahbai's son in law [*sic*] and nephew,

called Waziruddin. Mirza Mustafa Beg later on took
up a job in the Magazine and Waziruddin became
an officer in the Kanpur Court.

(Nizami, *Agony of Delhi*, p. 31)

114   Colonel Burn was made the Military Governor of the
City. He took residence in Chandni Chowk in the house
of Kutubuddin Sowdager (trader). He formed a company
of troops to find the people still resident in Delhi and
to bring them over together with their possessions. This
company of troops used this order to make unlawful
gains for themselves. They used to arrest the families
force the men to walk in front with their possessions on
their heads, and the women and children were all forced
to walk behind. Some women were carrying children
with others holding on to their hands or their shawls.
In this manner, they were made to walk. Some of the
women were not used to this type of hardship, others had
never come out without their veils, they were stumbling
all over the place but the soldiers just pushed them along
and forced them to march on.

When these people were presented in front of
Colonel Burn, they were ordered to surrender any
valuables they carried with them and the items, which
had no value, were returned to them. After this they were
taken under guard to the Lahori Gate, there they were
pushed out of the gates and thus thrown out of the City.
All these things have been stated in the history written
by Munshi Zakaullah.

It is worth thinking about how these poor people
managed with their children and families, being in a
state of utter destitution.

In short, there were thousands of families with no
cover, nothing on their feet and nothing to eat lying

outside the gates of Delhi. They had no place to sit and
no shelter from the Sun, and no water to drink. Some
kindly souls started feeding them with boiled pulses, but
it was not possible to feed such a large number of people.
Hundreds of children perished of starvation in the laps
of their mothers and scores of women committed suicide
to get away from their sorrowful state.
(Nizami, *Agony of Delhi*, pp. 29–30)

115 A special bracelet made of solid metal beads.
116 Bride money which the husband has to pay to his wife.
117 A town in present-day western Uttar Pradesh.
118 By Urfi Shirazi
119 Gami Khan was a well-known criminal and a British
informer. He had earlier been with the rebels, but soon
changed sides. He was 'responsible for the deaths of many
people and for destroying various families'. Gami was
feared even more than the British themselves, and people
used to shiver on hearing his name. However, in the end,
he was found out and the authorities hanged him for his
misdeeds. (Nizami, *Agony of Delhi*, p. 33)
120 A Muslim community found in Uttar Pradesh.
121 A numbardar was a privileged man with authority in
the area.
122 Zahir does not mention after how many days, just says '*ek
shab*'.
123 An invocation to God from Nizami Ganjavi's *Sharaf Namah*.
124 Probably those returning from Delhi after its fall.
125 They reached Rampur on 27 April 1858. He stayed here
till 1862. His son, Sajjad Mirza, was born during his stay
in Rampur.
126 She is the daughter of the Prophet (peace be upon him).
Saiyyeds claim direct descent from her.
127 Dada here means grandfather.

128 Dagh Dehlvi, the famous poet who had also taken shelter in Rampur after the mutiny.

129 Sahibzada was a title normally given to sons of nawabs.

130 Ameer Minai, the famous Urdu poet.

131 It is this same Lawrence who was the lieutenant governor and chief commissioner of Punjab during the ghadar. In 1864, he was appointed India's governor general after the death of Lord Elgin. He had written the review of the emperor's trial and recommended his exile. He was rewarded for his services during the ghadar as he had sent the Sikh forces to Delhi. He permitted the Muslims who had run away in 1857 to return to Delhi.

132 Arastu Jah Mir Maulvi Rajab Ali Khan Bahadur was the mir munshi of the governor general. His family lived here.

133 A breed of horse originating from Central Asia.

134 A community of Muslim Rajputs.

135 These were designations given to the men in charge of different horses/stables.

136 It was the royal residence of the Alwar royals till 1928.

137 Kalawants were members of an established family of musicians (believed to be direct descendants of Tansen) who specialized in vocal music, and were the chief musicians in the Mughal court.

138 An insurrection took place in 1866 and later in 1870, when the Rajputs rose up once again.

139 The Shila Devi temple houses the famous idol of Goddess Durga situated in the Amber Fort. It is believed that Maharaja Mansingh brought the statue of the Goddess Shila Mata from Jessore, Bangladesh, in 1604. Legends say that the Goddess appeared in his dreams and asked him to recover her statue lying under the sea near Jessore (now in Bangladesh) and install it in a temple.

140 'Tu' is the Indian informal way of addressing someone and generally considered impolite. The formal would be 'aap' for an elder and 'tum' for a peer or younger person.

141 A Persian emperor, famous for his sense of justice.

142 The chief queen would be the consort in favour at that moment. She wouldn't necessarily be the eldest.

143 Current ruler.

144 Peshwas are religious guides/priests.

145 A Hindu mendicant and penitent, who, having forsaken the world, leads a wandering life.

146 Observance of rituals connected with mourning in the month of Moharrum.

147 He was an adopted son.

148 There is no mention of any sales sahib in the list of British agents in Jaipur. Thomas Holbein Hendley was possibly an acting agent for Beynon in 1880, the year the Maharaja died. From 1881 to 1882, Adelbert Cecil Talbot was the agent.

149 By Saadi.

150 He was the consort of Nawab Shahjahan Begum.

151 Umrao Mirza died in Delhi in 1885.

152 The palace and village was called Samode and was the feudatory jagir of Maha Rawal.

153 In the north-east part of Rajasthan.

154 Nawab Shah Jahan Begum was the ruler of Bhopal (29 July 1838–16 June 1901), and Nawab Siddiq Hasan Khan was her husband.

155 This could be a reference to a town called Bairat located 52 km north of Jaipur. It has remnants of a Buddhist *chaitya*, an Asoka edict and some very strange and naturally formed rocks and boulders which resemble animals or human skulls.

156 A box with a domed cover, used for keeping paan.

157 He stayed in Tonk for approximately sixteen years.

158   A poem in which the second line of every distich rhymes with the same letter.

159   This was sometime in 1892–93.

160   Now known as Boraj.

161   Khandela is in Sikar district.

162   Syed Mohammad Husain Bismil.

163   Muztar Khairabadi. Bismil was Muztar Khairabadi's brother.

164   The Prophet's birthday is on the twelfth day of the Islamic month Rabi-ul-Awwal and is popularly called Barawafat in India. Milads or gatherings are held to celebrate it.

165   He went to Hyderabad a second time in 1910.

166   An Arab poet who lived in the sixth century and was famous for his extreme generosity.

167   Everywhere here would refer to the places Zahir was acquainted with such as Jaipur and Delhi.

168   Marsiya is an elegy recited to commemorate the sacrifice of Imam Hussain, the Prophet's grandson in Karbala. It is set in classical raga and is recited by highly skilled people called marsiya khwaan.

169   These are various kinds of poems.

170   Garam and Aseem would be the pen names of these two gentlemen.

171   The poet presiding over the mushaira moves a lit candle stand/lamp in front of the poet whose turn it is to recite next. The poets don't pull it themselves nor can they recite unless invited as per protocol.

172   Dagh Dehlvi always remained a well-wisher and gave great respect to Zahir Dehlvi. He had given strict instructions to his students to give due respect too.

173   Prof. Shamsur Rahman Faruqi kindly cleared my confusion on whether the emperor left the Qila on 17 September or 19 September. He said that the emperor left the Qila on the 17th and took refuge in the mansion of Mirza Ilahi

Bux, his father-in-law, in Hazrat Nizamuddin basti. This area saw a lot of looting by the local rogue elements and it was felt that the emperor's life was in jeopardy; so on the 19th, on Mirza Ilahi Bux's suggestion, he left for Humayun's tomb.

Mirza Ilahi Bux was also a spy and sympathizer for the British and perhaps he felt that that it would be easier for the British forces to arrest the emperor from an open space than a crowded residential area.

174 See: http://csridentity.com/districts/alwar.asp
175 Shama Mitra Chenoy, *Shahjahanabad: A City of Delhi 1638–1857* (New Delhi: Munshiram Manoharlal Publishers, 1998).
176 Ibid.
177 Zahir's complete poems along with their translations can be found with Rana Safvi. Some may even be available on her blog 'Hazrat-e-Dilli' at ranasafvi.com.

YOU MAY ALSO LIKE

Besieged: Voices from Delhi 1857

Compiled and translated by Mahmood Farooqui

**'Brilliant and revolutionary . . . *Besieged* is a marvel'
William Dalrymple**

This groundbreaking, first-time translation of the Mutiny Papers documenting the siege of Delhi shifts focus away from conventional understandings of 1857. Mahmood Farooqui's translations chronicle the lives of courtesans, soldiers, potters, spies, faqirs, doctors and harassed policemen, all trying to live through the turmoil of their city. They present a searing portrait of the hopes, beliefs, and failures of ordinary people who lived through the end of an era.

**'Brings forth the rich vibrancy and complexity of the historical event, mostly in the words of ordinary men and women'
Tabish Khair, *Mint***

**'If you want to know what Dilliwalas had to go through in 1857, you cannot do better than read this book'
Khushwant Singh**

**'Groundbreaking'
*The Hindu***

YOU MAY ALSO LIKE

The Last Mughal: The Fall of a Dynasty, Delhi, 1857

William Dalrymple

Winner of the Duff Cooper Prize for History 2007

Bahadur Shah II, the last Mughal emperor, was a mystic, a
talented poet and a skilled calligrapher who, though deprived
of real political power by the East India Company, succeeded
in creating a court of great brilliance, and presided over one of
the greatest cultural renaissances of Indian history. In 1857, it
was Zafar's blessing to a rebellion among the Company's own
Indian troops that transformed an army mutiny into the largest
uprising the British Empire ever had to face.

The Last Mughal is a portrait of the dazzling Delhi Zafar
personified, and the story of the last days of the great
Mughal capital and its final destruction in the catastrophe
of 1857. Shaped from groundbreaking material, William
Dalrymple's powerful retelling of this fateful course of events
is an extraordinary revisionist work with clear contemporary
echoes. It is the first account to present the Indian perspective
on the siege, and has at its heart the stories of the forgotten
individuals tragically caught up in one of the bloodiest
upheavals in history.

**'Captivating . . . It is rare indeed that a work of such
consummate scholarship and insight could also be so
accessible and such fun to read'
Amartya Sen**

'A splendid work of empathetic scholarship'
Times Literary Supplement